25.ᴺ

REVOLT
of the
FILMMAKERS

Post-Communist Cultural Studies Series
Thomas Cushman, General Editor

The Culture of Lies
Antipolitical Essays
Dubravka Ugrešić

Burden of Dreams
History and Identity in Post-Soviet Ukraine
Catherine Wanner

Gender Politics in the Western Balkans
Women, Society, and Politics in Yugoslavia and the
Yugoslav Successor States
Sabrina P. Ramet, ed.

*The Radical Right in Eastern and Central Europe
Since 1989*
Sabrina P. Ramet, ed.

The Culture of Power in Serbia
Nationalism and the Destruction of Alternatives
Eric D. Gordy

Russia's Liberal Project
State-Society Relations in the Transition from
Communism
Marcia A. Weigle

Revolt of the Filmmakers
The Struggle for Artistic Autonomy and the Fall of the
Soviet Film Industry
George Faraday

REVOLT
of the
FILMMAKERS

The Struggle for
Artistic Autonomy
and the Fall
of the Soviet Film
Industry

GEORGE FARADAY

The Pennsylvania State
University Press
University Park,
Pennsylvania

Library of Congress Cataloging-in-Publication Data

Faraday, George, 1964–
    Revolt of the filmmakers : the struggle for artistic autonomy and the fall of the
Soviet film industry / George Faraday.

    p.   cm.—(Post–Communist cultural studies)
    Includes bibliographical references and index.
    ISBN 0-271-01982-4 (cloth : alk. paper)
    ISBN 0-271-01983-2 (pbk. : alk. paper)
    1. Motion pictures—Soviet Union—History.   2. Motion picture industry—
Soviet Union—History.   I. Series.
    PN1993.5.R9F27 2000
    791.43'0947'09048—dc21   99-27360
                                                                                   CIP

It is the policy of The Pennsylvania State University Press to use acid-free paper for
the first printing of all clothbound books. Publications on uncoated stock satisfy the
minimum requirements of American National Standard for Information
Sciences—Permanence of Paper for Printed Library Materials, ANSI Z39.48–1992.

For my parents

In America there is no question about employee rights and creativity. These are simply not discussed. They just work over there.
     —Filipp Yermash, head of Goskino (1979)

Art is by nature aristocratic.
     —Andrei Tarkovsky (1986)

Now we don't have any censorship. But, then again, we don't have any films to censor.
     —Karen Shakhnazarov (1995)

CONTENTS

ABBREVIATIONS

CDSP   *The Current Digest of the Soviet Press*
CE   *Cine-Eye* (English-language edition of *Kino Glaz*)
IK   *Iskusstvo Kino*
KG   *Kino Glaz*
MN   *Moscow News*
MT   *Moscow Times*
SF   *Soviet Film*

ILLUSTRATIONS

Following Page 109

ACKNOWLEDGMENTS

Scholarship, no less than art, is ultimately a collective enterprise; this book could not have been written without help and encouragement from many people along the way. The present work began life as a doctoral dissertation at Duke University's Department of Cultural Anthropology. I would like to thank the members of my supervising committee, Jane Gaines, Thomas Lahusen, Mack O'Barr, Orin Starn, and in particular, the chair, Claudia Strauss, for their indispensable moral and intellectual support. The field research in Moscow on which much of this book is based was made possible by fellowships from the Department of Cultural Anthropology and Duke University's Graduate School of Arts and Sciences. Thanks also to my friends and colleagues at Duke, especially Alexei Yurchak and Borislav Knezeviç, for the late-night discussions that kindled my interest in life after the Party.

Living in Moscow in the mid-1990s would scarcely have been possible, let alone as enjoyable as it turned out to be, without the numerous people who offered me their hospitality and friendship while I was there, Nastya Goreva, Ira Tavitskaya, Yuri Nechiporenko, Amanda Chapman, Kostya Kamenev, Liza Faktor, Nastya Filippova, and most of all, Katya Vasilyeva. Zara Abdullaeva, Lev Karakhan, and Daniil Dondurei at *Iskusstvo Kino* played a vital role in helping me define my research agenda "on the ground." Without Sasha Chernykh's unstintingly generous help (and good-humored company) I could not have begun to put this agenda into practice.

The arguments and presentation of this book have benefited greatly from the advice and encouragement of Bruce Grant, Katherine Verdery, Caroline Humphrey, and Maya Turovskaya. I would also like to thank Thomas Cushman, editor for the Post-Communist Cultural Studies Series in which this book appears, for his invaluable help in revising this manuscript for publication and Peter Potter at Penn State Press for guiding me through the process. Any remaining shortcomings are, of course, entirely my own responsibility. Finally, nothing at all would have been possible without my wife Michele's peace, love, and understanding.

DEATH OF A CULTURE INDUSTRY

In June 1995 I attended the Kinotavr Film Festival to research a newspaper article on the state of contemporary Russian cinema. In the six years of its existence Kinotavr had established itself as the biggest event in the Russian cinematic calendar. Held at the huge Brezhnev-era *Zhemchuzhina* ("Pearl") Hotel in the Black Sea resort town of Sochi, its competition programs showcased most new movies produced in the countries that once made up the Soviet Union. For two frenetic weeks the festival provided a social venue for nearly anyone who was anyone in the post-Soviet film world. A good sampling of post-Soviet high society, including celebrities from the (often overlapping) worlds of big business, show business, politics, and organized crime could be seen rubbing shoulders with designer-stubbled actors and chain-smoking critics. Its stabs at cosmopolitan glamour inspired then prime minister Viktor Chernomyrdin to make the inevitable claim in his opening speech that Kinotavr had become Russia's answer to Cannes.

Cannes-like or not, the celebratory atmosphere at Sochi stood in stark contrast to the parlous situation of Russian filmmaking as a whole during this period. Indeed, Kinotavr's executive director, Mark Rudinstein, declared that he established the festival in 1989 with the intention of "stop[ping] all talk of the death of national cinema, which was useful for those who meant to turn everyone onto American crap, as I call the stuff which fills our screens. . . . So we had to put together some kind of institution, some kind of island, that could publicize and discuss our native cinema."[1] Judging by the deserted stalls at its film market, Kinotavr—which had soaked up a quarter of the Russian government's $20 million annual subsidy for film—was having little impact on the economic fortunes of the industry as a whole. At the festival's press conferences directors and producers constantly reiterated the impossibility of covering production costs from commercial distribution and prophesied the industry's total extinction if state support fell below its already meager levels. As Leonid Yarmolik, star and producer of *Moscow Holidays (Moskovskie kanikuly)*, warned sternly, "This festival is a social get-together [*tusovka*]. We can do what we like here but our films aren't reaching the public."

*   *   *

By the mid-1990s Russian filmmaking had entered a period of crisis whose scale and severity is perhaps unique in the experience of the world's major cultural industries. In the previous decade, a film industry that in terms of output and audience size had been one of the world's largest had been virtually liquidated as a medium of mass entertainment. In the late-Soviet period, Soviet studios turned out almost 150 feature films annually, a figure comparable to that of Hollywood, while, at almost four billion tickets sold a year in the mid-1980s, cinema attendance stood at three times the size of the domestic American audience in the same period. By the mid-1990s the theater audience for Russian films had shrunk a hundredfold, as average rates of cinema attendance declined from fourteen visits to one visit per person each year, and domestic production's share of what audience remained fell from two-thirds to one-tenth of the total. By 1996 the number of films produced within Russia had fallen to a mere twenty full-length features.[2]

Clearly, many of the causes of this collapse were external to the film industry itself, for most branches of Russian cultural production (and indeed of material production generally) declined precipitously over this period as well. As the head of a video distribution company put it to me: "It would be amazing if everything lay in ruins and only the film industry was working."[3] Broader factors at work included the drastic overall decline in most Russians' purchasing power and the proliferation of alternative sources of entertainment (for those with sufficient time and money) attendant on the breakup of the Soviet state's monopoly control over cultural production and distribution.

It can also be argued, however, that filmmakers themselves played a central role in bringing about the decline of their industry. Since the early 1930s Soviet filmmakers had worked within a system of production and distribution that differed fundamentally from those typical of the commercial cultural industries of the West. Creative workers in the Soviet Union were subjected to the direct supervision of the state, yet at the same time were insulated from the pressures of audience demand. In the name of creative freedom, the revolutionary Fifth Congress of the Soviet Filmmakers' Union of May 1986 dismantled the Soviet apparatus of control without establishing a market-led system in its place. As a result, the creative workers of one of the world's largest cultural industries achieved an unprecedented degree of autonomy from any form of external pressure. This gave rise to a paradoxical situation in which domestic cinema was exposed to foreign competition within the national market, but those who created it were not subjected to any economic mechanism capable of forcing them to orient their work toward mass public demand. The consequent displacement of "national cinema" (*otechestvennoe kino*) from domestic distribution was the direct result, many commentators within the industry argued, of the tendency of Russian directors "to make films for themselves," rather than for external audiences. As one distributor, Yevgeny Miropolsky, charged, "Our filmmakers produce such nonsense it is dull even for intellectual viewers. Instead of making good, clever, box-office films, filmmakers burst out sobbing: they go on about the dominance of American cinema! There is no such dominance! Simply Russian cinema occupies the place it deserves."[4] In a sense, therefore, a situation that bears the outward hallmarks of "cultural imperialism" can be seen as the outcome of a process more justly labeled *auto-colonization*. That is, the marginalization of domestic cinema production within its own market was in large part the product of indigenous forces, not least important of which being the vigor with which Russia's filmmakers claimed the status of autonomous "artist." Although not all post-perestroika filmmakers were as indifferent to public demand as Miropolsky claims, the effect of the industry's institutional transformation during perestroika was to ensure that for the many who did wish to make movies for themselves, very little stood in the way.

The central task of this study is to examine the nature, background, and consequences of the revolution in the name of art that took place in May 1986. In the first part of this book I consider the period before perestroika to ask, Why did filmmakers aspire to creative autonomy? How did the structures of the Soviet film industry work to simultaneously frustrate and enable its practice? What specific conceptions of cinematic practice did this aspiration stimulate? In the second part, I turn to the decade following 1986 to consider: first, the institutional changes initiated by the Fifth Congress and their effects on the structure of incentives operating within the industry; and second, the discursive and creative responses of Russia's filmmakers to the transformed conditions in which they now found themselves.

This book grew out of field research I conducted while living in Moscow from mid-1994 to mid-1995. In the course of my research I interviewed both individuals working in the post-Soviet film industry and people active in other areas of Russian cultural life. Supplemented by material from the Russian film press, these interviews form the basis of the account I present of the industry in the period during and after pere-stroika in the second half of this book. In the first half I draw upon exist-ing studies and published firsthand accounts to present an analysis of the social and institutional dynamics of the film industry in the late-Soviet period. My aim here is not only to throw fresh light on the origins of the industry's contemporary crisis, but to use the case of Soviet filmmaking to develop a general theoretical model of the distinctive characteristics of cultural production under socialism. In the remainder of this introduc-tion I discuss the theoretical approach I have taken in attempting these tasks.

RETHINKING THE STATUS OF "ARTIST" UNDER SOCIALISM

The moral and aesthetic relativism that now typifies academic study of the arts in the West has been slow to take hold in both "native" and Western accounts of cultural life under socialism. Unorthodox artists and intellectuals working within (or in exile from) state socialist countries tended to present cultural activity as a sphere that could—or, at any rate, ought to—express absolute "humanistic" values against the ideological distortions and political repression of the Communist state. In an essay on the political significance of art, Vaclav Havel declared, for instance:

> The more an artist compromises to oblige power and gain advantages, the less good art can we expect from him; the more freely and indepen-dently, by contrast, he does his own thing . . . the better his chances of creating something good. . . . The counterpart of power in this conflict is not an alternative political idea but the autonomous, free humanity of man and with it necessarily also art—precisely as art!—as one of the most important expressions of this autonomous humanity.[5]

This elevated and moralistic view of art's role under socialism has power-fully influenced Western accounts of the Soviet film industry. The open-ing sentence from a recent survey of East European cinema exemplifies the kind of rhetoric it has inspired: "The history of Soviet film is one of a struggle for truth—for the right of the individual filmmaker to create a work that presents reality honestly according to his or her own vision." The author continues: "By restricting both content and style, the Party *unnaturally* attempted to enforce a permanent state of infancy. To do so was not only to deny freedom of expression, but *to deny the artists their humanity*. This factor is what made being a film artist in the Soviet Union or any other Soviet bloc country an existence full of pain and anxiety" (emphasis added).[6]

This humanistic conception of art sets up an opposition within accounts of East European filmmaking between "good"—artistic, individualistic, humanistic, truthful—films (and directors) on the one hand, and "bad"— inartistic, conformist, immoral, and escapist—ones on the other. Take for instance the following characterization of Soviet cinema during the Khrushchev Thaw of the late 1950s and early 1960s: "Creativity was al- lowed a freer hand and new themes and styles, inspired by a general con- cern for the individual and his inner world, made their way to the screen. . . . After two decades of make-believe, audiences yearned for a measure of truth."[7] And describing the drive for commercialism in the cinema of the 1970s, the same author writes: "A few talented directors were able to rise above the level of grayish mediocrity and stand up for humanistic values and artistic integrity."[8]

Clearly such accounts employ a conception of culture out of step, to say the least, with the tendency dominant within Western cultural studies to view any absolute conception of aesthetic value as intellectually problem- atic and politically retrograde. Since the 1960s such ideals have been at- tacked for the contribution they are held to have made to legitimating the domination of privileged social categories within the sociocultural order of the modern West. Ironically, however, it is precisely this com- mitment to "antihegemonic" struggle that has led many Western com- mentators on cultural life under socialism to take up the humanistic interpretation of cultural value prevalent among East European cultural producers themselves. Thus Andrew Solomon writes in the preface to his account of the late-Soviet underground art world:

Where I have used the moral/aesthetic rhetoric of nineteenth-century humanism, I have done so because the nature of Soviet work, and my relation to it, seemed to me to require such language. Though this vocabulary has been often and reasonably challenged in the last thirty years, its aspiring universalism is more apposite to work born out of the resistance to ideology than is the rarefied and often morally neutral or even morally defensive diction of much contemporary criticism.[9]

That is, the appeal that "the moral/aesthetic rhetoric of nineteenth-century humanism" has held for both observers of and participants in cultural life under socialism stemmed from the particular significance cultural activity assumed in the context of a society where alternative forms of political representation and opposition were (largely) suppressed. Furthermore, as the passage from Havel indicates, the narrowness of the bounds that the political authorities attempted to impose on cultural life meant that forms of aesthetic activity that elsewhere might lack any explicitly political content (say, abstract painting) have been interpreted as acts of defiance toward the state.

From an evaluative perspective what we may call the *heroic artist paradigm* of cultural politics under state socialism was clearly hard to challenge as long as the Soviet system was still in existence. The late-socialist order was less dramatically inhumane than its Stalinist predecessor, but it continued to constrict the lives of its subjects in the name of an ideology that, by then, represented no one's interests or desires (arguably not even those of the ruling nomenklatura). Even in the relatively liberal post-Stalin period, professional cultural producers in the Soviet bloc labored under a system of ideological and aesthetic requirements more pervasive and restrictive than those imposed by the most illiberal regimes of the capitalist world.[10] The universalizing humanism espoused by heterodox East European artists and writers may well have been vulnerable to the deconstructive apparatus of Western poststructuralism. Yet at a time when a good number of East European intellectuals were risking unemployment, exile, or imprisonment in the name of individual moral-cultural autonomy, demystifying the ideological system that inspired their struggle can scarcely have been an attractive task for even the most relentless foe of humanism.

The collapse of socialism has radically altered the conditions facing East European cultural producers, raising new evaluative priorities and new questions for critical analysis. Today the most urgent threat to high culture in postsocialist countries is not repression but marginalization. The bulk of their population prefers to consume forms of mass culture to a large extent imported from the commercially-based culture industries of the West. The following lament from the Russian journalist Nadezhda Azhgikhina is fairly representative of how the educated elite of Eastern Europe reacted to the transformation of the postsocialist cultural order in the early 1990s:

About 90 percent of printed matter in the country today consists of pirated translations of foreign science fiction, detective stories, erotic novels . . . the population of the country is reading less. . . . Movie theaters and video stores are flooded with Arnold Schwarzenegger, Sylvester Stallone and erotica. Television is full of foreign and domestic soap operas and melodramatic serials. . . . The streets of Russian cities, once adorned with posters declaring "Glory to the Communist Party," now glitter with advertisements for Coca-Cola, which is accessible to most people, or for IBM computers which are not. . . . Pop culture is so active and aggressive that it seems to be forcing out high culture.[11]

To the extent that the importation of Western mass culture is stimulating the construction of a postsocialist cultural order more responsive to the experiences and concerns of the East European public, its role may be positive.[12] However, its globally disseminated products were not created in dialogue with the specific (and, we may assume, rather distinctive) needs of postsocialist cultural consumers. Their overwhelming dominance within Eastern European markets threatens, therefore, to hinder the development of a vital popular culture responsive to local conditions. Comparative experience suggests that when locally made cultural products of the right kind are available they tend to hold their own against foreign imports; the domination of imported mass culture in East Europe implies that local culture-producing elites have generally failed to respond to popular taste.

With the benefit of hindsight, therefore, the aspiration of East European cultural producers for the status of autonomous artist takes on a problematic aspect. While their struggle under the old regime for "the truth" was frequently justified, quite possibly sincerely, in terms of the need to "serve the people," we may suggest that there was always a latent contradiction between their pursuit of creative autonomy and their willingness to respond to the desires of the mass public whose effects only became fully apparent once both cultural producers and cultural consumers were freed of the restrictions imposed by the socialism. The incompatibility between radical artistic autonomy and national cultural autonomy exposed by the collapse of socialism demands that we reexamine the dynamics of socialist cultural production, treating the ideal of artistic independence as a problem for historical and sociological analysis rather than as a self-evidently attractive organizing premise.

I make no claim to be the first commentator on Soviet cultural life to depart from the heroic artist paradigm. Much recent work on Russian cultural politics has qualified or challenged this perspective from a number of directions. Historical accounts of the formation of the Soviet cultural order during the early Soviet and Stalinist periods have demonstrated the complex and often morally ambiguous character of the relationship between cultural producers and the political leadership.[13] Increased emphasis has been placed on the central role played within Soviet society by cultural forms outside the "high" cultural sphere upon which Western scholarship traditionally tended to focus,[14] a trend reflected in the renewed attention given to popular cinema.[15] And while most Western commentators gave an unequivocal welcome to the new cultural freedoms promised by perestroika, a minority struck a distinctly skeptical note regarding the practicality, or indeed, desirability, of the Russian cultural elite's desire for, as Nancy Condee and Vladimir Padunov sardonically put it, a society with both "full larders and revered poets."[16]

My most direct inspiration for adopting a "revisionist" perspective on this issue derives, however, from the skepticism a number of filmmakers, critics, and scholars within Russia itself now show toward the traditional paradigm. Commenting on the inability of Russia's filmmakers to compete with American cinema for the affections of the mass domestic audience, one contemporary critic, Yuri Bogomolov, states, for instance:

It had been generally accepted [before perestroika] that so-called "auteur" filmmakers, whose works are clear expression of individuality, suffered the worst wounds under the totalitarian dictatorship throughout the 1970s, and that talented craftspeople and professionals who made mass genre movies were better able to adapt to the film production system. In fact, however, we see now that what suffered most were the popular or mass genre movies. . . . [T]he professional level of cinematography was sharply degraded.[17]

A further indication that the crisis of post-Soviet cinema is forcing Russia's filmmaking community to rethink its traditional commitment to creative independence is that a number of the industry insiders I interviewed went so far as to invert the evaluative perspective of the heroic artist paradigm. Whereas traditional accounts of Soviet cinema viewed the Stalin era as the period when the artistic biographies of the pioneering directors of the 1920s were, as Herbert Marshall puts it, "crippled,"[18] several of my contemporary informants (none of whom appeared to be sympathetic to Stalinism as a political system) praised Stalinist cinema for its technical and entertainment quality.

> In the 1940s and 1950s we had excellent entertainment cinema: the movie was a spectacle with a captivating story, an ideological show like *Kuban Cossacks*. . . . After the fall of Stalin they decided this cinema was a lie. It was a lie but not only a lie.[19]

> Our films have got a lot worse since the 1950s. . . . Before then they made fewer films and every detail was checked by a lot of people. There were a few good ones in the 1960s like Bondarchuk's. His were immaculate. Today they're awful—every [technical] aspect of filmmaking here is worse now than in the West.[20]

By the same token, many saw the relative freedom of the post-Stalin Thaw, not as enabling a period of artistic renaissance, but as the source of the problems that contemporary Russian filmmaking now grapples with:

> Our biggest problem is not artistic freedom or the problem of money, but [lack] of professionalism. . . . After the fall of Stalinism we decided that these movies were a lie. . . . [W]e went to the dirty kitchens of communal apartments.[21] We wanted to show the truth. So we destroyed the school of lighting. We didn't want the camera-work to be beautiful.[22]

> In the 1960s our directors tried to get away from genre, influenced by French and Italians, and as usual took foreign ideas too seriously and thought the more naked truth the better and the more popular. And this destroyed the system and it lowered the level of professionalism. Every time [in Russian history] one generation overthrows the last and destroys their achievements. At the end of the Stalin period a lot of people stopped directing and others switched to neorealism.[23]

According to these accounts, the fundamental weakness of the late-Soviet film industry was not the "success" with which its administrators obstructed the quest of filmmakers for self-expression but its failure—relative, at any rate, to the major commercially based industries of the capitalist world—to ensure the production of "professionally made" films oriented toward the tastes of the broad public. Understanding the roots of this failure is one of the central goals of this study.

THEORIZING ARTISTIC AUTONOMY

What Western reappraisals of the relationship between cultural producers and the state under socialism have rarely done is consider the aspiration for creative autonomy within the context of a general theoretical model of the socialist system of cultural production. Katherine Verdery's study of cultural politics in Ceauşescu's Romania, *National Ideology under Socialism*, stands out as an important exception to this rule.[24] She sets out a model of the relationship between cultural production and the basic characteristics of socialist political economy that offers a number of insights into the dynamics of the Soviet film world—most particularly, her thesis that socialist cultural politics was driven by competition for centrally allocated symbolic and material resources. However, her assumption that theories based on Western conditions are inapplicable to East European societies owing to the unique character of the "laws of motion" of socialist political economy tends to foreclose possibilities for comparative analysis.[25] I assume that, while distinctive, the Soviet system of cultural production was not so exceptional as to render conceptual tools developed in relation to the Western experience entirely useless. Indeed, I argue that applying them allows us to reach a more precise understanding of exactly what it was that made the Soviet conditions distinctive. A comparative perspective can also be justified in terms of its topical relevance: understanding the relative weakness of the culture industries of the formerly socialist countries takes on an additional urgency now that they are subject to direct competition with those of the West.

From a historical perspective, the aspiration of cultural producers for creative autonomy is the outcome of a particular and relatively recent process of social and ideological development. While all class-stratified societies have possessed specialized cultural producers, before the modern period, artistic autonomy existed neither as a practical possibility nor even as a publicly expressed aspiration. In the medieval West, elite forms of cultural production depended on the economic support of the church, the monarchy, and the nobility and directly served the ideological and status needs of their patrons. The consolidation of art as a distinct "institution" (to use Peter Bürger's expression) within society—that is, as a sphere of symbolic production defined precisely by its nonutility to external social groups—took place through a series of ideological and practical breaks that began with the Renaissance and culminated with Romanticism. Each of these breaks was enabled by the emergence or consolidation of alternative sources of patronage with new ideological requirements; thus the secular character of seventeenth-century French theater, for instance, depended on the support of a centralizing monarchy, the socially reformist literature of the Enlightenment on the formation of an increasingly wealthy and ideologically self-confident bourgeoisie.[26]

The final consolidation of the ideal of the artist as a charismatic self-sufficient individual, expressing transcendent rather than socially functional values and indifferent, if not actively hostile, to the tastes of his or her public took place in response to the growth of an impersonal market for cultural goods in the late eighteenth and early nineteenth centuries. The Romantic ideal of art expressed the paradoxical combination of freedom and insecurity that cultural producers experienced once their direct dependence on individual patronage was ended. Once formed, it stimulated the development of modes of creative practice increasingly alien to the tastes of the largely bourgeois public for "high" cultural products.[27] From this perspective, the socialist order of cultural production had a contradictory aspect. On the one hand, as Boris Groys has argued, it can be interpreted as an attempt to return creative workers to the unalienated yet subjugated status they had occupied under feudalism. Their function was once again to act as eulogists of the political leadership and reproducers of ideological doxa. In return they were to be "freed" from the vagaries of the marketplace to bask in the generous and unwavering support of the state.[28] On the other hand, the Romantic view of the artist as unique, charismatic genius remained an important influence on official policy toward cultural producers. As the Czech writer Ivan Klinka puts it:

It is true that the system took a crudely ideological view of art. . . . On the other hand, the ideology which the system (at least initially) believed in, was an odd mixture of nineteenth century rationalism and

romanticism, incorporating something of that century's attitude to artists. As a result, the rulers . . . accorded great respect to the person of
the artist, and felt a need to possess their own recognized figures . . .
the ideologues dreamed of finding, or even creating, then decorating
with titles, their own Tolstoy or Dostoyevsky, or at least a Turgenev,
for which they were willing not only to use violence, but also to lavish
wealth and favors upon their chosen ones.[29]

We see here that the conception of the artist as moral exemplar and individual genius that informed the claims of heterodox cultural producers to
freedom shared basic assumptions with official views on the arts. Thus
the leadership's cultural policies fostered the cult of the autonomous artist by upholding its ideological value, while simultaneously attempting to
prevent its practice.

My approach to the dynamics of the Soviet film industry assumes that
the basic premise of the "production perspective" to the sociology of
culture—that all forms of cultural production are influenced by the immediate social context within which creative workers operate—is as applicable under socialism as under capitalism.[30]

As Howard Becker and others have shown, even forms of cultural production like poetry or painting, conventionally interpreted as the creation
of individual authors, are influenced by other social actors and institutions such as peer groups, critics, dealers, publishers, museums, academic
institutions, and so on. No individual can achieve social recognition as an
artist except by defining his or her creative projects in relation to the
norms established by this social context. This is as true of the most experimental or transgressive member of the avant-garde as it is of the conventional traditionalist. Not only does this social context influence the
artistic goals of creative workers, through the operation of formal or informal systems of selection, evaluation, and distribution, it ultimately determines what works are accorded the status of art. Art, as Howard
Becker has put it, is necessarily a "form of collective action."[31] In these
terms, what distinguished Soviet cultural producers from their Western
counterparts was not that they were subject to external social influences
but rather the particular form these influences took under socialism. Most
obviously, in addition to the expectations of peers, editors, and critics,
any Soviet cultural producer working within what I call the "authorized"

sphere had to negotiate a system of ideologically inspired censorship and patronage backed by the full authority of the state.

All forms of cultural production may ultimately be "collective," but not all are collective to the same extent or in the same manner. Most sociologists of the arts and mass media draw a clear distinction between the social dynamics at work within industrial as against nonindustrial spheres of cultural production. Pierre Bourdieu, for instance, proposes a division between a sphere of "restricted cultural production" and one of "large-scale production." In the former, production is subject to an "autonomous principle of hierarchization" under which the approbation of other cultural producers (and, we may add, culturally elite gatekeepers) determines the value of works and the status of their creators. The latter sphere he characterizes as "heteronomous," in that its products are consciously designed to conform to the tastes of a broad public outside the sphere of cultural production, generally in the interests of commercial profit. In conventional discourse the status of "art" is associated primarily with the autonomous sphere, while the products of the large-scale sphere are generally classified as "mass," or "popular" culture.[32]

Table 1 summarizes some of the basic contrasts between the two spheres as they exist within the contemporary West. Owing to the inherent technological characteristics of cinema, films are expensive to produce but relatively cheap to distribute and exhibit.[33] In capitalist countries much filmmaking, therefore, has taken place within the sphere of large-scale production organized by private corporations to maximize profits through distribution to the widest possible audience.[34] Creative authority within the commercial sector tends in a very direct sense to be "collective" and indeed bureaucratic in nature—the major decisions are made through complex negotiations between a variety of agents, the most powerful of whom are motivated by financial rather than artistic considerations.

Alongside this "commercial" sector, however, has grown up a tradition of "art" (or in the United States, "independent") cinema, which conforms more closely to the characteristics of the sphere of restricted production. In the art sector individual directors possess far greater creative control over their work, leading them to be termed *auteurs* (authors) within conventional film criticism. (I do not refer here to the usage of the term *auteur* within academic film theory, where it has generally been used to refer to directors working within the commercial industry whose work

Table 1.   Art versus mass culture in the contemporary West

	Sphere of Restricted Production	Sphere of Large-scale Production
Conventional classification	High culture / Art	Mass / Popular culture
Primary goal of production	Symbolic profit ("Artistic reputation")	Economic profit
Intended audience	Other cultural producers / cultural elites	Mass audience(s)
Social determinants on creative practice	Esteem of peer circles, critics, gatekeepers ("autonomous hierarchization")	Mass audience taste as interpreted by corporate management ("heteronomous hierarchization")
Aesthetic tendencies	Innovation, differentiation, negativity	Standardization and stability within proven genre conventions, affirmation

is held, nevertheless, to display an individual aesthetic.) Orientation toward financial profit tends to be weak in this sector, either because it receives subsidies from the state (as in Western Europe) or because costs are kept low enough to be returned through limited commercial distribution (more typical of "independent" cinema). In either case, the audience tends to be far smaller and better educated than that for mainstream commercial cinema. The dichotomy between art and commercial sectors should not be overdrawn: the organizational and technological complexity of film production and its consequent high financial cost place limits on the scope for individual creative autonomy within all but the lowest budget forms of art cinema, while creative workers retain some room for self-expression within even the most regimented commercial system.[35] Nevertheless, the conventional distinction possesses a degree of descriptive usefulness, since commercial and art cinemas are generally produced within different institutional contexts (or even countries), secure funding from different sources, and aim their products at different publics.

From this perspective, the nature of the Soviet film industry was thoroughly ambiguous. On the one hand, it was clearly the functional equivalent of the major commercial culture industries of the West, in that it was bureaucratically organized and created products disseminated to a mass audience that were supposed to embody centrally determined aesthetic norms. On the other, it was not ruled by the "law of profit" and was viewed by both the authorities and many of its creative workers as a site for the production of "art." To understand its social determinants, therefore, we must both employ the institutional and political-economic modes of analysis that those working within the production perspective have applied to the sphere of large-scale production in the West and consider the dynamics of the competitive struggle for symbolic prestige that Bourdieu sees as governing the restricted sphere of high art.

CULTURAL PRODUCTION AND CLASS IDENTITY

The emphasis of the production perspective on the influence of the immediate social conditions within which cultural works are created may be distinguished from an older theoretical tradition within the sociology of culture that interprets works as "reflections" of broader forms of collective consciousness—a tradition most highly developed in the work of Marxist cultural theorists such as George Lukacs and Lucien Goldmann, who concentrated on the issue of socioeconomic class ideology.[36] While this mode of analysis has informed sometimes highly sophisticated readings of cultural texts, its practitioners (perhaps because by taste and trade they tend to be philologists rather than sociologists) have tended to adopt an extremely simplistic model of the relationship between class consciousness and the ideological significance of cultural works. As Peter Golding and Graham Murdock point out in "Ideology and the Mass Media," the ostensible "materialism" of textually based attempts at ideological analysis is vitiated if they fail to take into account the determinations imposed by the immediate social and political-economic conditions within which these texts are produced. (Within film theory a classic example of extreme imbalance between hermeneutic subtlety and simplistic socioeconomic analysis is offered by *Cahiers du cinéma*'s interpretation of John Ford's *Young Mr. Lincoln*.)[37]

The primary focus of this study, however, is not the significance of cinematic texts themselves, but the discourses that their creators produced concerning their role and status as artists. That is, I do not ask what kinds of ideology were expressed by art but rather what kinds of ideology were created about art (although clearly the latter had some impact on the nature of the works themselves). While this approach still requires us to take into account the influence of the immediate social milieu within which filmmakers operated, I argue that there was a direct correspondence between their views on art and the ideology of the general social category to which, by virtue of their professional status and most typical sociocultural background, they belonged—the *intelligentsia*. Indeed, as I will explore in Chapter 1, the relationship between artistic ideology and the most prominent forms of "class consciousness" was particularly close under socialist conditions because social structure was defined by the possession (or lack) of, not private property, but what Bourdieu calls "cultural capital," that is, legitimate cultural knowledge and taste. We can, therefore, avoid the difficulties faced by traditional Marxian, class-based approaches to cultural production that attempt to explain the behavior of artists and intellectuals in terms of their positioning within a system of *economically* defined classes. In economic terms, under capitalism, nothing clearly distinguishes cultural producers from other elements of the educated middle classes. Under Soviet conditions, however, social hierarchy was defined primarily by possession of cultural capital. The claim Soviet cultural producers made to artistic autonomy, along with the elevated sense of the role and dignity of art that this implied, may be interpreted as a specific expression of the Soviet educated elite's consciousness of itself as a class. Central to this sense of identity was the belief that those who were culturally superior were also morally superior and thus entitled to leadership over society as a whole.

Taking this approach allows us to "demystify" the universalizing pretensions of the cult of the autonomous artist without going to the other extreme of reducing it to nothing more than an instrumental strategy deployed in the self-interested pursuit of prestige. That is, from a class perspective, these claims may be interpreted as expressing beliefs sincerely held at an individual level which nevertheless draw their strength from the sense of status characteristic of a specific, and highly privileged, sector of society.[38]

We should view, therefore, the claim filmmakers made to creative freedom as motivated by their allegiance to the class culture of the intelligentsia rather than the expression of a self-evidently attractive ideal shared by every (right-thinking) member of Soviet society. Whereas the most highly educated sections of society took a passionate interest in the struggle of nonconformist cultural producers for self-expression and the works that grew out of that struggle, the less educated majority was generally content to consume products that the intelligentsia viewed as trivial or mendacious. Indeed, in the Soviet Union as in other socialist societies, the cultural tastes of the political leadership were a good deal closer to those of the "masses" than to those of the educated class. As the dissident Czech intellectual Antonin Liehm wrote in the 1960s:

Our leaders didn't read books, didn't visit theaters or exhibits or concert halls . . . and yet they sat down once a week and examined films. And because the people who made these films read books, visited theaters and concert halls, traveled in the world—their experiences were remarkably evident in their films, especially in the better ones— misunderstandings naturally arose. I do not understand, shouted the centralized omnipotent power, and this of course meant that the film was the work of Satan. . . . And because the vast majority of people do not read books, do not visit theaters or concerts . . . the centralized power is convinced that its opinion is the opinion of the people and vice versa.[39]

We see here the origins of a disjuncture between the creative aspirations of the filmmakers and the cultural tastes of the mass public whose effects became glaringly evident when, following perestroika, both were liberated from official control.

PART ONE

BEFORE THE REVOLT

1

ART AND THE INTELLIGENTSIA

The theme of this chapter is the relationship between late-Soviet cultural producers' sense of their creative mission and a broader pattern of status consciousness characteristic of the Soviet educated class as a whole. I contend that the aspiration of cultural producers to the elevated, altruistic, and autonomous status of "artist" was a specific expression of a sense among highly educated Soviets that appreciation of high culture and moral superiority were inextricably linked. This ideological complex informed the intelligentsia's sense of superiority in relation to both the political-administrative elite and the popular classes. In the specific context of cinema, it shaped and motivated the claim by late-Soviet filmmakers that their activity should be free from the pressures of both political supervision and mass audience demand.

ART AGAINST OPPORTUNISM

In 1980, the prominent Soviet director Eldar Ryazanov gave a speech before the Filmmakers' Union whose major theme was the incompatibility between art and what he referred to as "opportunism" (*prisposoblench-estvo*):[1]

It is impossible to live from one official campaign to the next. There is only one concern—the state of the people's soul, their health, their stomach, their garb. And if all this does not inspire the artist, what kind of artist is he, anyway? He is simply making a living! . . . *The criterion of a master, an artist, a man of art has been substantially lowered and diluted by a great number of hacks and opportunists.*

Speaking of opportunists, *we are accustomed to think that an opportunist always desires to please the big bosses*, to do a picture or a book that appeals to the leadership. That is an oversimplified concept: there are for example foreign-travel opportunists, who make films which appeal to international festival audiences.[2] (Emphasis added)

Ryazanov was here following a tradition, going as far back in Russian cultural discourse as the nineteenth-century literary critic Vissarion Belinsky, within which the true artist is defined as someone who refuses to pander to the powers-that-be but is inspired, rather, by selfless concern for "the people." Within this tradition, as Isaiah Berlin puts it,

The man and the artist and the citizen are one; and whether you write a novel, or a poem, or a work of history or philosophy, or an article in a newspaper, or compose a symphony or a picture, you are, or should be, expressing the whole of your nature, not merely a professionally trained part of it, and you are morally responsible as a man for what you do as an artist. You must always bear witness to the truth, which is one and indivisible, in every act and in every word. There are no purely aesthetic truths or aesthetic canons. . . . [W]hat is intellectually false or morally ugly cannot be artistically beautiful, or vice versa.[3]

Ryazanov's contrast between the "artist" and the "opportunist" is indicative of a structural opposition within the field of late-Soviet filmmaking between the dual "principles of hierarchization" Bourdieu identifies within the field of (French) cultural production. On the one hand, the "autonomous" principle under which status is awarded by other cultural producers, and on the other, the "heteronomous" principle under which the criteria for success are established externally, either by the mass market or by the dominant class.[4] The manner in which these two principles worked to define rival criteria for status within the late-Soviet film world comes across in the following passage from a history of Soviet cinema written by the liberal film critic Neya Zorkaya during the perestroika period:

[Under Brezhnev a] process of unofficial stratification took place: filmmakers grouped around two poles.

One group willingly abided by the law of the Goskino, made "commissioned" films their superiors were sure to like, and thus earned "most favored nation treatment" as far as film shooting, funds, interesting trips, bonuses and other privileges were concerned. Alas, not only hacks but also some of the really gifted filmmakers who had begun successfully in the 1950s and the 1960s made the fatal choice. By doing so they gradually gave up their artistic positions.

However, neither official recognition nor laurels could ensure the progress of art. That's why I have no intention of dwelling on the officious first-night shows of many mediocre pictures that did not deserve their awards or nationwide "fame"; they were typical enough of the 1970s.

. . . I will be concerned only with the opposite group—searching and genuine artists who never betrayed their ideals and principles and who created immortal masterpieces. . . . Even in the 1970s their names were known to many true viewers, and they shine especially brightly now when the fresh winds of change have swept away the restrictions and bans.[5]

While this is clearly not an impartial account, it does suggest that alongside and in opposition to the officially established hierarchy among late-Soviet filmmakers, there existed an informal prestige structure within which rank was awarded on the basis of noncompliance with the authorities' demands. In practice the existence of these opposing principles of hierarchization did not result in as neat a division into two distinct groups as Zorkaya implies. As one scriptwriter put it to me: "People tend to oversimplify how we lived back then. In fact, there were a thousand ways of being a dissident and a thousand of being a conformist."[6] The vital point remains, however, that the more fully filmmakers complied with official demands the more likely they were to forfeit the esteem of their peers. In the revolution of 1986 the relationship between these hierarchies was reversed, as the informally recognized filmmaking elite displaced the figures elevated by the authorities under Brezhnev from positions of leadership and influence within the industry.

* * *

The ideology of artistic autonomy was not confined to cinema. It appears to have influenced creative workers across the spectrum of late-Soviet cultural production, including those who did not achieve star status in either the official or the unofficial hierarchy. The complexities involved in negotiating the contradictory demands between moral-artistic integrity and conformity to official demands are suggested by the recollections of a retired sculptor whose professional career spanned the period from the 1950s until perestroika. Although she had never held any managerial position in the cultural bureaucracy, she described herself, albeit somewhat ironically, as a "nomenklatura artist" (*nomenklaturnaya khudozhnitsa*) because she had been a member of the state-organized Artists' Union, through whom she was assigned her studio and apartment in central Moscow.

Most of her work was commissioned by *kombinaty*, state organizations to which a number of sculptors were attached that acted as middlemen between artists and buyers—assigning state commissions and providing materials. Some works, however, she produced at her own initiative for exhibition, where they might be bought by (state) museums and, occasionally, directly by private individuals. (Private sales were tolerated, but the market was too limited for them to provide an adequate source of income.)

(GF: What kinds of subjects did you depict?)
In what area—exhibitions or commissioned work for *kombinaty*? For *kombinaty* portraits, for instance, soldiers [laughs], Lenin, and so on. Stalin I never did. . . . A lot of Lenins because that was my bread and butter and I wanted to buy my own apartment. . . . It's not pleasant for me to remember that work. But what I did for exhibition was more free, more what I wanted to do. When you do Lenin it's not your own, it's always the same. In the beginning I thought that I would always make things I liked. But then I had a son and I divorced my husband. And then another girl came along and so I had to work for the *kombinat* and it was very unpleasant. . . .
(GF: What personal qualities did it take to be successful as an artist?)
One type of person, talented and energetic, will be successful under any system. But for an average artist—well, if I'd joined the Party it would have been a lot easier. But I had a tender conscience and I'd have felt that I had to approve of what happened in Hungary and

Czechoslovakia [the Soviet invasions of 1956 and 1968]. . . . Because of the principle of democratic centralism, it didn't really make any difference whether you approved or not. But it's a problem of separating inner character [*lichnost'*] from outward appearance [*vneshnost'*]. I don't know why some could do it and others couldn't. . . .

I had to do a portrait of Zhdanov [Stalin's much-hated minister of culture] and so I did some reading about him and discovered what kind of person he was. I didn't want to do it. I could have refused but I was going through a difficult period [financially] so I did it. But at the exhibitions that I did myself, I never once did a Communist leader. . . .

(GF: Did you feel a sense of solidarity with other people who were disenchanted with the Party?)

I wouldn't call it solidarity. We simply understood each other and were friendly to each other. But we tolerated those who joined the Party for convenience. It was a question for their own conscience [*sovest'*]. But if they did Lenin and Krupskaya [Lenin's wife] for exhibition then we didn't respect them—they'd sold their souls. For instance [X], who lives in our block, did Krupskaya. She collected many honors, got many commissions and the chance to sell to foreigners for a lot of money.[7]

She was forced by the state's position as a virtually monopolistic buyer of her work to spend most of her career turning out pieces she found both creatively unsatisfying and politically distasteful. (Her bread-and-butter specialty was Lenin-as-an-infant.) However, she also sees herself as having sacrificed her career advancement, specifically her possibility of receiving the most lucrative and prestigious commissions, by refusing to join the Party or demonstrate her "spontaneous" enthusiasm for official ideology by turning out pieces on orthodox subjects in her less-restricted exhibition work. And while she refuses to condemn her colleagues who did join the Party, she sees those who made Lenins "freely" as beyond the moral and aesthetic pale.

As her account suggests, the surest way for a cultural producer to win official favor was to take on the kind of "commissioned theme" (*zakaznaya tema*), of which Bondarchuk's films celebrating Brezhnev's deeds in World War II are particularly blatant examples. She also indicates the distaste that this decision could provoke among more scrupulous peers, that is, the inverse relationship between official and unofficial forms of prestige. A common motif of (noncommissioned!) late-Soviet film and literature was, in fact, the creative and moral bankruptcy suffered by cultural producers who succumbed to this temptation. For instance, Gleb Panfilov's shelved film *Theme* (*Tema*, 1980) portrays the emotional crisis of a playwright who reexamines his life choices while trying to work on a "patriotic" commissioned play about the medieval Russian hero, Prince Igor. Even the apparently "safe" Soviet genre of the production novel could be adapted to this theme, like for instance, Grigory Baklanov's 1975 novel *Friends* (*Druz'ya*), which contrasts an architect who conforms to bureaucratic demands with another who holds on to his professional and creative integrity.

Judging by the account given by Thomas Cushman in his ethnographic study of the Leningrad rock scene, *Notes from Underground*, the cult of artistic autonomy was also evident in the unofficial, "underground," sphere of cultural production, which emerged as an important force in the late-Soviet period.[8] Most rock musicians stressed that their work was a form of "art" and expressed a sense of creative mission similar to that contained in Ryazanov's discourse, one stating for instance that "all art ought to serve the purpose of making man's soul clearer and higher."[9] For Leningrad rockers, the equivalent of the conformist "hacks and opportunists" condemned by Ryazanov were members of the so-called Vocal-Instrumental Ensembles (VIAs), which with the approval of the Soviet authorities, purveyed an innocuous form of pop music (known derogatorily as *popsa*).[10] Unlike their counterparts in the rock underground, VIA performers enjoyed the status of professional musicians: they were allowed to play publicly and to release their music through the state record company, Melodiya. Whereas lyrics in the rock underground were generally elliptical in form and philosophically and morally "serious" in content, the lyrics of VIA compositions tended to be simple, clichéd, and on romantic or nostalgic themes. (We should note, however, that they were not usually explicitly ideological in content.)

In her examination of cultural politics in Romania, Verdery argues that the claim East European intellectuals frequently made for the independence of cultural and intellectual values from political direction was a response to the sense of marginalization many experienced within state socialism's peculiarly centralized system of cultural institutions:

> The Party sets up an education system that produces more intellectuals than its "ideological apparatus" can absorb. Those whose thinking is

congenial and whose ambitions permit a collaboration with power enter into alliance with it. The remainder, whose preference or unsuitability excludes them, are left with a sense that they are entitled to influence—on the basis of their knowledge—but they can achieve it only by claiming that their knowledge, or artistic creativity constitutes separate grounds for status. For them that is, influence depends upon their gaining recognition for their cultural authority as something independent of the political status to which the Party wants to restrict the exercise of cultural power.[11]

This model is helpful in interpreting the role that the claim to artistic autonomy played in structuring the factional struggles within the official apparatus of cultural production. It does not, however, explain why categories of cultural producers who had clearly opted out of the official sphere were equally insistent in opposing their elevated and moralistic conception of art to officially sanctioned cultural norms. There is no evidence, for instance, that Leningrad rockers turned to the underground only after being excluded from the official music establishment, yet their contempt for what they saw as the unchallenging diversions of popsa was at least as uncompromising as that of nonconformist filmmakers for "opportunist" cinema. That is, cultural producers appear to have adhered to the ideology of artistic autonomy even when they had no direct interest in furthering their status within the official sphere of production. Nor can it account for the willingness of some cultural producers who occupied, or had the potential to occupy, advantageous positions in the official cultural hierarchy to jeopardize their status by staking a claim to autonomy from the state (Ryazanov's 1980 speech exemplifies this tendency). This does not, however, imply that we have to accept at face value the universalizing humanistic significance Soviet cultural producers themselves attached to the status of autonomous artist. Rather, we should see the cult of the artist as a specific expression of a wider ideological complex that has played a vital role in defining the identity of the collective group to which cultural producers belonged by virtue of their social function and their typical family background—that is, the Soviet intelligentsia.

THE INTELLIGENTSIA IDEA: ORIGINS AND SIGNIFICANCE

Since it was first introduced in the 1860s, the term "intelligentsia" has occupied a central place in Russian public discourse.[12] Most simply, the term denotes the class of people possessing higher education and employed in occupations involving mental rather than manual labor. In late-Soviet social discourse this general category was frequently subdivided into the "creative intelligentsia," which included intellectuals and professional cultural producers, the "scientific intelligentsia," and the more numerous "broad" or "mass" intelligentsia, those working within the lower-status professions requiring a postsecondary education, such as medicine, engineering, and education. A notable feature of the term "intelligentsia" as it was officially defined was that it included within its bounds the social grouping referred to in nonofficial discourse as the *nomenklatura*, that is, Party and state officials. As we will see, this classification was symptomatically silent about the crucial division perceived by intelligentsia outside the nomenklatura between themselves and those within it.

The full significance of the term "intelligentsia" cannot be understood without taking into account the normative cultural, moral, and political connotations it has assumed since first popularized in the nineteenth century. For most educated Russians, to claim the status of *intelligent* it was not enough merely to be knowledgeable and refined, these capacities had, in one way or another, to be dedicated to the general betterment of society. As the Populist Pyotr Lavrov wrote in the 1870s: "[Just as] not every one that saith unto me, Lord, Lord, shall enter into the kingdom of heaven, not every educated person can become a member of the group of critically thinking individuals [that in his opinion constituted the intelligentsia]."[13] We should see the term, therefore, as a social signifier that attained its central place in Russian public discourse through its deployment in the cultural elite's historically continuous but never finally resolved debate regarding its identity and role within society. Each alternative normative definition of intelligentsia identity emphasized different kinds of responsibilities. Although many educated Russians did not share the Populists' definition of the intelligentsia as a "critically thinking" social group dedicated to achieving social justice through revolution, most appear to have assented to the general proposition that cultural and intellectual attainments carried with them *some* kind of wider duty to society; for an educated person to refuse to assume any kind of responsibility to society would imply forgoing his or her claim to the positively valorized status of intelligent. We should also note, however, that while this assumption of social responsibility was discursively presented as an act of altruistic self-denial (and in historical practice, a good number of educated Russians have sacrificed everything, up to and including their lives, for what they believed to be the general good), it also implied the claim that, as bearers of superior knowledge, they were entitled to, as George Konrad and Ivan Szelenyi put it, define social *telos*—that is, society's ultimate goals.[14]

Clearly, the idea that education carries with it the right and duty to assume social leadership has not been a uniquely Russian phenomenon. Nevertheless, by comparison with Western (and most particularly anglophone) societies, this conception defined the identity and aspirations of the entire educated class rather than those of a limited number of oppositional intellectuals. In their well-known work *Intellectuals on the Road to Class Power*, Konrad and Szelenyi trace this difference to the distinct path that Eastern Europe, and most particularly Russia, took toward modernization in the eighteenth and nineteenth centuries. In the modern West, the growth of secular education has been largely stimulated by the need of capitalist industrialization for trained technical and managerial labor. In Russia, by contrast, the formation of the educated class from which the intelligentsia arose was initiated by the state in the interests of international military competition and cultural prestige.[15] It came into being, therefore, in the context of a society still subject to the jealous rule of a determinedly autocratic regime; one that, moreover, was virtually the sole employer of educated labor, owing to the laggard development of capitalism. Given these conditions, the educated elite could not advance its particular interests as a class without challenging the entire sociopolitical order.[16] That is, the intelligentsia of tsarist Russia took upon itself the historical role that Marx predicted for the proletariat in the capitalist countries of Western Europe.

The autocracy's suppression of legal means for expressing political dissent had the further consequence of foregrounding literary fiction's role in expressing and forming the sociopolitical concerns of the nascent educated class. Adapting Louis Althusser's theory of "interpellation," under which ideology shapes identity through a process of "hailing" and self-recognition,[17] we may argue that by *addressing* its public as moral and social agents rather than as mere consumers of entertainment and diversion, literature encouraged the tsarist educated class to *recognize* itself as a distinct group with a particular social mission. As Belinsky wrote in the middle of the nineteenth century: "Our literature has created the morals of our society, has already educated several generations . . . has produced a sort of special class in society [composed] of people of all estates who have been drawn together through education, which with us, is centered exclusively in a love of literature."[18]

As Berlin and others have observed, the peculiarly prominent role literature played in tsarist society fostered an intensely moralistic conception of aesthetic value in the intelligentsia; we can also see this process as working the other way, however; that is, as encouraging the development of a discourse in which an individual's capacity to appreciate high culture was treated as intrinsic to his or her moral worth. This discursive association between cultivation and morality is evident in the intelligentsia's perennial hostility toward "philistinism."

THE INTELLIGENTSIA'S "SENSE OF DISTINCTION"

Although Russian intellectuals have rarely agreed on the positive content of the intelligentsia ideal, they have rarely differed in their definition of its antithesis. Since the nineteenth century this cluster of negative attributes, which includes narrow-minded self-interest, careerism, grasping materialism, and lack of cultural taste, has been labeled using the term *meshchanstvo*.[19] A Russian word with no exact equivalent in English (it is usually translated as "philistinism"), it originally denoted the merchant estate of pre-Petrine Muscovy. By the nineteenth century it had become a generalized term used by *intelligenty* of all ideological stripes to stigmatize nonintelligentsia modes of thought and behavior. R. V. Ivanov-Razumnik's 1906 *History of Russian Social Thought* offers a representative sample of pre-Revolutionary anti-meshchanstvo rhetoric: "Anything deep the *meshchanin* renders shallow, anything wide he makes narrow, anything brightly individual he converts into dull mediocrity."[20]

The following passage from a 1987 article "On the Traditions of Our Country's Intelligentsia," indicates the role that meshchantsvo continued to play as defining Other within late-Soviet intelligentsia discourse:

If . . . I were to search for the so-called dialectical counterpart to the concept of "intelligentsia," I would doubtless choose the notion of the philistine and petit bourgeois. When the inferior takes the place of the superior, and when idle talk, indifference to society's concerns, the cult of rank and conformist time-serving replace concern for getting the job done, one is faced with manifestations of philistinism. They are incompatible with membership of the intelligentsia, a philistine member of the intelligentsia, a money-grubbing member of the intelligentsia—can such a person exist? From a scientific, theoretical point of view, this is nonsense, a logical absurdity. But in real life, it turns out, one encounters such a "unity of opposites."[21]

Yuri Trifonov's Moscow novellas of the late 1960s, one of the best-known literary portrayals of the mores of the late-Soviet educated elite, explore and, to an extent, satirize the role that the association between cultural knowledge and moral worth played in structuring intelligentsia perceptions of social status.

In Trifonov's 1970 novella *Taking Stock*, the narrator and protagonist, Gennady, self-deprecatingly presents himself as a kind of intelligentsia Everyman, though his occupation of literary translator in fact places him rather close to the pinnacle of the Soviet cultural hierarchy: "Class: average intellectual of the late 1960s. Genus: literary proletarian. Species: failure, but usually manages to get by."[22] Looking back on his life from the vantage of a health-imposed exile in Central Asia, he recalls how he put his cultural knowledge to work for distinctly worldly ends:

> From the window of my room I look out at these former possessions of the Shah and think to myself: *Also sprach Zarathustra*. I have a passion for quotations and am always plucking them from books. *Also*, I think with satisfaction, *sprach Zarathustra*. A wonderfully concise quotation and one that has accompanied me my whole life. It suggests a philosophical attitude toward life, erudition, intellectuality, a knowledge of foreign languages and at the same time, nonsense and deception. For most of my knowledge is superficial, my intellectuality is only for show, and I've never seriously read any Nietzsche. . . .
>
> Once I managed to turn a certain girl's head. . . . The girl sat on the sofa . . . and recited her own poems, which struck me as beautiful. I in turn asked her, "Have you ever read *Also sprach Zarathustra*?" And afterward, on the basis of my petty deception, she responded to my boyish advances.[23]

The association between culture and human worth does not always work to Gennady's advantage, however. Criticized by his wife Rita for his failure to appreciate classical music, he voices his private skepticism about the moral value of culture:

Rita would blush and turn to me reproachfully, "Why is it you're so ignorant when it comes to music? . . . No, you really can't be considered a truly cultured person!" Nor have I ever thought of myself as one.

But not at all because I'm not an expert on music.

It's true that I don't understand serious music. . . . What can I do? It's a shortcoming, a defect, a flaw in my spiritual makeup—but why keep reproaching me for it? Good lord, a love of music doesn't reveal anything about a person. It doesn't determine his *humanity*. Snakes like music too. . . . One can love music and still be a cynic.[24]

That is, Gennady doesn't consider himself "truly cultured" in the sense employed by the Russian intelligentsia, not because he lacks cultural taste but because he feels that he lacks the moral standards that would make him genuinely worthy of the epithet. His wife appears to lack these self-doubts and becomes involved in a fashionable circle that turns to pre-Revolutionary religious philosophy not, according to Gennady's jaundiced account, as part of any yearning for spirituality but out of conformity to the latest intellectual fad.[25] She and her friends engage in a frantic competitive quest for icons. Having acquired one from the family's peasant maid (for whom we are told they actually are objects of religious veneration), she hangs it, in a nice satirical touch from Trifonov, in their apartment, "next to the large Picasso."[26]

Trifonov's 1968 novella *The Exchange* (*Obmen*) explores the relationship between culture and morality by contrasting the values and behavior of two families related by marriage, the Dmitrievs and the Lukyanovs. The Dmitrievs are an old intelligentsia family that still cherishes its revolutionary traditions; his wife Lena's family, the Lukyanovs, are a late-Soviet avatar of the *meshchane*. Despite their distinguished revolutionary past, perhaps even because of it, the Dmitrievs look down on the Lukyanovs in a somewhat lordly fashion for their lack of cultural sophistication and the openness with which they pursue self-interest: "[Dmitriev's] mother called her new relative [the father of Lena, her new daughter-in-law] 'the learned neighbor'—behind his back of course and considered that he was not a bad man, in some ways nice even, though of course not at all of the intelligentsia, unfortunately . . . of a different breed—those 'who know how to live.' "[27]

By contrast, Dmitriev characterizes his own family as suffering from an excess of intelligentsia disinterestedness, musing upon "their noble inability [to succeed in life] . . . which they are secretly proud of."[28] Lena herself lacks the scruples of her husband's family, and her contempt for their pretensions to moral and cultural superiority comes out during an argument with Dmitriev's openly snobbish cousin, Marina:

> There were some arguments about poetry, about how universal philistinism [*meshchantsvo*] was. Marina loved this theme and didn't miss a chance to trample on philistinism. Those philistines! When she was fuming about the existence of people who hadn't heard of Picasso or the sculptor Erzya, something coiled up in her mouth seemed to glisten.
>
> Everything that Marina hated about the word "philistinism," Lena hated about the word "hypocrisy" [*khanzhestvo*]. She declared, "All that's hypocrisy." . . .
>
> [Marina:] "Hypocrisy? . . . Liking Picasso is hypocrisy? . . . So you tell me then: what do you call hypocrisy?"
>
> [Lena:] "Well, everything that's done not from the heart, but with an ulterior motive, out of wanting to make oneself look good."
>
> [Marina:] "Aha! So that means you are being hypocritical when you visit Aunt Ksenya [Dmitriev's mother] on her birthday and bring her sweets?"[29]

In certain respects *The Exchange* displays Trifonov's adherence to the traditional intelligentsia belief that, as he put it in a published interview, "the world can only survive with altruists."[30] Yet at the same time, he is too scrupulous a social observer not to make clear the distinctly worldly advantages that *presenting* oneself as cultured and altruistic offered members of the educated class. Like many other intelligentsia commentators of the period he accuses his class of capitulating to the amoral pursuit of narrow-minded self-interest.[31] Whatever the empirical accuracy of these claims (and we might question whether the golden age of generalized intelligentsia altruism he found so lacking in the late-Soviet educated had ever actually existed), they do not indicate the demise of the intelligentsia ideal as a principle structuring social distinction within Soviet society. If anything, these accusations testify to its continuing relevance: *intelligentnost* retains its discursive importance so long as its meshchantsvo other is considered worthy of condemnation.

*   *   *

The dichotomy between intelligentnost and meshchantsvo has a particular significance for the manner in which cultural producers conceived of their relationship to society at large. By identifying moral altruism with elevated cultural taste, it creates an opposition precisely homologous to the one we identified between art and opportunism in Ryazanov and Zorkaya's discourse. That is, the opposition between art and opportunism may be seen as a translation of the more general opposition between intelligentsia and meshchantsvo from the realm of social discourse to that of cultural politics: like the meshchanin, the opportunist cultural producer was deemed both morally and culturally deficient. We can further argue that the fundamental role that this discursive complex played in defining the intelligentsia's sense of identity fostered a sense among the cultural producers that they were the guardians of moral-cultural values that neither the mass public nor their political masters understood or respected.

The following comments from a report on public filmgoing preferences illustrate the view educated Russians commonly took regarding popular cultural taste. Noting the popularity of films imported from India and Arab countries with the broad Soviet audience, the author comments: "It is not a secret that the majority of films of these countries which are shown in our theaters are not of a high artistic quality. The banality of the subject, the imitation of life's truths, the everyday down-to-earth quality, the melodramatic accent, the triteness in the use of expressive means, to a greater or lesser degree are typical of most of the Indian and Arab pictures. And the evaluation of such films by moviegoers is a quite definite indicator of the level of their artistic taste, aesthetic demands [and] general culture."[32] According to Cushman, similar sentiments regarding mass cultural taste were also expressed by members of the rock underground, most of whose members, as he notes, originated in highly educated cultural backgrounds.[33] One of his informants, for instance, a former graduate student given to references to Schopenhauer in his lyrics, spoke of his contempt for "philistine people" (meshchanskie lyudy) concerned only with worldly survival and advancement: "And the narrow-minded love [meshchanskaya lyubov'] for stability scares people away [from rock]. People of the level of the general masses. They go here and there, and then what?"[34] Clearly, cultural producers with this kind of conception of popular taste were unlikely to be especially active in searching for ways to accommodate its "primitive" demands.

*   *   *

As we shall consider below, the Soviet system of cultural production to a great extent insulated the creative intelligentsia from the need to satisfy consumer demand. For this reason, creative workers critical of the poverty of popular taste could nevertheless rest secure in the knowledge that it need impinge little upon their artistic projects. By contrast, those working within the official apparatus of cultural production, at any rate, could not avoid the necessity for constant dealings with the officials appointed to supervise their activities. Thus it was the "lack of culture" creative workers perceived in the bureaucracy that presented the most immediate obstacle to the fulfillment of their artistic aspirations. Indeed artists' and intellectuals' accounts of the injustices they experienced at the hands of officialdom frequently interpreted their problems as the result of this cultural gulf rather than pressures for ideological conformity. In one such memoir, the sculptor Ernst Neizvestnyi complained, for instance: "Nowhere have I met such a low level of culture and professional skill as above. And when I became familiar with these people, I felt an aesthetical [*sic*] fright which turned into a social one. . . . Apparatchiks perceive any actions—Plisetskaya's dances, Shostakovich's music, my sculptures—as personal insults and some inconvenience."[35]

Similarly, in his posthumously published diaries Tarkovsky wrote, "Dignitaries bedecked with honors and *incapable of stringing two words together* have demolished our cinema" (emphasis added).[36]

More generally, educated Russians (in talking to foreigners at any rate) continue to delight in anecdotes mocking the poor diction and grammar of late- (and post-) Soviet political leaders. Brezhnev, for instance, was notorious for his inability to decline his compound numbers correctly, a problem particularly disabling when it came to reciting industrial output targets for the next Five-Year Plan. Although under Western eyes Gorbachev appeared the epitome of urbanity by comparison with his predecessors, metropolitan Russian intelligenty are merciless in their scorn for his provincial accent and shaky grasp of the rules of standard grammar. He compounded these problems with his tendency to use what were perceived as pretentious, indeed nonsensical, neologisms. I was once told the story of how, in the early years of perestroika, he telephoned a theatrical producer to tell him that he and Raisa considered his new play a true *pirdukha*. The director was not sure whether to be flattered or alarmed: Although his epithet brought together the words for "feast" and "soul," the combination doesn't actually exist in standard Russian, making him fear that Gorbachev was using some provincial obscenity. (*Perdukha* is

Russian for "fart.") Apparently members of the cultural world took to using Gorbachev's expression as a label for something they viewed as pretentious.

Gorbachev's (apparently unappreciated) attempts to play the role of cultural connoisseur do not seem to have been typical of the official class to which he belonged. It appears that the nomenklatura's members were not only relatively lacking in high cultural competence but, in private at least, suspicious of those who were not. Take the following description of the problems of cross-cultural adaptation faced by an ambitious, young Komsomol[37] official with unusually "elevated" cultural tastes for someone pursuing a career within the Party administration. (His mother was a professor of literature.) "He had to hide his knowledge of foreign languages, for example, for fear of being considered an intellectual. Similarly he hid his fondness for jazz. 'I said all the right things. There was a show of modern art: I said it was good we had democracy to allow these things, but I like the good old Russian art, good old Russian soul.' "[38] We can suggest, therefore, that, the cultural gulf between nomenklatura and creative intelligentsia played a significant role in fostering cultural producers' aspiration for autonomy from an official apparatus they perceived to be dominated by philistine placeholders with no understanding of, or sympathy for, culture and the arts.

BOURDIEU'S THEORY OF CULTURAL CAPITAL

These observations suggest the existence of a striking parallel between the Soviet intellectual elite's sense of its position in relation to the rest of society and French social structure according to the analysis Bourdieu presents in *Distinction: A Social Critique of the Judgement of Taste.* The best-educated elements of French society, he argues, base their sense of superiority toward both to the masses, and the dominant political-economic elite on their privileged possession of "cultural capital," that is, legitimate high-cultural knowledge and taste. An aspect of Bourdieu's overall analysis of the relationship between culture and social hierarchy particularly suggestive of Soviet conditions is his account of the dichotomy between the French intellectual elite ("the dominated fraction of the dominant class") and the ruling political-economic elite ("the dominant fraction"). He writes: "The antagonism between the life-styles corresponding to the opposing poles of the field of the dominant class is clear-

cut, total . . . comparable to the gap between two 'cultures' in the anthro-
pological sense."[39]

Equally applicable to Soviet society is his argument that the French
intellectual class's tendency toward political radicalism is stimulated by its
members' urge to challenge their subordinate relationship to the ruling
political-economic elite—a subordination that the "universal" cultural
values on which their social status is based leads them to perceive as ille-
gitimate. As Bourdieu puts it: "Intellectuals and artists are so situated in
social space that they have a particular interest in disinterestedness and
in all the values that are universal and universally recognized as highest.
. . . The hope of an apocalyptic reversal of the temporal hierarchies which
arises from the lived experience of the scandalous disparity between the
hierarchy of 'temporal' greatness and the hierarchy of 'spiritual' greatness
impresses itself as a practical self-evidence on cultural producers."[40]

In terms of content, the ideological outlook typical of the late-Soviet
intelligentsia differed from that of the French intellectual elite in that it
was based on a defense of values that in the West would be classified as
"liberal humanism," rather than egalitarian leftism. Nevertheless, we can
see this ideological stance as a response to a structural position within
Soviet society that in many respects resembled that occupied by intellectuals in France. In both social systems the attraction that oppositional
forms of ideology and consciousness exercised on the cultural-intellectual
elite grew out of the contradictory nature of their social positioning, that
is, out of the conflict between their simultaneous experience of "spiritual"
dominance and "temporal" subordination.

Bourdieu's theory of the status of the French intellectual elite is based
on the analysis of a society in which economic capital is clearly the "dominant principle of domination."[41] If we are to apply his perspective to an
analysis of the position of the intellectual class in Soviet society, we must
explore how cultural capital functioned within the fundamentally different conditions present within socialist societies where not economic capital but *political status* dominated.[42]

THE OFFICIAL CONSECRATION OF HIGH CULTURE

On the inside cover of the workbooks in which the conduct of Soviet
employees was recorded were printed thirteen "instructions" advising

their bearers in socially constructive modes of thought and behavior. Alongside such improving exhortations as "Respect old people" was a point that suggested "If you have a free minute—pick up a book."[43] This juxtaposition illustrates the manner in which official discourse shared the intelligentsia's tendency to associate ethical and high-cultural values. It also indicates the pervasiveness (if not necessarily the effectiveness) of the authorities' attempt to improve the cultural level of their subjects.

The use of the term *kultura* within Russian public discourse to denote a combination of high cultural competence, moral probity, and refined manners predates the Revolution, first achieving general currency in the 1880s.[44] The official Soviet attempt to universalize culture in this sense can also be traced back to the pre-Revolutionary period, when following the emancipation of the peasantry in 1861, elements of the intelligentsia established schools and propagated respect for Russian literature in an attempt to raise the cultural level of the masses.[45] This project was informed by an ideal of cultural progress whose paternalism was shared by later Soviet cultural policy: As Sheila Fitzpatrick points out, neither the intelligentsia nor the Bolsheviks had any conception that "the culture that was best for the masses was the culture that the masses liked."[46]

The early Bolshevik movement was divided in its attitude toward the "bourgeois" cultural legacy of tsarist Russia. Lenin's views on cultural policy represented the conservative wing in this debate. He argued that the primary task of what he called the "cultural revolution" (a term that in his usage had none of the left radicalism it later acquired at the hands of Stalin and Mao) should be to teach the Soviet masses "that the earth is round, not flat, and that the world is not governed by witches and sorcerers and a 'heavenly father' but by natural laws. . . . For a start we should be satisfied with real bourgeois culture . . . we should be glad to dispense with the cruder types of pre-bourgeois culture."[47] His gradualist approach grew out of his opposition to the *proletkult* movement within the Bolshevik party, whose adherents advocated the development of a supposedly independent "proletarian culture" (one which was, in fact, their own utopian construction).[48] Faced by a society still overwhelmingly populated by largely illiterate peasants, Lenin was far more concerned with preventing a reversion to "barbarism" than with utopian dreams of building a nonbourgeois culture.[49]

His stance toward the pre-Revolutionary intelligentsia was similarly pragmatic. He firmly denied its members the right or capacity to criticize Party rule—it was Gorky's call for the preservation of intellectual freedom following the October Revolution that provoked Lenin's notorious outburst regarding "pathetic *intelligenty*, lackeys of capitalism who pride themselves on being the nation's brain [who] are not its brain . . . [but] its shit."[50] Otherwise, however, his approach toward the non-Bolshevik intelligentsia tended to be conciliatory, since he viewed its technical and organizational skills as indispensable to the task of building a new society.

The 1920s saw continuing debate within the Party regarding policy toward the intelligentsia and its cultural heritage. The controversy culminating in the short-lived triumph of the proletarian culture movement during the Cultural Revolution of 1928–31 and the brief but intense campaign of persecution launched against "bourgeois specialists" (i.e., representatives of the pre-Revolutionary intelligentsia). Nevertheless, from Stalin's cultural settlement of the 1930s onward, it was Lenin's view of Russia's cultural heritage that proved the dominant force within official Soviet cultural policy.

According to Stalin's pronouncements of the 1930s, measures against the intelligentsia were no longer necessary because, as he declared in 1939, "The remnants of the old intelligentsia [have been] dissolved in the body of a new, Soviet, people's intelligentsia firmly linked with the people and ready en masse to give it true and faithful service."[51] To make this claim required him to redefine the term "intelligentsia" itself, to denote all those with a higher or specialist education, regardless of social origins, cultural tastes, or ideological orientation, a definition that subsequently remained standard in official accounts of Soviet social structure. This definitional sleight of hand effectively foreclosed further debate on the relationship between class origin and ideological loyalty by subsuming both old intelligentsia and nomenklatura elites within the new, catchall category, "Soviet intelligentsia."[52]

The concomitant of the Stalinist regime's accommodation with the intelligentsia was its reaffirmation of pre-Revolutionary high culture's place within the Soviet cultural order. Avant-gardist and "proletarian" movements in the arts were reined in and respect for the works of Russia's pre-Revolutionary culture once more encouraged. Although artists and intellectuals were subjected to a minute and sometimes brutal supervisory apparatus, those who avoided official disfavor were heaped with highly publicized material and symbolic privileges. As Fitzpatrick puts it: "[The] populist spirit was not dominant in the culture of the Soviet period because the regime had made the basic decision to put its money on *kul'turnost'* and to honor the old non-Communist and nonproletarian intelligentsia. . . . [P]ower and cultural authority were in different hands under Stalin: the party had the political power to discipline the old intelligentsia but lacked the will or resources to deny its cultural authority. In cultural terms then, who was assimilating whom?"[53]

If anything, as the utopian militancy of Soviet ideology faded in the decades following Stalin's death, the status accorded to kultura and its intelligentsia bearers rose still higher. One of the clearest indications of official Soviet respect for pre-Revolutionary high culture was the mass publication of the classic works of tsarist-era literature. Not only were they printed in huge editions, in accordance with Lenin's dictum that even "bourgeois" culture contained "progressive elements" that could play a valuable role in educating socialist citizens, their study formed a central part of the school curriculum.[54]

One effect of these efforts was to ensure that in contrast to many Western countries today, knowledge of the classic literary canon has remained a vital element in the shared culture of Russia's educated. "Kitchen philosophy," articles on nonliterary topics, and even newspaper reports on politics tend to be laced with literary references (often unattributed, presumably because for the cognoscenti this should not be required).[55] While living in Russia, I often found that if the conversation turned to, say, differences between Russia and the West, my interlocutor would say words to the effect of "You can't understand Russia without reading this by Dostoyevsky (or Chekhov or Pushkin)" and rummage through his or her library to lend, on occasion give, me the book in question. Any familiarity I displayed with the Russian classics would be praised, any gaps in my knowledge treated as a severe—if, in a Westerner, only to be expected—shortcoming. Westerners were often criticized, not only for their ignorance of Russian classics, but also for ignorance of "their own" canon.

As a number of commentators have argued, the Soviet regime's attempt to co-opt tsarist literature toward its own legitimation may have backfired by introducing the Trojan horse of pre-Revolutionary intelligentsia ideology into the ramparts of Soviet official culture.[56] Pre-Revolutionary texts were supposed to be taught with a socialist gloss; Dostoyevsky's sympathy for the "insulted and injured" of tsarist society, for instance, was stressed over his enthusiasm for orthodoxy and tsarist autocracy. However, few of the most celebrated nineteenth-century writers had been sympathetic to the revolutionary socialist project, and their works conveyed ideological messages that accorded poorly with the worldview the Soviet authorities sought to encourage in their citizens. The remarks of a young director working today bear this out: "The more the soul was repressed in the Soviet Union, the more there existed an unofficial style of art, life, and contact. And everyone who tried to think about that was a dissident. Each person who read Dostoyevsky . . . because at school only some of his things, or of Gogol's, were taught."[57]

The inherent resistance pre-Revolutionary texts presented to official ideological co-optation may account for the capacity of the cultic belief in high culture to survive the general decay of belief in official ideology that took place in the late-Soviet period. Take for instance, the following hyperbolic but not atypical reaction of one writer to official plans to celebrate the 150th anniversary of Pushkin's birth in 1987: "[I was afraid of] any kind of campaign, at which we were so adept in the recent past, [but then] a saving thought occurred to me: love for Pushkin is no campaign! . . . It is Love for the one who expresses national feelings, for a spiritual Father, upon whom one can depend as on the Truth of earthly virtues."[58]

The logic of the argument presented above regarding the centrality of literature in forming the identity of the nineteenth-century intelligentsia applies, therefore, equally to the Soviet period. The continued relevance of the pre-Revolutionary literary heritage to the cultural life of the late-Soviet intelligentsia was caused not only by the specific encouragement it received from the authorities but also by the relative absence of alternative means for representing (or acting upon) unorthodox views and attitudes. Soviet conditions worked to reproduce high culture's traditional prominence as a means for the transmission and dissemination of morally valorized, antihegemonic ideals; sociomoral altruism was associated with high-cultural knowledge and vice versa: the high-cultural medium was the message.

EDUCATION, OCCUPATION, AND CULTURE

The key to understanding the distinctive role that cultural capital played in *differentiating* Soviet social structure must be sought in the interaction between the system of formal education and patterns of social mobility.

The Soviet leadership attached great importance to the expansion of the educational system, not only because of its need to fill the administrative and technical positions created by its breakneck pursuit of industrialization, but also because official ideology presented educational advancement as in itself one socialism's fundamental goals. Under Soviet rule, first elementary and then secondary schooling became universal, while the numbers of graduates from institutes of higher education increased as a proportion of the total population from 0.8 percent in 1939 to 9 percent in 1987.[59] While in absolute terms this quantitative expansion transformed the "cultural level" of the Soviet population by, for instance, virtually ending illiteracy, it did not—nor was it intended to—eliminate striking social disparities in educational attainment. In particular, the number of student places available in the highest-prestige institutions such as the "special schools" of Moscow and Leningrad and the elite training institutes and university departments whose graduates dominated the most sought-after professions remained extremely limited.

One effect of this unequal distribution of educational attainment was to render vain the official hope that a taste for high culture could be made universal among the Soviet public. Soviet sociological studies of the late 1960s established a correlation between level of education and cultural preferences broadly similar to that typical of Western societies.[60] One found, for instance, that in rural areas scarcely more than a tenth of unskilled workers read books regularly, as compared to around half of intelligenty (a category, we should remember, that was defined broadly in Soviet sociology to include all people with a postsecondary education).[61] Perhaps less troubling for the Soviet authorities was the strong correlation surveys of the period found between possession of high levels of education and a taste for unconventional or critical cultural works.[62] This presumably rendered cultural nonconformity less politically dangerous than it might otherwise have been and may account in part for the degree of de facto tolerance it was accorded in the late-Soviet period. This finding also suggests that the consumption of heterodox cultural works may have acted as a marker of high sociocultural status, reinforcing the association within late-Soviet intelligentsia culture between "good taste" and private disenchantment from official ideology.

Neither the unequal distribution of educational attainment nor its correlation with differences in cultural taste is particularly surprising (except in terms of the egalitarian claims of official Soviet ideology). In historical practice, these phenomena have characterized all industrialized societies. In other respects, however, the educational system's significance in structuring social hierarchy differed from the pattern characteristic of Western capitalist countries. As Caroline Humphrey has pointed out, under socialism individual rights and privileges were not based upon ownership of private property—as they are to a great extent in the West—but on one's position in the officially ordained division of labor. Soviet society was structured as a hierarchy of occupationally defined status groups or "administrative-production estates," as she terms them, rather than by socio-economic classes of the kind found under capitalism. In theory, and to a great extent even in practice, entry to the more privileged status groups was determined exclusively through achieving the appropriate educational qualifications. The role that inherited wealth plays in determining social reproduction within capitalist societies was entirely eliminated.[63]

The extent to which less educated Russians were aware of the link between educational success and advantageous occupational status (along with the mixture of envy and resentment this awareness provoked) is suggested by a passage from the memoirs of Anatoly Marchenko, one of the few Soviet dissidents of working-class origin. The son of railway workers, he recalls:

> We constantly heard the same warning from our parents: if you don't want to end up a greaser like your father for the rest of your life, then study! . . . [Nevertheless] I entered life with a firm prejudice against intellectuals. They were people who didn't work very hard and got paid for doing nothing . . . on the one hand, everyone knew that academics and writers were involved in absolutely useless, even ludicrous work: writers scribble lies, scientists breed some kind of flies. On the other hand, everyone worshipped their omniscience and omnipotence, except when it came to everyday life.[64]

The way in which professional cultural producers were recruited exemplifies the close relationship between educational credentials and occupational status in the Soviet Union. Employment in creative positions within the arts and media was dominated by graduates from the humanities departments of the major metropolitan universities, like Moscow State, along with a small number of specialized training institutes. In the film industry, for instance, virtually all directors throughout the Soviet Union graduated from the "All-Union Film Institute" (VGIK) established in Moscow in 1919 (the world's first film school).[65] In Western countries attending film school is neither a necessary nor a sufficient condition for a directing career—the real challenge being to obtain financial backing. By contrast, a graduate from VGIK's directing faculty was virtually guaranteed the opportunity to shoot films as the salaried employee of a state studio.[66] At this level, at least, the Soviet educational system saw little of the "inflation of qualifications" that has characterized the West since World War II—high-prestige degrees retained their value as passports to high-prestige careers. The intensity of competition for entry into such departments is telling evidence of the status intellectual and creative occupations enjoyed in Soviet society.

We see, therefore, that the Soviet educational-occupational recruitment system made attainment of what Bourdieu calls "the institutionalized form" of cultural capital the primary means of achieving entry into desirable occupational categories.[67] The particular value that cultural attainment held in Soviet society derived, therefore, not only from official preaching (which in other respects, Soviet citizens were quite capable of ignoring). The officially ordained mechanism of social advancement gave Soviet individuals powerful practical incentives to compete with one another for cultural status. Indeed, in the sphere of culture and education, the Soviet system established the effective system of personal incentives that it so signally failed to create in that of economic activity.

This emphasis on acquiring educational credentials did not, however, equalize opportunity within Soviet society, owing to the vital role played by what Bourdieu calls the "domestic transmission"[68] of cultural capital in determining who achieved educational success. Bourdieu makes the general proposition that the hereditary transmission of cultural capital "receives proportionately greater weight in the system of reproduction strategies as the direct, visible forms of transmission tend to be more strongly censored and controlled."[69] His argument is well illustrated by the Soviet case, where as we have seen, inherited economic capital played no role in the intergenerational transmission of social status.

The greater the status of a department of higher education the more likely its students were to originate in highly educated, metropolitan family backgrounds.[70] Such applicants possessed a number of advantages in the selection process. First, like their Western counterparts, they could deploy cultural capital acquired outside the educational system, that is, from their family, peer group, and so forth. Second, the strong role played by *blat* (pull) in Soviet educational selection meant that they benefited from the social connections their parents were likely to have to those in charge of the selection process. (Soviet academic departments administered their own entrance examinations, giving their faculty great personal discretion in making admission decisions.)[71] Finally, many of the best academically prepared applicants had already benefited from attendance at one of the highly selective "special schools" in Moscow or Leningrad where admission was itself strongly influenced by the operations of blat and inherited cultural capital (hence their sobriquet: "Schools for Talented Parents"). The only group capable of competing successfully with children from intelligentsia backgrounds were the offspring of the nomenklatura, whose suit was backed by the best blat of all. Such students were sardonically referred to as "sons and daughters."

A film critic recalls the situation regarding entry to VGIK when she was a student in the early 1980s:

> (GF: There must have been a lot of competition for film school.)
> Yes, because there was only one in the country. . . . It was practically impossible. You had to be involved like crazy inside it, *or you had to be son of somebody*. In Europe there are people [who make it into film school] who are just interested; in Moscow, if you were just interested, you would never get into VGIK.
> (GF: You needed connections?)
> Yes, or be very well prepared. But even if you were you might lose out to children with connections. In France I realized it's not like this. In August we had awful exams at the university [for admission] . . . *all the parents would start to phone their friends of their youth to see if they knew someone here or there.*[72] (Emphasis added)

The accounts of young film directors who entered film school during this period confirm the vital role family background played in developing and enabling their interest in a career in cinema. Valery Todorovsky, son of the well-known Soviet director Pyotr Todorovsky, recalls for instance: "I was born and raised in Odessa and I virtually lived in the Odessa film studios. And the disease entered my body from the moment of my birth. I could scarcely imagine myself pursuing any other kind of career. My parents were skeptical about my choice but fortunately I'm doing what I want to do."[73]

Marina Tsurtsumia's decision to enter the industry was similarly influenced by her family background. Her account also suggests the impact family support could make in determining success within this highly personalized admissions process:

My parents also worked in the cinema. My father was a cameraman and then became a director. He was a great cameraman. He shot with our very famous director [Sergei] Gerasimov and with [Sergei] Bondarchuk as a director of photography. My mother graduated from the cinema criticism department of VGIK, and worked as a critic. . . . I've lived in the world of cinema since I was six. So when I was a kid I wanted to be a director just like others want to be cosmonauts. But when I applied for film school everyone was against it except my father. I wanted to study with Gerasimov and my grandmother phoned him to stop him taking me. And they didn't take me. But the second year I got in [laughs], though to a different studio.[74]

Few Soviet citizens enjoyed such a head start in pursuing their childhood dreams. Of the younger filmmakers I interviewed, only one, Gleb Aleinikov, acknowledged no family background in the arts or humanities. (His parents were civil engineers.) Significantly, though interested in art from an early age, he did not even apply to an arts faculty, assuming that without family connections he stood no chance of being admitted. Instead, he and his brother began shooting independently on 8mm in the mid-1980s, going on to become pioneers of what became known as the "parallel cinema" (i.e., underground) movement of the perestroika period. Entry into the upper reaches of the creative intelligentsia was not, of course, entirely hereditized. Vasily Shukshin and Vladimir Menshov are examples of prominent late-Soviet film directors from working-class, provincial backgrounds. Notwithstanding such exceptions, it is clear that children from intellectual families enjoyed a vastly better likelihood of entering the creative professions than the children of collective farmers or coalminers.

A further implication of this tendency toward intelligentsia hereditization is worth noting. Despite the tribulations the survivors of the pre-Revolutionary intelligentsia suffered under Stalin,[75] we can argue that the basic rules for social advancement within Soviet society worked to place its offspring in a strong position in the competition for privileged occupational status. The majority of the late-Soviet intelligentsia was not drawn from individuals with intelligentsia family backgrounds, simply because of the rapid expansion in its total numbers.[76] However, it seems likely that descendants of the pre-Revolutionary intelligentsia were disproportionately represented in its ranks, particularly at the highest, most educationally selective levels. This in turn may have contributed to the degree of cultural continuity observable between the late-Soviet and pre-Revolutionary intelligentsias.

A DIVIDED ELITE

In Humphrey's terminology, both creative intelligentsia and nomenklatura can be conceived of as elite "administrative-production estates." They were primarily distinguishable from each other, not by degree of material privilege (the nomenklatura's standard of living was on average higher, but there was considerable overlap between the two groups in terms of both cash income and access to noncash benefits), but by the function assigned them within the Soviet division of labor. The Soviet state delegated the task of producing cultural value to the creative intelligentsia, while entrusting its executive authority—that is, the right to tell people what to do—to the nomenklatura. With respect to political power, the nomenklatura were clearly the dominant group within society. In terms of publicly recognized social status, however, the relationship between the elites was reversed; official discourse celebrated the rewards attendant on intellectual and cultural (and sporting) achievement while remaining systematically silent regarding those accompanying high office in the bureaucracy. This is not to say that the average Soviet citizen was unaware that these privileges existed, but it does imply that, unlike those enjoyed by Western economic elites, they were not held up as models for public emulation.[77]

The origins of the cultural gulf between the intelligentsia and nomenklatura go back to Stalin's policy in the 1930s of promoting a new generation of often sketchily educated working-class Party activists—the so-called *vydvizhentsy*—into leadership positions. This cohort, which included Khrushchev and Brezhnev, continued to dominate the upper echelons of the Party until the beginning of perestroika.[78] Their rapid rise within the Party hierarchy was facilitated by the particular weight with which the purges fell on "old Bolsheviks," most of whom had intellectual social backgrounds. Thus in sharp contrast to the policy of accommodation Stalin followed in relation to the intelligentsia *generally*, this period saw the systematic deintellectualization of the Party leadership. While it is hard to know whether this trend was the product of a deliberate policy decision, it is possible to argue on deductive grounds that excluding highly educated, "critically thinking individuals" (to recall Lavrov's definition of the intelligentsia) from positions of power may have helped preserve the ideological unity and policy-making coherence of the Party-State. A cynical remark by Anatoly Lunacharsky, Bolshevik commissar for enlightenment in the 1920s, a figure generally regarded as well disposed toward the intelligentsia, suggests that elements of the Party leadership understood this logic all too well: "The more lacking in ideas a person is, the more valuable he is."[79] Certainly, many autocratic regimes of the past, including that of early modern Muscovy, have sought to preserve their monopoly on power by entrusting executive authority to elites of their own creation rather than relying on individuals with an independent status in society.

As the Soviet system evolved, levels of formal education among new entrants to the nomenklatura rose markedly. By the 1980s almost all possessed postsecondary, and many even graduate, qualifications. In this formal sense (and in this sense only) the official system of social classification that placed the late-Soviet nomenklatura within the intelligentsia was accurate. For Konrad and Szelenyi, this trend portended the eventual merging of intellectual and political elites into a technocratic ruling class.[80] However, as we have already seen, the *relative* cultural difference between the best-educated elements of the intelligentsia and the nomenklatura persisted. It was this, rather than the general rise in the latter's level of formal education, that played the crucial role in determining the relations between the two groups.[81]

Two major factors operated within the Soviet system of social advancement that worked to reproduce the cultural gap between intellectual and political elites into the late-Soviet period. First, although it was necessary to achieve a minimum level of educational certification to gain entry to the nomenklatura, academic qualifications had to be supplemented by a conspicuous record of (loyal) Party activism. An émigré's description of one aspiring *nomenklaturshchik* at MGU in the 1950s indicates the sociocultural characteristics that this system tended to select in new entrants to the Party apparatus:

In his first year at the philology faculty of Moscow University, A was a square peg in a round hole. He was crude, spoke with a strong northern accent, and read very little. The son of a regional party official in the Urals, he had managed somehow to enter a university which annually turns down from 19 to 24 applicants for every candidate accepted. [The author is hinting that he used connections.] He was by no means stupid. He learned his way around quickly and realized that he would never qualify as a scholar or a teacher. Accordingly, he took up Komsomol work: he was forever organizing, rallying, "working people over," "discussing." He said he planned a Party career.[82]

In the late-Soviet period, university students whose academic abilities guaranteed them access to other kinds of advantageous positions in Soviet society appear to have been little attracted to the onerous task of "forever organizing" their peers. In practice, therefore, most entrants into the late-Soviet nomenklatura continued to originate in relatively marginal sociocultural backgrounds and tended to be educated in applied scientific subjects (notably engineering) rather than higher-status fields such as the humanities and pure science.[83]

A second factor tending to undermine the nomenklatura's capacity to accumulate cultural capital was the systematic tendency of the nomenklatura's own offspring to pursue careers within intellectual professions rather than follow their parents into the official bureaucracy.[84] Given Soviet society's general tendency toward nepotism, we can assume that had they (or their parents) so chosen, they would have had little difficulty in following in their parents' footsteps. The fact that they opted not to do so constitutes perhaps the most telling evidence of the low prestige enjoyed by the nomenklatura by comparison with elite intellectual occupations. At the same time, what we may call this rejection of hereditization ensured that the nomenklatura's ranks remained far more open to ambitious Soviet citizens of relatively humble social backgrounds than were the upper reaches of the intelligentsia. The result of this system of social advancement was that, as Shlapentokh puts it: "The [political] elite consists primarily of people with very mediocre education and cultural tastes. In this sense rulers and apparatchiks are really much closer to ordinary people than to intellectuals."[85]

INTELLIGENTSIA IDENTITY AND THE MISSION OF ART

This analysis of the dynamics of social hierarchization under state socialism allows us to understand more fully the peculiarly high status occupied by the Soviet intelligentsia by comparison to their counterparts in the West. The Soviet system was rather successful in making the acquisition of institutionalized cultural capital the chief condition of access to social status and privilege. However, cultural capital has inherent properties that make its distribution within society resistant to total external regulation. To a great extent, cultural capital is *embodied*, as Bourdieu puts it, in the intellect, personality, and even physicality of its individual bearers.[86] Unlike, say, political authority or even private property, it cannot simply be awarded or removed by an outside force. To function as capital in society, that is, as a means to make status claims, it must of course be recognized by others, but what kinds of people receive this recognition and what kinds of criteria are used to award it cannot be completely determined by official institutions. As a result the Soviet state was unable to control fully either the process by which cultural capital was acquired or the informal definitions of what constituted legitimate cultural capital operating within Soviet society. The ultimate result of its focus on education as the means to social advancement, therefore, was to concentrate cultural authority in the hands of an elite whose members refused to view the system to which "objectively" they owed their privileged position as embodying their definition of moral-cultural excellence.

By contrast the Soviet authorities *were* successful in determining what kind of people achieved access to executive power. Within the realm of culture, this success carried a price, however. It stimulated antagonism between the producers of culture, on the one hand, and the administrators of culture, on the other. The former not only created but embodied cultural values; yet their autonomy was restricted by the Party's claim to ultimate authority over their activities. The latter, on the other hand, were drawn from a class whose members were incapable of embodying the cultural values they were assigned to control. In the light of this argument, Soviet cultural producers' valorization of "art" as an autonomous moral force fundamentally incompatible with "opportunistic," conformism, can be interpreted as a specific expression of the intelligentsia's privileged yet subordinate status within Soviet society. Contrary to Marx's assertion that in every society the ruling ideas are the ideas of its ruling class, we can say, therefore, that under socialism there was a profound disjuncture between the dominant cultural values and the culture of the dominant.

2

The main outlines of the Soviet filmmaking system as they persisted until perestroika were set in place during the First Five-Year Plan (1928–32). For the first ten years of their rule the Bolsheviks presided over a turbulent and fragmented cultural field continuous in many respects with that of late-tsarist Russia. In particular, the relative economic prosperity of the NEP period (1921–28) allowed the restoration of a vital, commercially based popular culture oriented toward the urban proletariat and petite-bourgeoisie.[1] For radical Bolsheviks this was a disturbing situation, in part because much of NEP popular culture was imported from the capitalist West. This was particularly true of cinema, where Soviet films made up only 23 percent of new releases during the 1920s, while those homegrown products capable of competing with imports for the mass urban audience were accused of pandering to "bourgeois" needs for entertainment and diversion.[2] By the same token, the great showpieces of revolutionary propaganda produced in the period, such as Eisenstein's *October*, no matter how critically successful, were little watched by a mass audience more eager to catch the latest Mary Pickford release. Although the Party was successful in preventing the importation or distribution of anything directly subversive, it was clearly not going to be able to use the mass media to construct the "New Soviet Person" so long as cultural production was even partially organized on a commercial basis. As the head of the Party's Agitprop department declared in 1928:

> The Soviet cinema must not follow in the wake of its audience, but must move ahead of it; it must lead the audience, support the beginnings in it of the new man, instill into it new views, tastes, habits which correspond to the tasks of the socialist reconstruction of the whole of society. In this we can see the striking difference between the Soviet cinema and the bourgeois cinema, which in its relationship to its audience, indulges and supports in it views, tastes and attitudes that are reactionary . . . and are cultivated by capitalism in its own interests.[3]

It was this utopian aspiration to remold subjectivity that explains why, unlike its fascist contemporaries, which in this respect were less ambitious, the Soviet state could not tolerate the existence of a commercially based, entertainment-oriented cultural industry.[4] All available media were to be used to educate, enlighten, and indoctrinate, rather than pander to the corrupted desires of the actually existing cultural consumer.

The leadership's solution to this problem was to organize all sectors of cultural production, both "high" and "popular," along the same command-administrative lines being applied to the economy generally during this period. The system that resulted, which we may term the *socialist mode of cultural production*, came to govern the arts and mass media of not only the Soviet Union but all Soviet-dominated and state socialist societies. In its "ideal" form (which in the Soviet Union was in historical practice most closely approximated under Stalin) it was characterized by the following features:[5]

1. *State Monopoly*: The Party-State assumed responsibility for all aspects of cultural production, distribution, and exhibition. In most sectors access to this cultural apparatus was restricted to creative workers who had been admitted to corporate institutions established by the state (in particular the "creative unions"). All loci of production and distributional flows outside what I shall call the *authorized sphere*, such as private production or foreign imports, were suppressed.

2. *Bureaucratic Control*: Each sector of cultural production was administered through a system of bureaucratic institutions in which, in

theory, senior management exercised complete authority over both creative and organizational questions. Managers were appointed by, and were ultimately answerable to, the supreme political leadership.

3. *Aesthetic-Ideological Orthodoxy*: All authorized cultural producers were expected to conform to a single system of aesthetic and ideological norms established by the Party leadership.

In certain respects the position of creative workers within this system paralleled that of their counterparts within the corporate sector of cultural production in the West. Both groups worked within large bureaucratic organizations according to vertically imposed and narrowly defined norms of what kinds of work were considered desirable. Most accounts of the dynamics of such corporations in the West quite reasonably see their character as profit-making capitalist institutions as having more effect than the aspirations and mentality of their creative personnel on the character of their output. That is, in general, the industries' internal disciplinary mechanisms operate with sufficient rigor to result in products whose character is determined far more by the need to sell them to a wide public than by the creative urges (or class identity) of their makers.[6]

At first sight, it might seem that Soviet cultural producers' room for creative autonomy under the socialist mode of cultural production should have been far more restricted than that of their counterparts in the Western cultural industries. No film director, for example, could receive professional training, be employed by a studio, begin shooting a film, or see it released to the public without receiving approval from above. Unlike Western cultural producers, those of the Soviet Union had no alternative options for professional work, as the institutions within which they worked made up a single, monopolistic apparatus. Furthermore, their activities were subject to a system of rewards and sanctions emanating ultimately from the state itself: if they provoked official displeasure they could be denied foreign travel privileges, have their work banned, be prevented from working within their profession, and in the most extreme cases, suffer police harassment and imprisonment.[7] If their work found favor, on the other hand, they could be elevated to almost the very summit of Soviet society.

For all the range of controls at their disposal, the ability of the state authorities to determine the character of Soviet cultural production was, in practice, surprisingly limited. The case of the film industry demonstrates that they were unable to ensure the production of works that embodied official interpretations of ideological orthodoxy, artistic excellence, and mass appeal on a scale sufficient to satisfy public demand. The contradiction between the industry's qualitative and quantitative goals is apparent in the contrast between its mode of operation before and after the death of Stalin.

From the effective nationalization of the industry in 1930 to Stalin's demise in 1953, the creative autonomy of the filmmakers was effectively eliminated. Soviet filmmaking became subject to an elaborate and time-consuming process of preproduction censorship, exemplified by the case of Ivan Pyriev's *The Conveyer-Belt of Death*, which was remade fourteen times before its release.[8] Given the intense personal interest that Stalin took in film, and the general climate of terror created by the purges, "errors" became potentially lethal. (In practice no film directors were imprisoned or executed during this period but many managers were less fortunate.) The general climate of fear and ideological mobilization suppressed any open expression of resistance to official control.

As a result, the films that did eventually reach the public were ideologically orthodox, technically well-made, and in some cases possessed genuine "mass appeal." On the other hand, the rigor of this supervisory process caused a slump in output that continued until Stalin's death in 1953: 128 films were produced in 1930 but only 35 in 1933, with a further drop after World War II to a low of 9 in 1951.[9] In Maya Turovskaya's words: "To the question often asked by Soviet publicists at this time, why could the industry not fulfil its plans and provide the public with enough films, there was an easy answer: It became almost impossibly difficult to make a film in the Soviet Union."[10] In 1951 official policy abandoned the hopeless commitment to quantitative increase altogether; the declaration that only "masterpieces" were to be produced and only "acknowledged masters of the art" were to make them,[11] recognized in principle what had long been the case in practice. Meanwhile, as the system of exhibition steadily expanded through the policy of "cinefication," the public's growing demand for cinematic entertainment had to be satisfied through the bizarre expedient of putting into distribution "trophy films" captured from Nazi Germany at the end of World War II.

Even before the death of Stalin, dissatisfaction was being voiced publicly with the virtual standstill in film production. After his death in March 1953, a renewed drive for increased output began. This time it was successful, with numbers of new films released annually increasing tenfold in the period up to the late 1960s.[12] While the basic institutions of the system that had been constructed under Stalin remained in place, the workings of the supervisory machinery were relaxed sufficiently to allow a faster pace of production.

As a 1954 press article revealingly put it: "A large part of the blame [for the film industry's problems] falls on our top cinema officials. In planning film production they have not taken account of the interests and the individual artistic bent of the director. And how is it possible to disregard the creative inspirations of the artist?"[13] Although official controls became stricter once more from the late 1960s onward, they remained far looser than under Stalin, and an expanded rate of output was maintained.

From the authorities' point of view this quantitative expansion came at a heavy price, however. First, a proportion of late-Soviet film directors created works that in one way or another may be regarded as *heterodox*: in theme, some were implicitly critical, or at least not actively supportive of the Soviet order; in form, some broke away from "realist" aesthetic conventions, thereby, according to the authorities, ceasing to be popularly accessible. The reemergence of the filmmakers' claim to autonomy as artists was signaled by the currency that the expression *avtorskoe kino* (auteur cinema) achieved in the Soviet film world from the 1960s onward. While only a minority of directors pursued heterodox forms of creative practice, the importance of their resistance was magnified by the second weakness of the late-Soviet filmmaking, its tendency to produce large numbers of "gray" works. This term was used by Soviet critics to refer to films that although ideologically unexceptionable, lacked both artistic interest and popular success.[14] In combination, these two trends severely restricted the size of the pool of artists that the Soviet authorities could rely upon to produce works that were both competently made and orthodox in form and content.

It is here that we see the weakness of the Soviet film industry by comparison to the corporate capitalist mode of cultural production. In the culture industries of the West, management rarely has much difficulty ensuring that a steady stream of works are produced that are both made to a minimum level of professional competence and "orthodox" (i.e., marketable) in form and content. The Soviet film industry was unable to achieve this combination despite the conscious intentions of its managers. The roots of this failure must be sought in the fundamental characteristics of the socialist mode of cultural production, which militated against the *large-scale* production of films combining ideological and aesthetic orthodoxy on the one hand with technical competence and mass appeal on the other.

THE CULTURAL ECONOMY OF SHORTAGE

No less than the economy in general, the Soviet market in cultural goods was characterized by permanent and structural consumer shortage. As Yassen Zassoursky puts it: "Stalin's principle, put forward in the 'Economic Problems of Socialism,' prevails: Demand must always exceed supply. Therefore, Soviet mass culture does not reflect the taste of the public, or, if you will, is not determined by public taste because there is insufficient access to many cultural products."[15] We may term this phenomenon the *cultural economy of shortage*.[16] Its existence was a direct consequence of the state's monopoly control over large-scale forms of cultural production. Given this monopoly's existence, if the public wished to consume mass-produced cultural works at all, it had to select from whatever the state chose to make available to them. The process was circular in that the more limited the range of cultural products being offered, the greater the state's freedom to ignore actual public demand. Paraphrasing Ferenc Feher, Agnes Heller, and Gyorgy Markus's characterization of the overall socialist political economy as a "dictatorship over needs," we can say therefore that the cultural economy of shortage allowed the state to exercise a *dictatorship over cultural needs*.[17]

In her analysis of the establishment of consumer shortage within Soviet cinema during the 1930s, Turovskaya points to the dramatic disjuncture between the rise in the numbers of filmgoers and the restriction of the cinematic repertoire.[18] In this situation, Turovskaya argues: "Given the general shortage of entertainment facilities (cafes, dance halls, 'parks of culture,' sports grounds, etc.), it was not specific films but cinema as a whole that became the target of increased demand."[19] As a result, the size of a film's audience was influenced more by how widely the state had decided to distribute it than by how much the public "really" wanted to see it.[20] Turovskaya proposes that by depriving the public of other options for diversion, the Stalinist state was able not only to ignore audience taste but also effectively to force audiences to watch films with a high degree of ideological content. We can say, therefore, that the particular intensity of cultural shortage during the Stalin era allowed the Party's dictatorship over cultural needs to be exercised with maximum effectiveness. It enabled the creation of a film industry that in the words of the 1927 official report cited by Turovskaya could be at once "100 percent ideologically correct and 100 percent commercially viable."[21]

In the late-Soviet period the range of cultural products available to the public became increasingly diverse. The regime's administration of the official apparatus of cultural production became more liberal, while the same period saw the emergence of what I call an *unauthorized sphere* of cultural production and exchange. This process was self-reinforcing in that the more cultural options the Soviet public possessed, the less able the authorities were to ensure the consumption of particular approved works. In this sense the state's dictatorship over cultural needs had become untenable by the 1970s.

At the same time, however, the development of the unauthorized sphere demonstrates that the disjuncture between the supply of "authorized" cultural products and consumer demand persisted into the late-Soviet period. Research conducted in the 1960s and 1970s into the tastes of the cinema audience found that films that were filled with spectacle, simple and conventional in form, and populated by sympathetic and good-looking characters appealed to the broadest section of the Soviet public.[22] That is, the mass audience wanted to be diverted and entertained according to criteria broadly similar to those employed by its counterparts in the rest of the world. Relatively little of the Soviet industry's output satisfied this need. According to one estimate, for instance, of the 1,750 films available for exhibition in 1970, three-fourths concerned "weighty subjects," while most of those in "light entertainment" genres were foreign imports.[23] The 1970s saw an officially sponsored campaign for the production of more entertainment-oriented films. But although this drive produced some notable hits, they were relatively few in number: During the 1970s, 15 percent of the 150 or so films the industry produced each year accounted for 80 percent of ticket sales.[24]

The cultural economy of shortage had profound effects on the system of incentives and sanctions operating within the film industry. For the officials in charge of production decisions, achieving box-office success took second place to fulfilling the quantitative targets for the production of films on particular subjects established by the Ministry of Culture in consultation with Goskino (the *templan*).[25] Looking back on this system, a film promoter whose career in the industry began during the Soviet period contended, "The state financed all films and no one ever cared if they sold the films. If it made you feel good you could say, 'my films are in distribution,' but who cared? Because the next time your films were subsidized [anyway] . . . but the state was never interested in this money. Who counted this money? . . . Film production and distribution were never connected."[26] This account is something of an oversimplification in that, by the late-Soviet period, the regional film-distributing organizations, which were under pressure to sell enough tickets to fulfill planned revenue targets, did care about the box-office potential of new productions. Indeed, they frequently refused to carry films they deemed lacking in audience appeal.[27] However, the very frequency with which distributors rejected Soviet studios' output suggests that her contention that their interests (and hence those of the public) had minimal impact on production decisions is fundamentally correct.[28] The Soviet system stands in strong contrast, therefore, to the American system, in which distributors' estimation of public demand plays a vital role in determining the character of films produced. As we will see, this disjuncture between the incentive structures operating on producers on the one hand and distributors on the other was to play a significant role in the dissolution of filmmaking as a mass-cultural industry in the post-perestroika period.

The Soviet leadership clearly intended that the film industry should turn a profit for the state.[29] The existence of the cultural economy of shortage ensured that, at least until the immediate pre-perestroika years, it was able to do so, despite its relative inattention to the problem of pleasing the mass public. The industry's overall profitability contributed to the tendency for particular production decisions to be made under what Janos Kornai has termed "soft budget constraints." Under such conditions the financial disincentives for decisions that under capitalism would be economically irrational—such as the manufacture of unsalable goods or the production of unwatchable films—operated weakly or not at all.[30]

The cultural economy of shortage and the soft budget constraint meant that filmmakers were relatively free from the financial concerns that dog their Western counterparts. By the same token, they were under less pressure to consider the likely public demand for their work. To the question, "Were there any advantages to the Soviet system of filmmaking?" one director active during the Soviet period, replied: "There were no problems with money. Directors didn't even understand it could be a problem. . . . The state paid."[31]

This insulation from the market is apparent in the method by which the state assigned financial awards to film directors. The level of compensation they received for the completion of each film depended on which of five distribution categories it was assigned by Goskino: "Directors got a regular salary plus a commission depending on the category of film. The officials said it if was first, second, or third category. If it was first, you got 8,000 [rubles], second was 6,000, third, 2,500, and fourth nothing. (That was when 6,000 was enough to buy a car.) . . . Of course there was a special small group of directors like [Stanislav] Rastotsky, and Bondarchuk who made films for the government, and they got an extra high category paying 12,000."[32] The higher the category, the more copies of the film were printed and the more widely it was distributed. Thus filmmakers' financial rewards were determined, not by how many people in fact saw the movie, but by how many people the authorities considered *ought* to see the movie.[33] The wealthiest directors were those like Sergei Bondarchuk who were selected to film projects on high-priority "commissioned themes" (*zakaznye temy*). These films were awarded a high distribution category whether they turned out to perform well at the box office or not, and their makers prospered accordingly. Bondarchuk lived in a six-room apartment in Moscow, not remarkable luxury by Western standards, but enough nevertheless to attract the envy of his less fortunate peers.[34]

A similar pattern was apparent in other sectors of cultural production. In book publishing, for instance, royalties were awarded on the basis of print runs rather than retail sales. The works of officially approved authors (derisively known as "secretary literature") were printed in huge editions, much of which, after languishing for a while on store shelves, were returned unsold for pulping. Between 1980 and 1987, for instance, 39,685,000 copies of titles by the first secretary of the Writers' Union, Sergei Mikhalkov, were printed.[35] Such writers were among the wealthiest individuals in Soviet society.[36]

Thus in Bourdieuian terms, by accepting heteronomy in relation to the state, consecrated "conformist" artists could enjoy the benefits of autonomy from public demand without paying the price (i.e., relative poverty) this status exacts on cultural producers under a market system of cultural production. No rewards were handed out for producing work that had wide public appeal but which failed to respect the official orthodoxies. (The stake that officially consecrated artists had in the socialist mode of cultural production may explain the vigor with which the "patriotic" wing of the Writers' Union opposed perestroika.) On occasion, officially approved cultural producers chose to create works capable of appealing to a large public. However, they made this decision as a response to the authorities' tendency to approve of cultural production they considered popularly accessible rather than out of direct—that is, economically enforced—conformity to mass market demand.

The cultural economy of shortage also affected the relationship between less orthodox artists and their audiences. Whereas its dynamics allowed officially approved artists to remain oblivious to the real structure of public demand, it gave the less orthodox a tendency to think there was no inherent contradiction between the aspiration to work as autonomous artists and the problem of appealing to a market. They experienced an immediate harmony between their creative aspirations and what they believed to be a widespread demand for cultural products challenging or evading the official norms. (I shall examine specific examples of this perception in more detail in the next chapter.)

Late-Soviet conditions of cultural production gave this perception an element of validity. During this period the authorities generally attempted to minimize the public impact of cultural products they did not fully approve of by restricting their scale of distribution. (Outright bans or imprisonment of their creators were reserved for cases judged extreme.) Print runs of heterodox books, for instance, tended to be small, while unorthodox films were assigned low distribution categories. The effect was to create a strong unsatisfied demand for such works, albeit one largely restricted to the intelligentsia public.[37] Indeed, the rumor that the authorities had only reluctantly approved a film's release virtually guaranteed that urban intelligenty would stampede to see it.[38]

The result was that even though the state's treatment of heterodox cultural producers was discriminatory rather than protective, official control over the distribution of cultural products enhanced their autonomy from the market by intervening between them and the "real" structure of demand. This created a paradox: for good immediate reasons, nonconformist cultural producers experienced the socialist mode of cultural production as the chief obstacle to their wider communion with the Soviet public. Yet at the same time, the existence of the socialist mode of cultural production was the condition of possibility for their perception that there was an unforced, that is, autonomous, correspondence between what they wanted to produce and what the (largely intelligentsia) public wanted to consume. That is, the excess demand for artistically sophisticated and socially critical cultural products depended ultimately on the state's "artificial" restriction of the scale on which such works were distributed. When the state's monopoly over the cultural economy was dismantled during perestroika, politically imposed limitations on cultural distribution vanished and with it excess demand for truth-telling cultural products. As a result, Russia's "critically thinking" creative intelligentsia faced the painful prospect of joining their Western counterparts in being tolerated but largely ignored by a society with ample alternative means of distraction.

A NON-WEBERIAN BUREAUCRACY

Although the state claimed absolute authority to direct the creative output of cultural producers, the bureaucratic disciplinary mechanisms it used to do so proved to be surprisingly weak once the threat of terror was lifted following the Thaw. Two major factors were at work here: first, the rigor and regularity of the cultural bureaucracy was undermined by the "non-Weberian" nature of the Soviet administrative structures in general—that is, the tendency for decision making to depend more on personal relationships than on the formal hierarchy of office. Second, owing in large part to the "soft budget constraint" under which film production, like all Soviet industrial activity, operated, the authorities were unable to regularize and discipline the film production process.

The title and exact responsibilities of the main institution entrusted with the supervision of the film industry changed over the years in accordance with the Soviet predilection for attempting institutional solutions to systemic problems. From 1972 until the end of perestroika, the film industry's ruling body was named Goskino.[39] To filmmakers, perhaps as a way of sidestepping the need to constantly revise their nomenclature, it was informally known as "The Committee." The following is an account of Goskino's role and characteristics in 1970s. In its main outlines, however, it is applicable to earlier periods also.[40]

From its imposing office building in central Moscow, Goskino controlled most aspects of the Soviet film industry. Its central responsibilities included supervising the main film studios of the Russian Republic, approving films for distribution, determining film production budgets, vetting scripts, managing film import and export, arranging foreign coproductions, and developing industrial infrastructure; it also ran film archives and creative and technical training institutes (most important, the central film school VGIK in Moscow), organized film festivals, and published professional, critical, and popular film journals. The most important areas of the film industry outside its supervision were production and distribution within the non-Russian national republics (controlled by republic-level Goskinos under the authority of the local political leadership), and the management of film theaters (which were run by city and district councils).

Like other parts of the Soviet bureaucracy, executive authority within Goskino and its subordinate institutions was formally organized according to the Leninist principle of one-person management (*edinonachalie*), that is, as a pyramidal hierarchy of administrators, assisted by, but not in practice answerable to, an equivalent structure of committees.[41] At its upper levels, appointments were made according to the nomenklatura system. According to Soviet theories of organization, such bureaucratic structures were supposed to behave according to a "cybernetic" model, with orders flowing down the administrative hierarchy and only information up.[42]

The formal and hierarchical nature of Goskino's "corporate culture" is captured by the following description of its operations in the 1970s: "Every mistake 'may be the last,' so there is great emphasis on protocol, rank, and paperwork. The highest administrators maintain great social distance. Except for Sergei Bondarchuk and Stanislav Rastotsky, all film directors must make an appointment and can expect to wait four weeks for a formal interview with the 'boss.' An atmosphere of suspicion precludes certain behavior: 'private' opinions cannot be expressed, criticism in general must be circumspect, and documentation is needed at every step."[43]

In theory, this multilayered system subjected filmmakers' creative activities to minute supervision. Pyotr Todorovsky describes the lengthy vetting process scripts had to survive before being approved for filming:

> Let's say I'm a script writer working at the Odessa film studios. I give a director a script. He gives it to an editor who can make corrections, then it's re-written and discussed by the editorial council of the studio. If they don't make corrections (and it was unusual that they didn't) then [it went] to the director of the studio, then to Goskino Ukraine where there's a special editor for the Odessa studio. If no corrections,

then to the vice-minister, then to Moscow to the all-Union Ministry where there's someone in charge of Ukraine. . . . It was a harsh, very harsh system.[44]

Approval of the script was just the first step in the process of getting a film made and released to the public. Once the first cut was completed, it went through another series of checks. First, the film was viewed by the editorial committee of the creative team to which the director belonged, then by that of the studio as a whole, then by the studio chief. If problems arose, the director might be asked to reedit or reshoot parts of the film. The studio then offered up the film for initial clearance by Goskino; it then went to Glavlit (the government organ with overall responsibility for censorship in the arts and media) and finally was checked by the Repertory Control department of Goskino. Only then could it be copied and sent out to local distribution offices.[45] Lower-level organs were held accountable for failing to preempt problems noticed further up the chain. The higher the level a problem was spotted at, the greater the scandal.

Certainly this system was harsh enough in its operations to provoke a good measure of alienation in the film industry's creative personnel. For many, dealing with the Goskino bureaucracy was a stressful and humiliating experience that they still recall with a good deal of bitterness. One scriptwriter recalls: "My friends and I dreaded having to go to Goskino. We used to take tranquilizers before each visit. One scriptwriter I knew would have a nervous breakdown each time she went: it got to the point where she had to have someone go instead of her to speak on her behalf."[46] She is now on the committee of Roskomkino (the body that succeeded Goskino after the fall of the Soviet Union) which decides on funding for film scripts and says: "Just the building still has awful associations for me. A lot of the same old people are working there but now they're a lot more respectful. It's great to be able to go there and 'feel like a white' [*chuvstvovat' sebya belim chelovekom*]."[47]

Beneath the surface, however, the actual process of decision making within the film industry administration, in common with other areas of the Soviet bureaucracy, was less formal and rigorous than such accounts may suggest. First, it seems that the lower levels of the film administration, particularly within the studios, were often sympathetic to the directors and writers under their charge. Maya Turovskaya, for instance, characterizes Mosfilm's editorial department as active in helping creative workers present their projects in such a way as to make them acceptable to the higher (and generally less sympathetic) authorities.[48] Similarly, scriptwriter Valery Zalotukha recalls: "In fact, we knew these people [the studio editors] and they told us how to write so as to fool their bosses. We knew them and they knew us. There was trust between us."[49]

A second factor tending to weaken the rigor of official supervision was the role that personal whims, favors, and connections could play in overriding the outcome of the formal bureaucratic process. Within the administration of the film industry, as in all Soviet bureaucracies, there was no ultimate delegation of responsibility: decisions made by film industry administrators could be reversed by more senior officials, whether or not they had ordinary jurisdiction over cinema.[50] According to Val Golovskoy, in 1979, for instance, the complaints of a general were responsible for the cutting of "insufficiently patriotic" songs from a film starring the celebrated "bardic" singer, Vladimir Vysotsky.[51] No decision, therefore, could be assumed to be final. The arbitrariness of the system is indicated by Pyotr Todorovsky's account of how a film of his that seemed to have passed all the official hurdles ran into trouble at the last moment before release:

To illustrate with an example from when I was working in Odessa. The studio officials said the film I had just completed, *A City Romance* (*Gorodskoi roman*), was okay but then they got a call from Moscow saying that head of Goskino [at the time, Alexei Romanov] wanted them back in Moscow, so they returned. But his secretary said he was away, so they had to hang around for a week. The director of the studio went away because no one would talk to them. After a week the first assistant minister gives them a memo through his secretary saying, "We really like it, but either you or we missed one theme, incitement to adultery" [laughs]. The plot of the story is that a young man meets a girl. They go to the movies, go to his place and spend the night together. The problem was that she spent the night with him without being married. The chief said the picture had to be redubbed so that the guy addresses her as "my dear wife." They said as a big confidence that the movie was shown at the dacha of first assistant prime minister, Polansky, the KGB chief. He was away so only his wife and daughter saw it and [when she saw it] his wife said, "It was terrible! My daughter saw them go to bed together without being married." That was the kind of system we had.[52]

Todorovsky alludes here to the common practice whereby the highest-ranking Party chiefs previewed new films *na dache* (at the country house), a custom practiced by the leadership since Stalin.[53] Whatever the outcome of the regular vetting process described above, the *na dache* viewing could make or break the fate of the film and the official reputation of its maker. Valery Zalotukha (VZ) and director Alexander Chernykh (AC) sardonically recall this custom:

> VZ: In those [Soviet] times all the good films were watched "*na dache*" and everyone waited to see if they went down well there.
> AC [humorously]: They sat down with vodka and girls, to watch the movie. They watched Tarkovsky this way and so of course they fell asleep and they were very disappointed.
> VZ: Yes, it was a kind of Stalinist tradition. And after that, if they liked it on the dacha, it meant it would get wide distribution.
> AC: These are people who had private movie theaters at their dachas.
> (GF: Did Gorbachev do this too?)
> VZ: Of course. He considered himself a connoisseur.[54]

The tendency of Soviet leaders to override the decisions of the film bureaucracy in approving or banning films could also work to a filmmaker's advantage. The refusal to delegate responsibility could provide filmmakers blocked by Goskino with a kind of informal appeals process.[55] This required the mobilization of the informal networks of patron-client ties that pervaded all official structures. Films that had run into trouble with the cinema bureaucracy could be offered up via a chain of intermediaries for the supreme leadership to pass judgment on. Tarkovsky refers to one such incident in his diary. He had just refused to make the extensive cuts to his 1972 film *Solaris* ordered by then head of Goskino Alexei Romanov and was in despair about his future as a director. A few days later,

> Romanov came to the studio on the twenty-ninth and *Solaris* was accepted without a single alteration. Nobody can believe it. They say that the agreement accepting the film is the only one ever to be signed personally by Romanov. Someone must have put the fear of God into him.
> I heard that Sizov [chief of Mosfilm, Tarkovsky's studio] showed the film to three officials whose names we don't know . . . and their author-

ity is too great for their opinion to be ignored. It's nothing short of miraculous.[56]

Thus, in any given case, the informalization of the bureaucratic process could work either for or against filmmakers' interests. Its overall effect, however, was to rob the system of its consistency and therefore its effectiveness in subjecting creative practice to regular disciplinary norms. Such a system fostered a sense of injustice among late-Soviet filmmakers without being capable of fully controlling their activities.

THE FAILURE TO RATIONALIZE THE FILM PRODUCTION PROCESS

From a comparative perspective, one of the central weaknesses of the Soviet system of film production was its failure to subject the production process to the modes of "rationalized" control typical of Western film industries, in particular that of Hollywood.

The development of rationalized methods of film production in early-twentieth-century Hollywood was motivated by its financial backers' interest in turning out films swiftly and cheaply, yet at a consistently marketable level of quality. As what David Bordwell, Janet Staiger, and Kristin Thompson call the "classic Hollywood mode of film production" evolved, directors were subordinated to a producer answerable to the film's financial backers, who exercised overall control over not only budgetary and organizational questions but also even the creative aspects of the project.[57] Through such practices as the "production board," a costed schedule in which the cost, time, place, and personnel for each subtask are precisely specified,[58] the labor process was subjected to the maximum possible degree of managerial supervision.[59] By organizing the production process in this manner Hollywood has succeeded in turning out a high volume of films of a consistently "professional" standard of technical (if not always aesthetic and intellectual) excellence.

The perception that the technical standards of Soviet film were lower than those of the West was frequently expressed by my informants. Pyotr Todorovsky for instance: "Even bad [artistically?] American movies have a very high level of professionalism: you can see it in every camera movement, let alone their special effects. Here it's impossible to achieve this."[60]

Those who have had experience of both Soviet and Western production methods commented on the underdevelopment of specific filmmaking professions in the Soviet system. Maria, a production assistant working today, remarks, "Our filmmaking doesn't have line producers [the designation given in the Western system for the person responsible for organizing the actual shooting]. Instead, the director has a big mass of assistants who aren't professionalizèd. Also it doesn't have a photographer—someone who studies locations before shooting to make sure that as well as it looking right, there's electricity to run the equipment off of."[61] Maria's comments indicate the relative lack of functional specialization within Soviet film crews. Of course, these functions still had to be carried out, but from her account it would seem to have been the direct responsibility of the director to have them seen to. Given a competent director, this might not necessarily lead to a worse final result but would tend to slow down shooting. A Russian production manager who had recently worked on an American film shot in Moscow (*Police Academy VII*) confirms this picture: "Our crews are less than half the size of American film crews, maybe fifty people. So people are used to being able to do different people's jobs. Titles and responsibilities are rather different. They don't have special tools for everything but can patch things together from two planks and a bit of rope."[62]

Others, however, suggest that Soviet system of filmmaking provided opportunities for directorial authority and creativity they see as limited by the more regimented Western system. Ivan Maximov, a director of animated films,

> (GF: Do you think the decline in professionalism since perestroika people comment on is due to lack of money?)
> *Before everyone worked just for the sake of art*, the writer, the cameraman and so on. It was like a company of friends. The money came from the government. . . . *Now people have to think about money, about future work and we've lost that atmosphere of creativity.*
> (GF: I suppose that in the West creative workers are used to having to worry about money, but Russians don't have that experience?)
> *The main style of work under capitalism is very narrow specialization.* For instance in Russia the final edit was made by the director but no one would let me do it in America because I don't have enough training in that area.[63] (Emphasis added)

The manner in which the nonrationalized nature of the Soviet film production process enabled an "auteur" model of filmmaking to be practiced in the late-Soviet period is suggested by the working methods of Andrei Tarkovsky. Between 1965 and his departure from the Soviet Union in 1982, Tarkovsky completed only four films. This is not to suggest that he was in any sense incompetent: he was evidently ferociously committed to his work, open to the creative input of the others on his team, and presumably an inspiring enough figure to work for (despite the official disfavor under which he labored) to keep many of his key collaborators from film to film. Although he spent longer on shooting than was typical in the West, he completed his films on budgets small even by Soviet standards that nevertheless bore few marks of their low cost. He was not, however, by Western standards, a "professional," that is, adapted to working according to regularized norms and methods, and in this sense he was a typical product of the late-Soviet system of filmmaking.

Vida Johnson and Graham Petrie describe his working methods thus: "His films underwent a process of constant rethinking, rewriting, and recreation at every stage—pre-production, shooting, dubbing, mixing, and editing."[64] They suggest that his tendency to improvise rather than follow the script functioned in part as a way of resisting official supervision over his work. Such a strategy made sense because, despite the minute attention paid by censors to the script and the completed film, during the actual shooting "remarkably little supervision was provided either by the studio or by Goskino. No one from Goskino was present to make certain that the director shot what was approved in the script."[65] The censorship system not only failed to compensate for the lack of financial discipline, it contributed to what post-Soviet director, Valery Todorovsky (son of Pyotr), refers to as "a major sickness in our cinematic tradition . . . lack of respect for the scenario."[66]

The strains and stresses inherent in this kind of work method are conveyed by this excerpt from Tarkovsky's diaries concerning the shooting of his last Soviet film *Stalker*: "1. Faulty film three times running. . . . 2. After the cameraman and the production manager were replaced Kalashnikov refused to go on working and walked out. . . . 3. I sacked Boim for being a drunk. 4. I sacked Abdusalimov for behaving like a bastard."[67]

It is notable from this passage that, while avoiding supervision from above, Tarkovsky seems to have attempted to exercise absolute managerial as well as artistic authority over his crew. We may assume that, just as he proved adept at avoiding dictates from above, his subordinates had their own mechanisms for evading his control, thus contributing to the general unpredictability of the production process.

The link between the unpredictability of this working environment and the degree of authority Soviet directors sought over the production process is suggested by the account Johnson and Petrie give of Tarkovsky's difficulties in adapting to production methods in the West.[68] His producer in Sweden complained that "she found it impossible to pin him down in advance or even to hold him to certain commitments he had already made."[69] Tarkovsky in his turn expressed frustration at the *regularity* of his Swedish crew: he accuses them of being "bad workers" for only being prepared to work nine to five (as per union rules). In his view, this hindered his ability to pursue new inspirations or to exploit the possibilities offered by changed shooting conditions.[70]

The Soviet failure to limit directorial authority by rationalizing the production process was not due to official unawareness of the problem. As Richard Taylor has shown, the first head of the fully nationalized Soviet film industry, Boris Shumyatsky, a figure best known for his harassment of the directors of the montage school, was also an acute analyst of organizational problems within the industry that were to prove perennial. His opposition to the cinematic avant-garde was motivated not merely by aesthetic and ideological narrow-mindedness (although this may have been a factor) but also by his admiration for Hollywood's capacity to produce large numbers of popular films swiftly. He criticized Soviet film directors for privileging, in both their theory and practice, their individual authority over that of both the creative team and industry management. Shumyatsky's explanation for the slow pace of Soviet film production in relation to, for instance, that of Hollywood remained applicable throughout the Soviet and indeed post-Soviet periods: "When they make a film our directors are achieving a synthesis of [the functions of] various authors . . . but they are overburdened with administrative and organizational functions and this turns them into 'Jacks of all trades' without proper conditions and qualifications. This situation hinders the creative development of the director and similarly obstructs the development of the other co-authors of the film, subjugating them in administrative terms to the director."[71]

Prefiguring the ideas of many of my informants (particularly those who were not directors!), Shumyatsky proposed that to increase productivity, the Soviet industry follow Hollywood by encouraging the "direct creative participation of the management in a film."[72] In other words, he advocated what would now be termed a producer-led model of filmmaking.

Although Shumyatsky was successful in the negative sense that he was able to frustrate the creative aspirations of the experimental directors of the 1920s, he was completely unable to put the constructive aspects of his program into practice. With his fall from favor and execution in 1938, his attempt to rationalize the industry's production methods was abandoned, as it turned out, for good. His failure parallels the general inability of the Soviet leadership to introduce the principles of "scientific management" developed by Ford and Taylor within the manufacturing industry as a whole.[73] As David Stark argues, the rationalization of a particular production organization can only be accomplished if the organization is subject to a system of rewards and sanctions originating in *external* forces, in particular the financial pressure imposed by market competition. In socialist countries, however: "The attempt to manage an economy scientifically as if it were one factory prevent[ed] the scientific management of any one factory"[74] because production organizations were subject to no disciplinary mechanisms truly external to the state bureaucracy. The Soviet attempt to introduce scientific management everywhere meant that it could never became a reality anywhere. Similarly, the monopoly character of the Soviet film industry prevented the operation of the system of economic incentives of the sort that stimulated the development of the rationalized modes of discipline typical within Hollywood.

While the other aspects of the socialist mode of cultural production that I consider here affected state control over all cultural sectors, the failure to rationalize the production process was particularly important within cinema, owing to the inherently complex, quasi-industrial nature of filmmaking. Lacking the financial-organizational controls wielded by their Western counterparts, the authorities were unable to force filmmakers to work effectively and consistently on externally commissioned projects. Instead, the state was doomed to what we might call a non-Foucauldian exercise of power over film production; it could forbid but not enable, punish but not discipline.[75] This failure contributed to two of the industry's most characteristic features—on the one hand its generally poor technical quality and slow rate of completion, on the other the capacity of the more committed directors to arrogate to themselves full control over production (but not distribution) decisions. Under Stalinist conditions the failure to rationalize the film production process manifested itself in a low rate of output, under those of the late-Soviet period, the production of auteur cinema on the one hand and "gray" cinema on the other.

OFFICIAL CORPORATIZATION, UNOFFICIAL SOLIDARITY

From the 1930s on, the Party-State attempted to confine legitimate intellectual and cultural activity to those working within state-funded and supervised institutions.[76] To perform in public a musician, for instance, had to be employed by a *filarmonia*; an actor had to join a repertory theater. There were no freelance musicians or actors, or dancers or journalists—contracts were permanent. Through these organizations, all forms of artistic activity could be subjected to pre-production censorship, with their output governed by a "theme plan" (*templan*) established by state-authorized supervisory institutions. In sectors of cultural production like painting and literature, where works are created in an immediate sense by individuals rather than by production organizations, state control was exercised primarily through the system of "creative unions" called for in the Central Committee's 1932 resolution "On the Restructuring of Literary and Artistic Organizations."[77] Through these means, the Soviet state not only assigned rewards and sanctions to the cultural producers, it also attempted to determine who was permitted to occupy the status of artist.[78] In literature, for instance, writers were not accorded professional status unless they had been admitted to membership of the Writers' Union—as Joseph Brodsky's celebrated 1964 trial made clear, to follow one's muse outside the official system exposed one to the charge of "social parasitism," punishable by imprisonment.[79]

By making all cultural producers dependent on a bureaucratic system of patronage and control dominated by those most trusted by the authorities, this system would appear, and was no doubt intended to have minimized opportunities for creative autonomy. In certain respects, however, the corporatization of cultural production enhanced autonomizing tendencies through the manner in which it fostered possibilities for informal communication between participants in official cultural institutions. Golovskoy, for instance, recalls the sense of community that he experienced as a member of the Filmmakers' Union. Next to its offices in central Moscow, the Union maintained a "House of Cinema" (*Dom kino*) around whose plush bar, restaurant, and private 2,000-seat cinema much of the social life of Moscow filmmakers revolved.[80] At an invitation-only screening of a foreign film at Dom kino he recalls, "Acquaintances wave and it seems that everybody knows everybody else in the audience—one big fraternity."[81] When asked what he most missed about the Soviet film world, he stated: "The creative atmosphere amongst filmmakers. The opportunities for discussion . . . in the House of Cinema . . . opportunities for genuine discussion [better] than in some other countries that produce motion pictures."[82]

As another Soviet film critic recalls, such informal social contact between colleagues could play a crucial role in developing a sense of solidarity in the face of demands from above:

> During the period of "developed socialism" [an ironic reference to the Brezhnev era] there was a struggle within the journal because we tried to resist the pressure of the bureaucracy. We never wrote anything in support of the authorities. . . .
> (GF: Were the staff of the journal united in resisting this pressure?)
> It wasn't official, we tried to unite in our souls and we understood each other very quickly. There were a lot of young people [on the staff] . . . and we often met in the kitchen, as you know![83] We didn't have to work as hard [as today] and we had a lot of time for unofficial meetings to discuss all our problems. It was a time of talking and not of hard work. We had a lot of spare time. Because now it's impossible to find time to go to a café.[84]

Thus the manner in which the Soviet state concentrated, corporatized, and pampered its cultural producers did not merely subject them to the authorities' "whip and gingerbread"[85] but fostered the formation of a kind of hidden "public sphere," within which opinions were freely exchanged and a sense of community created. This in turn encouraged the development of the kind of *unofficial, internal* hierarchies of prestige that characterized the sphere of late-Soviet cultural production.[86] Once the leadership loosened the bonds of "democratic centralism" by allowing the free election of officers, the creative unions offered ready-made institutional platforms from which disaffected cultural producers were able to challenge the Soviet system of control.

ART AND ORTHODOXY

The official Soviet requirement that all cultural producers adhere to a theoretically unitary conception of aesthetic orthodoxy has no direct equivalent in Western societies. In the modern West, cultural production, at least in peacetime, has not been directly subjected to state ideological dictates.[87] At the same time, however, the Soviet doctrine of aesthetic orthodoxy can be seen as arising from functional needs that the Soviet apparatus of cultural production to a great extent shared with the cultural industries of the West. First, owing to their public prominence, large-scale cultural industries have a particularly intense need to justify their mode of organization and the character of their output, both to the public and their own staff—that is, they need to be able to claim a legitimating purpose. In the case of U.S. network television this purpose might be the provision of fun but wholesome "family entertainment," in the case of public broadcasting, the fostering of an informed and enlightened citizenry.[88] The legitimating goal of the Soviet cultural industry was the formation of the "New Soviet Person" through the aesthetic method of "socialist realism." Second, all bureaucratized institutions of cultural production in the West, whether motivated by profit or public service, attempt to regularize and discipline the activities of creative workers through the use of "formatting"—that is, relatively stable, stereotyped, and widely understood formulas for creative output.[89] As an aesthetic ideal operating to direct artistic activities and inform editorial and censorship decisions, socialist realism can be regarded as the functional equivalent of these formatting techniques. The difference of course was that the single format of socialist realism was applied across every sector of cultural production, including those, like literature, easel painting, or "art cinema," that in the West are not directly subjected to bureaucratic modes of control.

Interpreting the impact of the socialist realist ideal of aesthetic orthodoxy on Soviet creative practice is a difficult undertaking. Its concrete outcomes in particular media depended on their inherent characteristics, while whatever stylistic unity Soviet cultural production possessed under Stalin largely dissipated after the dictator's demise. I shall concentrate, therefore, on those aspects of socialist realism that, even if formulated under Stalin and applied to other sectors of cultural production, affected cinema during the late-Soviet period.

There is an important distinction to be made between socialist realism as an official discourse concerning the goals of cultural production, and socialist realism as a positive style characterizing actual Soviet aesthetic practice.[90] Even in the period of high Stalinism, official aesthetic discourse never became capable of giving cultural producers a fully stable or coherent system of directions: in one year a campaign for "conflictless" literature might be launched, in the next this ideal would be subjected to bitter polemics.[91] What the official discourse of socialist realism did do, however, was consistently express the claim that *orthodoxy itself* was expected of all loyal Soviet artists. As Bourdieu remarks (presumably with state socialist culture in mind), cultural production "can never be dominated by one orthodoxy without continuously being dominated by the general question of orthodoxy itself."[92] Thus the charter of each of the creative unions contained a clause declaring their members' allegiance to socialist realism, even though the official interpretation of what this meant in terms of aesthetic practice shifted constantly. Ultimately, the fundamental quality required of the orthodox Soviet cultural producer was *partiinost*—the subordination of one's creative projects to political direction, whatever specific form this direction might take.

In one sense, this doctrine was a direct negation of artistic autonomy: Stalin's chief of ideology, Andrei Zhdanov, indicated his hostility to the ideal of artistic freedom in his 1946 declaration that "beginning with Belinsky, all the best representatives of the revolutionary-democratic Russian intelligentsia repudiated so-called 'pure art' and 'art for art's sake.' They were heralds of art for the people, of art of high ideological and social significance."[93] More typical of official discourse on artistic autonomy than Zhdanov's outright rejection of the concept, however, was the claim that Soviet conditions of cultural production in actuality enhanced artists' creative freedom by releasing them from the dependence on the market. This argument goes back to Lenin's pre-Revolutionary pamphlet, "Party Organization and Party Literature," in which he justified his call for the subordination of literature to Party control on the grounds that the "freedom of any bourgeois writer, artist, or actress is simply masked (or hypocritically masked) dependence on the moneybags, on corruption, on prostitution."[94]

Official discourse also represented the very subordination of artists to Party direction as the achievement of the "true" freedom that in the Marxist-Hegelian tradition can be secured only by throwing in one's lot with the forces of historical progress. Thus in his speech before the founding congress of the Soviet Writers' Union in 1934, Maxim Gorky declared that the intention behind the union's formation was "harmoniously to merge all aims in that unity which is guiding all the creative working energies of the country. The idea, of course, is not to restrict individual creation but to furnish it with the widest means of continued powerful development."[95] The argument parallels the Party's general claim to establish "people's" as opposed to "bourgeois" democracy and to offer its subjects concrete rather than "abstract" rights. Within official discourse, Soviet artists were free to the extent that they recognized the necessity of serving the construction of socialism. As we have seen, in the case of the film industry the claim that socialist conditions of cultural production offered artists more creative freedom than their Western counterparts turned out have been truer than the authorities perhaps intended.

The political leadership's imposition of orthodoxy on cultural producers did not, therefore, imply any public diminution in the prestige accorded to the position of "artist" within Soviet society. Indeed, at a discursive level, this status was strenuously upheld. Even under Stalin, official cultural criticism showed an obsessive concern with the identification and canonization of new Soviet "masterpieces," capable of matching the consecrated works of the past. The creators of these modern classics were elevated into a pantheon of "cultural authorities" and admitted to the highest circles of the Stalin-era *beau monde*.[96] This concern with artistic excellence may explain the relative (if always unpredictable) leniency with which the most prominent nonconformist cultural figures were treated even during Stalinism's most repressive phases. Evidently some artists were considered too indispensable to purge. Similarly, in the late-Soviet period, the leadership's need for the outside world to recognize the greatness of the artistic achievements under their tutelage tended to strengthen the hand of those heterodox cultural producers who had won renown in the West.[97]

The manner in which the state attempted to normalize the activities of creative workers while reproducing the ideology of the artist as charismatic individual genius, significantly exacerbated the problems it faced in subjecting cultural production to the kinds of disciplines typical of Western cultural industries. Cultural producers were encouraged to develop a sense of social status that conflicted with the subordinated position they were assigned within the official apparatus of cultural production. At the level of discourse the state upheld the nobility of Art, yet in its actual administration of cultural production it treated Soviet creative workers as dependent hacks.

To an extent, this contradiction is also present in Western cultural industries, which attempt to subject their creative workers to bureaucratic modes of control yet exploit, and thereby reproduce, the cult of the inspired, unique, and charismatic artist in marketing even their most standardized products to the public.[98] Artists and performers with sufficient (perceived) market draw are not only able to demand a large share of the profits but also to secure creative control over the projects they are involved in. In contrast to the Soviet situation, however, in commercial culture industries the autonomy of the (star) artist remains dependent on the same principle motivating bureaucratic control, that is, the market. Within such industries, the authority of individual artists is recognized only so long as they use this authority in a manner that is compatible with market demands; it does not, therefore, present a challenge to the system's mode of operation or to the character of its output.[99]

During the Thaw, the official conception of aesthetic orthodoxy was redefined so that the freedom it accorded to the artist depended less on the subtleties of the dialectic and more on an increased, if still limited, acceptance of stylistic and thematic diversity. The requirement that Soviet art represent society "in its revolutionary development"—that is, as the leadership wished it to appear, rather than as it actually was—was dropped, branded as the "varnishing of reality." Even a measure of social criticism was considered valuable so long as it was not aimed at the central institutions or symbolic underpinnings of Party rule. The greater flexibility of the new aesthetic regime is indicated in this 1964 passage from *Kommunist* (a journal whose function was to provide a forum for theoretical-ideological "debate").

> From the standpoint of Communist ideology, our art reflects the most varied aspects of life and distinct human characters and fates, and reveals the processes and events of life with all its complexities, color and inconsistencies as well as an aspiration towards a Communist future. The wealth of everyday observation and the variety of themes and artistic ideas naturally give rise to the diversity of styles, fads, individual mannerisms, and creative approaches, i.e., to a practically inexhaustible diversity of our realistic forms of art.[100]

Such statements signaled the end of the Stalinist attempt to impose socialist realism as a coherent aesthetic style. Nevertheless, they did not imply that the Party leadership had abandoned the requirement of orthodoxy itself, merely that the authorities had broadened the range of creative practices that it was prepared to consider orthodox. True, this passage calls for an "art [that] reflects the most varied aspects of life," and so on, but this call for diversity is still authorized in terms of the necessities of Communist ideology. In the post-Stalin era, periods in which the limits of the artistically permissible expanded alternated with spells of contraction, but the leadership's basic claim to monopolize the authority to define those limits remained in place.[101] For the actual administration of cultural production, the post-Stalin loosening of aesthetic orthodoxy signaled a shift in emphasis from positive toward negative forms of censorship. The cultural bureaucracy's task became less to elicit the production of "ideal" works (although this was still occasionally attempted) than to prevent the distribution of those the leadership considered threatening. As a format capable of routinizing and disciplining cultural production, socialist realism was breaking down.

MASS APPEAL

Within capitalist cultural industries a central function of the practice of formatting is to ensure that creative workers conform to the assumed expectations of a consuming public. In some respects, the official conception of aesthetic orthodoxy can be seen as playing a parallel role in the Soviet Union.

Jeffrey Brooks suggests that the primary intended public of Stalin-era cultural production was the class of upwardly mobile workers from which the Party bureaucracy was increasingly being recruited, known within official discourse of the time as the "active Soviet public" (*sovetskaya obshchestvennost'*).[102] According to Evgeny Dobrenko, the formation of the high-Stalinist socialist realist aesthetic was significantly influenced by the authorities' wish to create a culture that would answer to this class's firmly "middlebrow" cultural tastes. In literature, for instance, he finds that the requirements of "worker-readers" in the 1920s and early 1930s included the following:

1. "The book should be recognizably useful, it should instruct."
2. "The book should be accessible to, even cultivate the reader."
3. "Literature should be realistic, yet optimistic and heroic."
4. "Poetry should be free of 'futurism' [i.e., avant-garde experimentation]."
5. "Literature should not be obscene."[103]

These preferences are remarkably similar to those characteristic of similarly positioned social strata in the West.[104] They exhibit similar hostility toward both "vulgar" forms of popular entertainment and modernist experimentation. What is distinctive about the relationship of Stalin-era socialist realism to the consuming public is not so much that it was oriented toward middlebrow taste, but that it categorically denied legitimacy to alternative taste cultures, whether "above" or "below" this imperial middle. Stalinist cultural production can be characterized as a form of "mass culture," therefore, insofar as it aimed to disseminate centrally produced works to the widest possible public. It was not, however, a form of mass culture in the sense critics of the Western cultural industries once deployed the term, for in no way was it aimed at the "lowest common denominator" of taste. Rather, it aimed to universalize exposure to, and appreciation for, an essentially middlebrow interpretation of high cultural excellence.

Socialist realist culture was required, therefore, not only to be imbued with optimistic moral uplift (qualities which in the Soviet context meant unqualified support for official ideology) but to exhibit the quality of maximum formal clarity and accessibility known in official discourse as *narodnost*. As Zhdanov declared: "Not everything that is accessible is great, but everything that is authentically great is accessible, and the greater it is, the more accessible to the masses."[105] In practice, this meant a return to the formal techniques of the mid-nineteenth century, less perhaps because they are intrinsically more "accessible" than those of any other era, than because they were familiar to a culturally middlebrow Soviet leadership and the middlebrow public it sought to address.

As we have seen, the intensity of the cultural economy of shortage in the Stalin period means that we have little way of knowing how popular the socialist realist "format" actually was (or more precisely, how popular it would have been had alternatives been available). Certainly there is evidence of genuine enthusiasm for works it would be hard to imagine finding a public under other conditions.[106] Even when the Russian cultural consumer became fully liberated after perestroika, however, Stalin-era films and songs continued to enjoy considerable popularity. While we can accord socialist realism a genuine capacity to satisfy the demands of a large section of the public, it nevertheless differed from the formats of capitalist culture industries in the crucial respect that it attempted to use essentially the same formula to appeal to all tastes. Even in the late-Soviet period, official cultural discourse either refused to recognize differences in public taste or, when it did acknowledge their existence, to accord them legitimacy. Highbrow culture was derogatorily branded "elitist" (*elitarnaya*), while the continued existence of lowbrow taste was seen as requiring not the redirection of state cultural production, but intensified efforts to educate the masses culturally.

Socialist realism's cult of mass accessibility had a particular impact on the development of Soviet filmmaking owing to the specific role cinema was assigned in the Soviet order of cultural production. Because socialist realist aesthetics privileged the written word as the clearest expression of meaning, cinema, like other aural and visual art forms, was treated essentially as an auxiliary medium to literature.[107]

Insofar as cinema was the "most important of all the arts" to the Soviet leadership, it was not because of the role it could play in formulating Soviet culture and ideology. Rather, it was considered to possess an unrivaled ability to popularize a system of meanings already worked out in textual form. This conception of cinema's contribution is displayed in a published speech of Khrushchev's, "The Great Mission of Literature and Art." In appropriately short sentences, he declared: "The cinema is a very important and interesting field of the Party's ideological work. Films are an effective ideological weapon and a mass medium of education. When a book appears not everybody reads it. Some books are within reach of only the advanced reader, and besides it takes a good deal of time to read them and to grasp their meaning. Films are easier to understand. That is why cinema is the most popular of the arts."[108]

The effect of the campaign against "formalist" cinema under Stalin was to put an end to the montage school of directors' attempts to develop film's expressive potential as a medium distinct from literature and theater. As Boris Shumyatsky, who spearheaded this campaign in the 1930s, declared, "We are obliged to require our masters to produce works that have strong plots and are organized around a story-line. Otherwise they [the works] cannot be entertaining, they have no mass character, otherwise the Soviet screen will not need them."[109]

The authorities' steadfast preference for popularly accessible cinema created problems for those late-Soviet directors who—albeit along very different lines from the early-Soviet "formalists"—resumed explorations of film's distinctive formal potential during the late-Soviet period. In the 1970s and 1980s, Alexander Sokurov (known as one of Tarkovsky's leading disciples), for instance, had all his feature films banned from distribution. In a later interview he claimed that this was purely because of their aesthetic qualities rather than any anti-Soviet thematic content:

> The problems the government film institutions had with me—they had no political grounds. Because I had no questions about the Soviet system. I had, let's say, no interest. So I wouldn't even bother myself with criticizing it. . . . I was always driven by visual aesthetics. . . . The fact that I was involved in the visual side of art made the government suspicious. The nature of my films was different from [those of] others. They didn't actually know what to punish me for—and that confusion caused them huge irritation. . . . On the one hand, the films that I made were forbidden to be shown publicly; on the other, my new ideas were always approved.[110]

Although Sokurov claims to have had no intention of challenging Soviet ideology, the authorities' opposition to formal experimentation tended to reinforce the perception among officials, artists, and the intelligentsia public that aesthetic difficulty and ideological heterodoxy were intrinsically linked. Indeed, officials' distaste for "elitist" forms of cinema may have been exacerbated by their (often correct) suspicion that part of the attraction formal complexity held for artists and their public was the possibility it created for subversive messages to be slipped past the censorship apparatus. The intertwining of thematic and formal concerns comes across in the official criticisms directed against Tarkovsky's 1972 film, *Solaris*. The picture concerns a scientific expedition from Earth to investigate an enigmatic planet which communicates with its human observers by conjuring up visions of their past. Like Tarkovsky's other work, *Solaris* is slow-paced and meditative in style. Its central theme is a critique of the possibility and desirability of scientific rationality, a distinctly unwelcome message for a regime that based its claim to legitimacy on the allegedly scientific properties of Marxism-Leninism. In his diaries, Tarkovsky records:

> Yesterday Sizov [head of Mosfilm] dictated comments and criticism of *Solaris* collected from various bodies—the cultural department of the Central Committee, Demichev's office, the Committee [i.e., the

Goskino executive] and the governing board [of Goskino]. . . . The comments go like this: 1. There ought to be a clearer image of the earth of the future. The film doesn't make it clear what it's going to be like. . . . 3. What form of society was the starting-point for Kelvin's flight—Socialism, Communism or Capitalism? . . . Cut out the concept of God (?!) . . . 8. The conference. Cut out the foreign executives. . . . 10. The notion that Chris is an idler should be unfounded. . . . 12. As a scientist Sartorius lacks humanity . . . 19. There should be a written introduction from [Stanislav] Lem [the author of the story on which the script was based] explaining it all (?!) . . . 28. Is science human or not? . . . 35. Take home message: "There's no point in humanity dragging its shit from one end of the galaxy to the other."[111]

Although Tarkovsky saw these comments as foolish, and they might appear so to most Western observers, they show, in fact, a shrewd enough understanding of the implicit challenge his film presented to official ideology. Both Tarkovsky and his official critics were playing something of a double game here. Tarkovsky hid his actually rather clear rejection of one of the central pillars of Soviet ideology behind a veil of formal obscurity. However, the authorities perceived the veil itself as contrary to orthodox aesthetic norms and effectively challenged him to lower it. Had he done so, he would probably have lost the possibility of working within the official Soviet filmmaking system altogether. As it turned out, his refusal to make the film's implicitly oppositional message explicit allowed him to appeal successfully to higher authorities (who were perhaps less perceptive concerning its message than the industry chiefs); the film was released and he continued to work with practical, if grudging, official backing.

By treating formal experimentation as inherently inimical to aesthetic-ideological orthodoxy, the Soviet authorities rather thoroughly erased the faith of early-Soviet avant-garde directors that the Revolution and artistic progress could be served simultaneously. Until the very end of his life Eisenstein, for instance, was at least outwardly loyal to the Revolutionary cause. His 1936 film *Bezhin Meadow*, which celebrated a boy's decision to inform on his "kulak" parents for hoarding grain during the collectivization campaign, might be considered egregiously so. It was banned not for any perceived ideological deficiencies but for its aesthetic "formalism." When the possibility of artistic experimentation reemerged in the Khrushchev years, it was from the first at least implicitly opposed to the Party-State's direction of cultural production.

THE DISTRIBUTION OF AUTONOMY

Under Stalin every sector of cultural production was subjected to a system of supervision whose (always high) degree of strictness varied little from one sector to another. This uniformity was achieved by the use of police methods, since almost any cultural producer, however and wherever he or she worked, could be effectively cowed by the threat of imprisonment or death. The relative liberalism of the Brezhnev regime created a considerably more complex situation: in this period, the extent to which a particular area of cultural production was characterized by orthodoxy depended, first, on the priority the authorities attached to controlling it, and second, on the extent to which its inherent technological characteristics made the state's institutional control practical to maintain.

The importance the state attached to maintaining control over a particular medium depended in part on how directly its output impacted the ideological basis for the regime's legitimacy: thus the news media were more closely supervised than fictional or nonrepresentational forms of cultural production. An additional factor was the breadth of the medium's potential audience:[112] television was kept under particularly tight control whereas supervision over theater was relatively lax.[113] In media such as book publishing and cinema where the scale of distribution varies from one title to another, the authorities allowed quite heterodox works to reach the public but ensured that their scale of distribution remained limited. The leadership's belief that few cultural products were intolerable if their dissemination was sufficiently small is suggested by the custom of allowing members of the Filmmakers' Union to attend closed viewings of a wide variety of otherwise undistributed Western films.[114]

The capacity of the late-Soviet state to maintain monopoly control over a particular sector of cultural production depended on its ability to prevent public access to alternative means of production and distribution. The more technologically intensive the medium, the better it was able to do this. In television and radio broadcasting the state's monopoly was absolute. Until the beginnings of the "parallel cinema" movement in Moscow and Leningrad around 1984, the same was true of cinema.[115] In other, less technologically intensive sectors, however, the state's monopoly was harder to maintain, allowing the creation of an unauthorized sphere of cultural production.

The component of the sphere best known to the West was *samizdat* (self-published) literature, which took the form of typescripts circulating across informal social networks. A tradition that originated in attempts to avoid government censorship during the tsarist era, samizdat reemerged in the Soviet Union in the mid-1950s when such activity, although still subject to repression, at least no longer carried a potential death sentence. From the mid-1960s onward, as the Brezhnev regime retightened the ideological screws on officially published literature without returning to the full rigors of Stalinist Terror, it became a central part of the intelligentsia's cultural life.[116] Through samizdat, a wide range of works deemed unacceptable for official publication could find a readership, albeit a limited one.

In the sphere of music, the "underground" scene, as it was known to its participants (the Russian term being merely a phonetic transliteration of the English), occupied a position in some respects analogous to that of samizdat in literature. The music underground was stimulated less by the Soviet state's demands for political-ideological conformity than by its reluctance to allow the performance or distribution of new genres of popular music, in particular, modern jazz and rock. The cultural bureaucracy was suspicious of both musical genres, regarding them as symptoms of Western degeneracy that threatened to weaken the moral and social discipline of Soviet youth. However, the leadership was unable to prevent new styles of popular music infiltrating the country through such channels as foreign students, returning seamen, and foreign radio broadcasts.[117] Even though these flows were restricted in scale, their effects were greatly amplified by the intensity of Soviet youth's demand for the forbidden fruits they provided. (Here again we see how the conditions created by the cultural economy of shortage stimulated "subversive" forms of demand.) By the late 1960s these imports had stimulated the birth of an indigenous rock scene which blended the musical forms of Western rock with a distinctively (high cultural) Russian emphasis on lyrical meaning and complexity.

Owing to official disapproval, performances were furtive and irregular, and generally took place in private. Nevertheless, both domestic and imported rock, along with songs by the "bardic" movement, reached wide audiences through the circulation of home-recorded tapes (*magnizdat*).

Very likely magnizdat dwarfed samizdat in terms of its breadth of distribution. Whereas samizdat publication was restricted by the hours of toil necessary to type and retype manuscripts, the unofficial distribution of music was facilitated by the mass dissemination of tape recorders among the Soviet public from the 1960s onward.[118]

The existence of the unauthorized sphere of cultural production posed a significant challenge to the state-controlled apparatus of cultural production. By providing the intelligentsia (in the case of samizdat) and youth (in that of magnizdat) publics with alternatives to official cultural production, it undermined the state's ability to impose approved works on the cultural needs of the public. In the case of literature this may have contributed to the Brezhnev regime's otherwise surprising level of tolerance for heterodox works.[119] In music, the authorities responded to the evident popularity of rock by fostering the creation of the so-called VIAs (Vocal-Instrumental Ensembles) to purvey anodyne pop to Soviet youth. By the mid-1980s, three-quarters of Melodiya's output was pop rather than classical.[120]

At the same time, we can argue that the unauthorized sphere, in particular samizdat, provided official cultural producers with a model of fully independent cultural production that helped keep their own aspirations toward autonomy alive. As Tarkovsky wrote in his diaries of the 1970s: "The great thing is to be free in your work. Of course it's important to print or exhibit, but if that's not possible you still are left with the most important thing of all—being able to work without asking anyone's permission. However, in cinema that is not possible. You can't take a single shot unless the State graciously allows you to."[121]

This account of the distribution of official control and monopoly may explain why filmmakers were particularly active by comparison with creative workers in most other sectors of cultural production in dismantling the state apparatus of control during perestroika. Filmmaking differed from broadcasting and news journalism in that the authorities tolerated the expression of a certain degree of heterodoxy; although nonconformists had a difficult time of it, they were not successfully excluded from entering the profession, and once admitted, were rarely ejected altogether. On the other hand, as Condee and Padunov have pointed out, heterodox filmmakers differed from their counterparts in say literature or painting in that if they were dissatisfied with their treatment at the hands of the authorities, they had no choice but to stick it out within the state sector—at any rate, if they wished to continue to make films.[122] Denied the luxury of "internal migration" (i.e., withdrawal from officially sanctioned aspects of life) so common among other members of the late-Soviet intelligentsia, when given their chance by Gorbachev in May 1986, filmmakers came up fighting.[123]

3

THE CINEMATIC FIELD UNDER BREZHNEV

Under Brezhnev, the authorities discouraged the trend toward formal complexity and thematic "sincerity" characteristic of cinema during the Thaw period. In its place they promoted a model of filmmaking that combined ideological orthodoxy with entertainment qualities. The leadership sought to achieve this change of course not through a return to Stalinist-style preproduction censorship but by systematically privileging the more compliant directors. This policy was successful in reinforcing official control over cinema without compromising levels of output. However, by creating a division between the favored and the marginalized within the film world, it strengthened the perceived connection between the moral integrity of the film "artist" and the social pessimism and aesthetic difficulty of his or her films. This unintended consequence of Brezhnevite cultural retrenchment was to play a vital role in conditioning filmmakers' response to perestroika.

The renewed emphasis on aesthetic and ideological orthodoxy within cinema was signaled by the imposition of distribution bans on a number of films completed in 1967 (including Askoldov's *Commissar*, Andrei Konchalovsky's *Asya's Happiness*, and Kira Muratova's *Brief Encounters*). In the next eighteen years around sixty films were to end up "on the shelf," few compared to the total number produced, but a significant share of the output by the more heterodox, and arguably more talented, directors.[1] The other major strategy used to encourage cinematic orthodoxy in this period was the co-optation of a number of the more prominent directors of the post-Stalin period. Compliant directors enjoyed privileged access to scarce resources such as imported film stock, were assigned higher shooting budgets and more leisurely shooting schedules, and were given the opportunity to shoot coproductions abroad. Furthermore, they were appointed to managerial positions within such institutions as the secretariat of the Filmmakers' Union, the studio and Goskino artistic advisory councils, and professorships at VGIK. From these posts they exercised authority over their less fortunate colleagues, not only on strictly professional questions such as approving scripts for shooting and so forth, but also on such mundane issues as access to union housing.[2]

Conversely, the more "difficult" directors found their access to official resources restricted. The authorities' treatment of Tarkovsky exemplifies this policy. He was never completely prevented from working, but the slowness with which his projects were approved, the niggardliness of the shooting budgets he was assigned, and the low distribution categories his few completed films were awarded, kept him in a perpetual state of financial insecurity. Indeed, in public at least, he maintained that it was his indebtedness that forced him to defect to the West. (Although his diaries suggest a degree of disenchantment from the regime, in public he continued to deny that he was "dissident" even after his defection.)

The following passage from his diaries is representative of his frustration at his poor financial situation: "I wonder if I shall ever earn enough to pay off all my debts and buy the most basic essentials—a sofa, the odd bit of furniture, a type-writer, the books that I'd like to have of my own? Then there are repairs to be done in the country [house]—that means more money."[3] He is clear enough about who was to blame for his predicament: "In a good period I could have been a millionaire. Making two films a year from 1960 on I could have made twenty films. . . . Fat chance with our idiots."[4]

The authorities were not so unyielding, however, as to deny heterodox directors a way out of this situation. On several occasions Tarkovsky was encouraged to bring his talents to bear on what was known in Soviet parlance as a "commissioned theme," that is, to shoot a film on a subject assigned by the authorities. One of the more bizarre moments in his war of attrition with the film industry leadership came in 1975. At the conclusion to a protracted and bitter battle over the release of one of his films, the Goskino head suggested, in a spirit of conciliation, that he make "something about Lenin."[5] And again, in 1979, when Tarkovsky discussed his plans for a filming trip to Italy with Nikolai Sizov, head of Mosfilm, the latter it seems, "was all for a topical theme, for something on the dissidents."[6] However strange, even comical, it might be to imagine Tarkovsky taking on such projects, had he done so, they would have made him rich instantly.

Brezhnevite policies toward cinema were not purely repressive. The 1970s also saw an attempt to address at last the industry's long-standing failure to produce films of mass entertainment. The inception of this policy was a response to a decline in cinema attendance, which began around 1970 owing to the spread of television ownership. It would seem that a Soviet leadership striving, in Brezhnev's immortal words, to "make the economy more economical" was reluctant to see the substantial revenues generated by cinema ticket sales reduced. Golovskoy states that it was Alexei Romanov's resistance to the new policy of commercialism that led to his replacement as Goskino head in 1973 by Filipp Yermash, an admirer of both the products and production methods of Hollywood. Under Yermash's leadership the cinema "repertoire [became] dominated by the mass, lightweight film aimed at everyone—the golden dream of the administration not only of the film industry but also of the Party ideologists."[7] Perhaps the crowning achievement of the new policy was the fleeting appearance of a bared female breast in Alexander Mitta's disaster thriller *The Crew* (*Ekipazh*).[8]

The attempt of Soviet cinema to head off the challenge from television would seem to have been relatively successful. The decline in audience size in this period was rather gradual compared to the experience of other countries at a similar stage in the spread of television ownership: at the end of the 1970s, cinema attendance actually rose.[9] Despite the spectacular success of some pictures, however, the industry was becoming increasingly reliant on foreign imports to retain its overall profitability.[10] Most imported films were produced in India and the Middle East because the Soviet state's ideological sensitivities and shortage of hard currency precluded it from buying rights to more than a handful of Hollywood productions each year. This effectively eliminated the competitive threat that U.S. cinema could potentially have presented to domestic production. Although the most popular Soviet films outsold any imports, this may well have been because domestic releases received wider distribution and heavier promotion whether or not their box-office potential merited it. Even so, by the 1970s, imported films accounted for 35 percent of ticket sales.[11] Even on these highly unequal terms, the domestic industry was barely able to hold its own.

By the end of the 1970s Yermash's outspoken admiration for Hollywood cinema had attracted opposition from both liberals and conservatives. From the conservative side, for instance, a Soviet general arguing (successfully) for cuts in a 1979 thriller about the army asked: "Why do our films always imitate American hits . . . why are our soldiers depicted as vicious fighters? Why not devote more attention to their patriotism— their love of our Soviet motherland?"[12] The manner in which Yevgeny Surkov, then chief editor of *Iskusstvo Kino*, characterized Yermash's policies in an interview given during perestroika exemplifies the distaste they provoked in many liberal *intelligenty*: "I felt they were steering our cinema toward an abyss, toward a glut of lowbrow, stupid pictures."[13] The similar terms in which those from both orthodox and heterodox camps attacked the products of the commercialization campaign suggests the extent to which both shared the belief that cinema's purpose was to enlighten rather than to entertain. Following the controversy surrounding Andrei Konchalovsky's family saga *Siberiade* (intended as a showpiece for the new model of cinema, it was branded as ideologically unsound after its release) and the decline of his political patron Andrei Kirilenko, Yermash's opponents seized the opportunity to block further moves toward commercialization.[14]

The story of Yermash's ultimate failure to enforce an entertainment orientation on the film industry exemplifies the general failure of the authorities to increase the responsiveness and efficiency of the economy in the late-socialist period. In cinema as in other fields of production, apparently reasonable initiatives that enjoyed high-level backing ran aground as they came up against the fundamental structural constraints imposed by the Soviet system.[15] Yermash attempted to impose a policy of commercialism without altering the institutional or economic structures of the industry. Like all other Soviet films, even the "blockbusters" produced under his leadership, such as *Moscow Does Not Believe in Tears* and *The Crew*, were made "like handicrafts," as Maya Turovskaya puts it.[16] Equally, Yermash did nothing to increase the economic incentive of filmmakers and production officials to respond to audience demand.[17] In these circumstances there was no mechanism by which commercial cinema could overcome the distaste of its opponents and achieve a dominant place within the industry.

THE ARTISTIC IDEOLOGIES OF LATE-SOVIET FILMMAKERS

Despite the impression given by Zorkaya and most other Soviet commentators writing during the perestroika period, filmmakers could not be clearly divided into two mutually exclusive and hostile camps under Brezhnev. Since filmmaking lacked an unauthorized sector of production, one could say that the mere decision to become or remain a director implied a degree of willingness to work within the system. Conversely, no establishment late-Soviet filmmakers, no matter how much they owed their positions to a record of conspicuous loyalty to the authorities' requests, were prepared to forswear the status of independent artist. In later years, even the archetypal "opportunist," Sergei Bondarchuk, claimed to have had difficulties getting his projects past the Brezhnev-era Goskino bureaucracy.[18]

Rather, we should follow Bourdieu in seeing the autonomous and heteronomous principles of hierarchization as establishing a range of relationally defined positions available to participants within the field of filmmaking. Each position within the overall structure offered a different balance of officially and unofficially conferred symbolic rewards to its occupants. In their creative practice and discursive self-presentations, therefore, filmmakers adopted a variety of "position-taking strategies," to use Bourdieu's expression, depending on their willingness or capacity to pursue success under autonomous or heteronomous principles. Here I consider three of the major strategies pursued by late-Soviet filmmakers, which represent alternative attempts to negotiate the fundamental opposition between "art" and "opportunism." Moving from the autonomous to heteronomous poles of the spectrum, I label these strategies *messianic elitism*, *populism*, and *commercialism*.

Within the fields of activity like cultural production, where status depends on public recognition rather than objectified advantages like economic capital, Bourdieu argues that agents consolidate their own positions by stressing the differences between their own conceptions of creative practice and those of others. Very often, indeed, they deny that their opponents are legitimate participants in the field at all. Positions within the field are defined through mutual opposition, a struggle in which the ultimate stake is the definition of the field itself.[19] This is espe-cially evident in a field of cultural production like Soviet filmmaking, in which participants are joined in competition for symbolic and material rewards emanating from a unitary, or at least highly concentrated, source. These strategies did not, therefore, exist simply as alternative conceptions of filmmaking; they were presented by their proponents as not only the best but also the only legitimate ideal of filmmaking.

The existence of alternative position-taking strategies within the late-Soviet cinematic field helps explain the capacity of some Soviet films to achieve genuine popularity with certain audiences despite the overall un-responsiveness of the system to public demand. Bourdieu argues that even the most self-consciously autonomous cultural producers may find an audience through what he terms the "effect of homologies." Works created in response to a particular position in the field of cultural produc-tion tend to appeal to cultural consumers who occupy an analogous posi-tion within society at large. As Bourdieu puts it: "By obeying the logic of the objective competition between mutually exclusive positions within the field, the various categories of producers tend to supply products ad-justed to the expectations of the various positions in the field of power, but without any conscious striving for such adjustment . . . the encounter between a work and its audience is, strictly speaking, a coincidence."[20] Thus the internal divisions within the cinematic field fostered the cre-ation of a variety of works capable of appealing to a range of audience types, from the few but dedicated highbrow viewers of Tarkovsky's films to the 100-million-odd public for Vladimir Menshov's *Moscow Does Not Believe in Tears*.

MESSIANIC ELITISM: ANDREI TARKOVSKY

From the late 1960s onward, Andrei Tarkovsky emerged as Soviet cine-ma's dominant exponent of the ideal of filmmaker as individual creative genius and exemplar of uncompromising moral integrity. Despite the dif-ficulties he faced in his dealings with the authorities, in terms of the au-tonomous principle of hierarchization, his was clearly a winning strategy. After his death in exile in 1986—which coincided with his official rehabil-itation—his reputation among filmmakers and the intelligentsia public became still stronger and his "creator cult" remains a central feature of the post-Soviet cinematic field. In 1995 a scriptwriter described him to me as "the most important figure for our generation. It seemed to us that he knew things we will never know. . . . For us in some mystical sense he was more than just a director, he was a modern philosopher and an 'outstanding citizen' [*velikii grazhdanin*]."[21]

Tarkovsky's status as preeminent late-Soviet auteur within the national cinematic field depended crucially on the appeal his work had for cinematic cognoscenti outside the country (which may be measured in terms of the steady stream of prizes his films won at international cinema festivals). His international artistic reputation eclipsed that of any Soviet director since Eisenstein, a fact of which he himself was keenly aware, writing in his diaries, "If anyone in Europe, or indeed anywhere, asks who is the best director in the USSR, the answer is TARKOVSKY. But here—not a word, I don't exist, I'm an empty space."[22]

The other key to the iconic significance Tarkovsky assumed for post-Soviet filmmakers was the "moral capital," to use Verdery's expression, he derived from his unyielding stance in the face of official disapproval for his work. From *Andrei Rublev* onward, all the films he made in the Soviet Union were shot and released only after prolonged and bitter struggles with the authorities. His chief weapons in these conflicts were his highly placed connections within the Soviet cultural establishment and his unrivaled ability to secure, as he put it, "international artistic triumph[s]"[23] for his country. Unlike the literary dissidents of the period (who had no equivalent in filmmaking), Tarkovsky's difficulties with the authorities stemmed primarily from his wish to pursue creative work without official interference. There are few indications that he had any wish to challenge the overall political order and certainly he was no great enthusiast for Western liberal capitalism.[24] Circumscribed as his resistance was in aim, it was nevertheless sufficiently dogged and uncompromising for many of his contemporaries and successors to accord him the moral integrity central to the Russian intelligentsia's definition of the "true" artist.

Although Tarkovsky's refusal to accommodate his work to official goals for cinema made him a dominant figure within the unofficial hierarchy of symbolic prestige, this position-taking strategy involved a high degree of risk and personal cost. Ultimately his war of attrition with the authorities led him to defect from the country in 1982 and may indeed have contributed to his premature death at the age of fifty-four. Tarkovsky's capacity and will to sustain this struggle bears out Bourdieu's thesis that individuals from the more privileged sectors of society are best placed to identify and occupy positions within the field of cultural production, which though potentially the most symbolically "profitable," entail the greatest risks.[25] In terms of cultural capital, Tarkovsky came from "old money." This both disposed him to assume the creative intelligentsia's traditional mantle of cultural-moral leadership and helped ensure that other members of the intelligentsia would recognize his claim. Take for instance the manner in which Zorkaya characterizes his social origins and the link between them and his moral-artistic aspirations:

Andrei Tarkovsky, in his understanding of the role of art, adhered to Russian cultural tradition and its basic principles. *He inherited them both figuratively and literally.* . . . [S]on of the talented Russian poet, Arseni Tarkovsky, who was a younger contemporary of Anna Akhmatova and Boris Pasternak, a grandson of a nineteenth-century Russian revolutionary (Narodnik), and *a descendant of many teachers, doctors, and professors, that true elite of society* . . . [he] absorbed his country's cultural tradition and applied it to the cinema.[26] (Emphasis added)

At certain points in his diaries—particularly in passages where he is expressing his frustration at his bureaucratic masters or at colleagues whom he regarded as less uncompromising than himself—Tarkovsky displays more than a tinge of cultural aristocratism. We have already seen evidence of his low opinion of the cultural level of Goskino officials. Following conflicts with Vadim Yusov, his director of photography during the shooting of his semiautobiographical film *Mirror* (*Zerkalo*), he wrote: "He's spiteful. He is filled with class hatred for the intelligentsia. . . . In his lower-middle-class way he was infuriated by the fact that I was making a film about myself.[27] . . . Vadim always had a need for success and professional acclaim. He is a pleb and hates anything original or independent . . . his views epitomize the attitude of the masses towards the intelligentsia. He has a class hatred of able creative people with a personality of their own."[28] Tarkovsky sees Yusov's lowly sociocultural background as making him more susceptible to official blandishments than "able creative people with a personality of their own." Conversely, he implies the latter were more likely to be found among those—like himself—who possessed a high degree of inherited cultural capital.

* * *

As we have seen, the central criticism the authorities had of Tarkovsky's work was that it was inaccessible to the "broad masses." The secretary of the Filmmakers' Union, Lev Kulidzhanov, remarked in a speech before the union in 1981, for instance: "He is a talented director and I have to say that frankly it is regrettable that he should aim at what is called an elite audience. What a joy it would be for us all to see Tarkovsky make a new film . . . which could move millions of people and which they could understand."[29] Perhaps because of these criticisms, in his diaries and his public writings Tarkovsky devoted considerable attention to the issue of communication between artist and audience, both in general and as it affected cinema in particular. In his discussion of this issue in *Sculpting in Time*, he begins by acknowledging cinema's dual character as individually conceived artwork and industrially produced commodity. "All manufacture, as we know, has to be viable; in order to function and develop, it has not merely to pay for itself but to yield a certain profit. As a commodity, therefore, a film succeeds and fails and its aesthetic value is established, paradoxically enough, according to straightforward market laws."[30] Immediately, however, he forecloses further consideration of consequences of this tension by treating cinema's commodified character as merely an obstacle standing in the way of its full attainment of artistic status: "As long as cinema remains in its present position, it will never be easy for *true cinematic work* to see the light of day, let alone become accessible to the wider public" (emphasis added).[31]

Tarkovsky's insistence that cinema should achieve independence from all nonaesthetic determinations led him to see both ideological and commercial pressures as inimical to its development: "Nothing could be easier than to substitute for aesthetic criteria purely utilitarian measures of assessment, which may be dictated either by the desire for the greatest possible financial profit or for some ideological motive. Either is equally far from the proper purpose of art."[32] His tendency to identify Soviet demands for ideological orthodoxy with purely economic pressures makes sense as a reaction to Yermash's campaign for the production of popularly appealing films in the 1970s; it betrays, however, a degree of naïveté regarding the very different dynamics at work within the Soviet and Western film industries.

Tarkovsky's uncompromising attitude toward the conventional expectations of the popular audience comes across both in his creative practice, which was characterized by long takes and minimal narrative development, and his writings on cinema aesthetics. In *Sculpting in Time* he declared that he had "no interest in that section of the cinema-going public that uses films as entertainment and as an escape from the sorrows, cares and deprivations of everyday life" (a section of the audience that he estimated at 80 percent of the total).[33] Furthermore, he had little respect for those filmmakers who were prepared to subordinate form to the need to communicate with this audience: "At the present time cineastes use editing rhythm to gild the pill that has to be swallowed by the unfortunate audience. According to me, entirely to make money."[34]

Nevertheless, Tarkovsky was far from advocating an aesthetic of art for art's sake. On the contrary, he shared with Ryazanov the belief that the film artist was obligated to address the spiritual and moral needs of the public: "The artist becomes the voice of those who cannot formulate or express their view of reality. In that sense the artist is indeed *vox populi*. That is why he is called to serve his own talent, which means serving his people."[35] Ultimately, then, Tarkovsky conceived the untrammeled creative autonomy he sought not as an end in itself but as the precondition for the assumption of a higher kind of heteronomy. Unconstrained by the worldly masters of state and market, film artists would be free to dedicate their muse to the people's spiritual welfare, "to turn and loosen the human soul, making it receptive to good."[36]

Although Tarkovsky refused to tailor his work toward the assumed taste of the mass audience, he showed a keen interest in Soviet filmgoers' reaction to his work. He toured the country constantly, giving lectures and discussing his work with the general public, and recorded viewers' responses to his films in his diaries.[37] The powerful chord his work struck with some sections of the Soviet audience evidently reassured him that the authorities' accusation that his films were unintelligible was fundamentally unjust. On the other hand, while recognizing that "art is by nature aristocratic," Tarkovsky did not explicitly acknowledge that, in practice, enthusiasm for his work was largely confined to the urban intelligentsia.[38] In *Sculpting in Time* he deployed a number of arguments to deny the class-determined nature of his films' appeal. Pointing to the existence among his audience of individuals "who could boast no particular knowledge or education," he contended that the highly developed aesthetic sensibility his films demanded was not confined to any particular social class.[39] He also appears to have believed that the state's philistine distribution policies unnaturally restricted the size of his audience and, more generally, were responsible for "corrupting" public taste by exposing it only to inferior work.[40] Finally, he claimed that his work could not be considered unintelligible to the Soviet people on the grounds that "I am part of my people: I have lived with my fellow citizens, been through the same bit of history as anyone else of my age, observed and thought about the same happenings and processes." That is, he argued away the possibility that a disjuncture existed between his creative aspirations and the mass audience's expectations by assuming that both were expressions of a shared cultural and historical experience. He may well have been correct in suggesting that his films dealt with themes whose relevance was not confined to the creative intelligentsia. Appreciation of the formal means through which they were explored, however, required a degree of cultural competence that few outside the intelligentsia's ranks possessed.

Clearly Tarkovsky is more likely to be remembered for his contributions to filmmaking than to the sociology of culture. His refusal to recognize the seemingly obvious—and for Western cultural producers not especially shameful—fact that distribution of cultural capital influences the character of an audience was symptomatic of the general tendency among the creative intelligentsia to treat their tastes and values as normatively, if not actually, universal rather than the product of particular social privileges. Under Soviet rule, cultural producers seeking creative autonomy from official direction drew considerable strength from this ideology; autonomy was understood and presented not as a selfish sectional goal but as the precondition for their self-assumed task of providing moral direction to the general populace. As Tarkovsky put it: "It is not a question of safeguarding particular advantages, what is at stake is the very life of our intelligentsia, our nation, our art."[41] Within the discourse of artistic autonomy, what was good for Art was good for Russia.

At the same time, we can argue that this ideology encouraged a tendency in Russian directors to underestimate or misinterpret the problems inherent in creating work relevant and accessible to a large audience. From the messianic-elitist perspective, if the capacity to appreciate film art was not universal, then it *ought* to be universal, and it was certainly not the director's task to accommodate his or her vision to the corrupt or primitive tastes of those who did not share it. The number of late and post-Soviet directors who fully shared Tarkovsky's aspiration to provide moral leadership through the development of an uncompromisingly esoteric film language was relatively small. Nevertheless, his refusal to accommodate his vision of artistic integrity to actually existing audience taste had an important influence on the distribution of prestige within the filmmaking field as a whole.[42]

THE POPULIST STRATEGY: ELDAR RYAZANOV AND VASILY SHUKSHIN

Adherents of the *populist* position-taking strategy shared the messianic elitists' view that filmmaking should be free of official control and dedicated to the moral improvement of society. However, they rejected formal experimentation in favor of an aesthetic of maximum (or at any rate, widespread) popular accessibility. These features of the populist strategy can be seen in the aesthetic discourses and creative practices of Eldar Ryazanov and Vasily Shukshin. Like Tarkovsky, both directors belonged to the generation of filmmakers that entered the profession during the Khrushchev Thaw. Although both came into conflict with the authorities for their oversatirical or overgrim depictions of Soviet life and sometimes found their projects blocked, unlike the messianic elitists, their work was not subjected to distribution bans. Their films also won far larger audiences: Shukshin's final release *The Red Guelder Rose* (*Kalina krasnaya*), for instance, was seen by 50 million viewers in the Soviet Union, as opposed to 3 million for Tarkovsky's *Stalker*.[43] Shukshin died in 1974, prematurely but of natural causes, whereas Ryazanov is still working today.

In the late 1960s and 1970s Ryazanov established a reputation as one of Soviet cinema's leading practitioners of the genre known as "sad comedy."[44] His greatest popular success was 1975's *Irony of Fate* (*Ironiya sudby, ili s legkim parom*), in which the hero, after getting blind drunk on New Year's Eve, inadvertently takes the night train from Moscow to Leningrad. Upon arriving, he fails to realize he is in a different city and lets himself into the apartment of a woman whom he has never met before which happens to have the same number, an identical-looking location, and even the same lock as his real home. Naturally he and the stranger fall in love. Despite the comic and sentimental satisfactions Ryazanov's films of this period offered the audience, they had socially critical undertones—the protagonist's confusion over his location in *Irony of Fate* can be seen, for instance, as an implicit commentary on the soulless unifor-

mity of the Soviet urban landscape. Nevertheless, the generally emotionally reassuring character of Ryazanov's production in this period drew
criticisms that he allowed his audiences to escape from the unattractive
features of Soviet reality, a charge that concealed the graver accusation
of opportunism.

In a press interview he responded to this accusation with two defenses:
"First of all, to reassure, to encourage the viewer, in order to make it
easier for him, to cheer him up, to help him believe in himself—it's not
such a sin in my opinion."[45] By stating that offering the viewer consolation was an ethically respectable decision, he implies that the conditions
of Soviet life created a need for such reassurance, a not-altogether-wel-
come proposition from the point of view of official ideology. He further
distances himself from the accusation that his films aimed to please the
authorities by claiming that their optimistic character was not "forced"
but the product of a spontaneous creative process: "And secondly, when
I work with Braginsky [his cowriter] on our stories we do not force a
happy ending upon them. Perhaps, we are so disposed that it's more interesting to us to talk about what unites people rather than what separates
them."[46] In these remarks, we see Ryazanov attempting, not without
some difficulty, to retain his claim to the status of artist.

His 1980 film *Garage* may have been intended as a more decisive answer to these criticisms. The film uses squalid wranglings over the allocation of parking rights at the fictional "Research Institute for the
Protection of Animals against the Environment" as a fairly transparent
allegory for the moral degradation of Soviet society. By comparison to
his earlier works the mood is bleaker and the satirical element far sharper.
Although (somewhat surprisingly) the film was approved for general distribution, it was nevertheless banned by some local party chiefs and
opened Ryazanov to sharp criticism from Yermash for the "fading artistic
taste" and "loss of responsibility" he displayed in making it.[47]

It was Ryazanov's boldness in *Garage* that authorized him (in terms of
the unofficial prestige hierarchy, at any rate) to speak out so forthrightly
against perils of opportunism in the 1980 speech quoted above. As we
saw, Ryazanov used the speech to set out his ideal of filmmaking as an
"art," whose value was dependent on the disinterested concern of its
makers for "the state of the people." Like Tarkovsky, he wanted cinema
to assume the role of "conscience of the nation" that he believed literature had played in pre-Revolutionary Russia.[48] However, his conception
of what kind of cinematic text was best able to play this role stood in

marked contrast to Tarkovsky's aestheticism. Indeed his condemnation of the type of filmmaking in which, as he put it, "Aesopian language is used for conveying all sorts of strange hints . . . not out of conviction but merely because by doing so [filmmakers] can rake in the money" suggests that he explicitly opposed the Tarkovskian model.[49]

Instead, Ryazanov proposed a cinematic aesthetic aimed at "real communication" between the socially concerned artist and "the people": "I've been to a film theater and observed that the audience applauds ten or twelve times during the picture [*Garage*]. . . . I attribute the audience reaction to the fact that *the people are perpetually longing for honesty, for truth, for real communication.* We smooth over a lot of things. We make pictures that resemble truth but are not truthful" (emphasis added).[50]

Ryazanov's conception of filmmaking as an art form inspired by concern for the people and capable of communicating this concern *to* the people should not be interpreted as advocacy for a directly commercial model of cinema. In his conviction that "the people" want honesty, truth, and sincerity, he suppresses the possibility that the largest public of all might be won by films devoid of any socially critical content. Judging by the kind of films which received the largest audiences in the late-Soviet period, like *Moscow Does Not Believe in Tears* (*Moskva slezam ne verit*) and the adventure film *Pirates of the Twentieth Century* (*Piraty XX veka*), this seems indeed to have been the case.

Also significant is the way in which he describes his intended public using the morally charged and unitary category of "the people" (*narod*), rather than speaking of a mere "audience," let alone breaking this public down into "mass" or "educated" elements. In practice, Ryazanov's work appealed primarily to the tastes and concerns of the broad intelligentsia.[51] Nevertheless, in his discursive contribution to filmmakers' struggle for creative autonomy from the state, Ryazanov parallels Tarkovsky in basing his arguments on universalizing claims about the yearning of "the people" for (his interpretation of) authentic art. Again we see the manner in which intelligentsia ideology suppressed the expression of more nuanced analysis of the relationship between cultural production and public taste.

Shukshin's rural social background made him an unusual figure among late-Soviet filmmakers. He grew up in a village in the remote Altai Mountain region of Siberia before coming to Moscow, where in 1955 he entered Mikhail Romm's workshop at VGIK after Romm recognized his potential as an actor and writer.[52]

Thematically, his films and stories concentrated on the lives of people from the rural social milieu within which Shukshin himself originated. As a writer he was considered one of the most prominent figures within the late-Soviet literary movement known as the Village Prose school, which presented a more naturalistic and downbeat vision of rural life than had been possible within the confines of Stalin-era socialist realism.

In his creative work and public statements Shukshin showed little of the resentment against the urban intelligentsia that characterized many of the Village Prose writers. Shukshin's public stance toward the intelligentsia was most clearly expressed in his 1972 film, *Shop Crumbs* (*Pechki-lavochki*), in which the main character, a tractor driver named Ivan Rastorguev, travels from his isolated Siberian village via the intellectual salons of Moscow to a Black Sea holiday resort. By playing the part of Rastorguev himself, casting his own daughters as Rastorguev's, and using his own birthplace as the hero's home village, Shukshin emphasizes the identity between himself and his fictional protagonist. Rastorguev, with little formal education and a sense of cultural inferiority in relation to sophisticated city folk, is nevertheless self-assertive and nobody's fool; he might be described as Shukshin (or, at any rate, Shukshin's image of himself) without the VGIK degree.

Along the road, Rastorguev and his wife encounter two representatives of the educated class, the first a minor Party functionary described by a Soviet film writer as a "self-satisfied and self-confident philistine [*meshchanin*] traveling on state business . . . the very personification of bourgeois mentality."[53] Antagonized by the condescension this man displays toward him, Rastorguev is at first suspicious when he later meets a Moscow-based professor conducting research into Siberian folk-dialects. The professor turns out to be genuinely respectful and friendly, however, and invites the Rastorguevs to stay with him in Moscow. In the big city Rastorguev's views on the state of the rural educational system are earnestly sought out by an intelligentsia circle selflessly concerned with such matters of the public weal.

Shukshin stated that in *Shop Crumbs* he wished to show that "if anyone has a right to feel at ease in their own country it is the people who do the work, whether that means Ivan Rastorguev or the professor of linguistics he meets on the train."[54] He accomplishes the precarious feat of identifying the cultural interests of workers and professors by splitting the educated class into false, *meshchanye* and genuine, *intelligentnye* components. The intelligentsia's cultural-elitist tendencies (and we must presume that as a former peasant in the big city Shukshin could hardly have been un-aware of them) could thus be detached from the genuine intelligentsia and pinned onto the cheap suits of minor bureaucrats. By so doing, para-doxically, Shukshin implies that it is precisely the *most* culturally privi-leged members of the intelligentsia who have most in common with the culturally subaltern masses, because they, being the most cultured, are most likely to adhere to the traditional intelligentsia values of altruism and social responsibility. We can further suggest that, by identifying gen-uine *intelligenty* with the common people, Shukshin expressed and to an extent ideologically resolved the dilemma that faced him personally as he attempted to bridge the sociocultural gulf between his humble origins and his privileged profession.

In his views on cinema theory, Shukshin shows a faith in the identity between popular appeal and artistic autonomy in many respects similar to Ryazanov's. (In the speech quoted above, the latter, incidentally, refers admiringly to Shukshin—who had died a few years before—as an exem-plar of a "true artist," who had worked himself to death in his eagerness to serve the people.) Like many other Soviet directors of his generation, Shukshin's work displayed the influence of Italian neorealism, stressing location shooting and the integrity of the *mise-en-scene* rather than relying on the studio sets and editing techniques of 1930s Hollywood (and Mos-film). He was also an uncompromising advocate of the auteurist ideal of filmmaking as the product of an individual creative will.

> *The important thing is the personality of the author*, the man who con-ceives and then creates the film. . . . *The trend toward "the author's film" is bound to grow, because viewers like such films.* This all goes to show that filmmaking is becoming more and more an art, an art in which it's possible for the author to make his own "revelation.". . . A well made film without the author's heart in it makes one really sad. . . . The ability to make a film well is nothing special. What is special, what makes people sit up and take notice, is an unexpected idea, a new point of view and some kind of personal conclusion.[55] (Emphasis added)

Up to this point Shukshin's discourse parallels Tarkovsky in its emphasis on filmmaking as an art and as a medium for personal expression. The difference between their ideals of cinema comes across in this passage from the same interview:

Q: But don't you think that films of a poetic nature that are often unpopular with the viewers are largely responsible for development in filmmaking?. . .

Shukshin: Possibly. But personally I see art not as an experiment but primarily as a means of conducting a rewarding dialogue.[56]

In another published interview he states that his conception of art was influenced by that of the villagers he grew up with:

> I grew up amongst the peasantry where people had their own ideas as to what art was and who it was for. And these ideas were such that art was considered more as song, story, story-telling and even convincing blarney of a very creative nature.
>
> I well remember that . . . there was no reaction at all or else a very hostile one to everything they felt to be empty of feeling, to the cold play of the mind and all that kind of thing. The popular conception of art had no time for all that.[57]

Just as Shukshin argued in *Shop Crumbs* for the essential identity between the aspirations of true intelligenty and those of the people, so he maintains here that the creative method of genuine art should be based on that of folk culture.

Thus, like Ryazanov but unlike Tarkovsky, Shukshin sees the expressive need of the author and the hunger for truth of the audience as meeting in film content rather than film form. Both he and Ryazanov, therefore, are closer in their conception of filmmaking to socialist realism's formal (or anti-"formalist") prescriptions than to Tarkovsky's project of aesthetic experimentation. Ryazanov and Shukshin share a faith that the audience demands authentic communication rather than directorial "tricks" and "deceptions." Evidently, despite their shared distaste for official control, there was some antipathy between populist and elitist filmmakers, owing to their different conception of film aesthetics and perhaps also the different audiences toward which their work was in practice oriented. Ryazanov's remarks regarding an "Aesopian" form of opportunism may have reflected a degree of jealousy at Tarkovsky's decisive superiority over other late-Soviet filmmakers in winning acclaim on the international festival circuit.

* * *

In its aspiration to "conduct a rewarding conversation" with "the people" and to reflect their daily life and concerns, late-Soviet cinematic populism adhered to at least the second two terms of the leadership's triadic prescription that cultural production combine "Party-spirit," "serious thematic content," and "mass character" (*partiinost'*, *ideinost'*, and *narodnost'*).[58] The populist creative strategy can be seen, therefore, as representing a viable, if tense, compromise between the rival demands of artistic autonomy and conformism, which constituted as it were a loyal opposition within the field of Soviet cultural production. While populist cinema risked the accusation that it lacked Party-spirit, its socially critical stance could be justified on the grounds that the Party's progressive goals for society were better served by artists motivated by true concern for "the people" than by hacks who merely conformed to "official campaigns" and the whims of the "big bosses." This faith in the constructive role of socially critical discourse underlay Gorbachev's policy of glasnost (openness) itself. At the same time, as the high esteem in which figures like Shukshin were held within filmmaking and intelligentsia circles indicates, pursuing the populist strategy did not involve sacrificing one's prestige as an autonomous, truth-speaking artist, even if the truths that were spoken were in actuality the outcome of a complex process of negotiation and compromise with the authorities.[59]

The prominence of the populist strategy in late-Soviet filmmaking was an important factor in giving many movies of the period the "human" or "humanistic" (*chelovecheskii*) character both Western and Soviet observers point to when contrasting it to mainstream Hollywood cinema. Mark Slater, an American director and producer who had been working in Russia for several years when I interviewed him, in general expressed considerable antipathy to what he saw as Soviet and post-Soviet directors' lack of market orientation and consequent tendency toward didacticism and "masturbation." Nevertheless he found this feature of Soviet filmmaking attractive:

(GF: Is there anything you value about Soviet cinema traditions?) They've just showed some of their best films about the War. There's an emotional depth that I miss in American films. You find yourself empathizing with the characters in Russian films more than you do with characters in American movies. The humanity of them comes across more. I'd say emotional depth. There's less violence. Meaningful rich portraits of the average man's experience. You don't have films about Everyman in America: they're all fantasy films.[60]

Slater's views on the particular value of Soviet cinema coincide closely with those of some contemporary Russian directors:

If you want to find something in general about Soviet films that I especially value it's their humanity. Partly maybe because scenes of violence were banned. So they had to get more human ideas. Maybe it was naive but it had its own charm. And this is the basic difference from European or American films. . . . And now [in America] it's the company that has the major role, not even the producer. And the company is something not somebody. So that's why there are a lot of monsters in U.S. movies.[61]

(GF: Do you think there was a distinctive tradition of Soviet cinema that had its own value?)
Definitely, and it's being wasted, but there are some directors who uphold it. Soviet cinema of the last period before perestroika had a kind of spiritual quality and dealt with what happens to humans. [This happened] the more the soul was repressed in Soviet Union, because there existed an unofficial style of art, life, and contact. . . .
(GF: Do you think this kind of cinema exists in the West?)
I think very little, very little. . . . Maybe it's the way Russians think. . . . We're used to life not being a party but a struggle. Maybe it's [the effect of] a damaging Soviet upbringing [laughs].[62]

Despite populist filmmakers' ability to win large audiences, their ability to do so while continuing to aspire to the status of autonomous artists who, as Shukshin put it, "make their own 'revelation,' " depended on the existence of a spontaneous correspondence between their concerns and the tastes of their intended audience. For this reason the populist strategy proved particularly vulnerable to the manner in which post-perestroika upheavals undermined the homologies between artist and audience that characterized the late-Soviet period. Contemporary populist filmmakers face the task of identifying new homologies between themselves and the Russian public which are effective in connecting artist and audience in the novel and uncertain conditions of post-Soviet society. In contrast, the purist strategy has proved more robust in the face of post-Soviet conditions: because its goals do not depend on communicating with a mass audience it is less vulnerable to changes in the character and taste of this audience. The international film festival circuit toward which it is objectively oriented has not been effected by the fall of the Soviet state.

THE COMMERCIAL STRATEGY: VLADIMIR MENSHOV

At the "opportunist" pole of the filmmaking spectrum we may identify two major position-taking strategies, which I shall label *propagandist* and *commercial*. The directors who pursued the first of these strategies were those prepared to take on commissioned projects given high priority by the Party leadership. For this they were paid handsomely and showered with official honors. The leading practitioner of this strategy was Sergei Bondarchuk, who in the 1970s employed the talent for epic cinema he had shown in his adaptation of *War and Peace* to make a series of films glorifying Brezhnev's supposed exploits during World War II. The latter films were greeted with derision by other filmmakers and apathy by the general public.[63]

The renewed emphasis under Brezhnev on the creation of a cinema of mass entertainment created an alternative position within the orthodox camp during the late-Soviet period, which I shall term (following the practice of Soviet critics) that of *commercialism*. This policy brought to the fore a new breed of filmmakers who seem to have flung themselves with a will into the project of combining ideological correctness with popular appeal. One such was Alexander Mitta, director of the 1980 airplane disaster thriller *The Crew* (*Ekipazh*). At a 1980 debate on the direction of the Soviet film industry, Mitta argued that "movie makers must be on the same plane as the audience and not higher." He justified the turn toward more explicit representations of violence on the grounds that, given the continuing threat from capitalist countries, the Soviet people must see themselves as "very strong and brave."[64] His defense of Soviet commercial cinema is interesting in that he attempts to decouple the long-standing association in Soviet official discourse between artistic value and ideological correctness and relink the latter concept with that of popular entertainment. This can be seen as an attempt to modernize (or better, perhaps, postmodernize) Soviet ideology by freeing it from its association with obsolescent notions of cultural value derived from nineteenth-century bourgeois traditions.

The most celebrated example of late-Soviet commercial cinema was Vladimir Menshov's hugely successful 1980 release, *Moscow Does Not Believe in Tears*. The film follows the life of Katya, who as a young woman in the 1950s arrives in Moscow from the provinces hoping for a better life but is instead seduced and abandoned by an untrustworthy intelligent. She recovers from this blow to work her way up to the position of factory manager. Some twenty years on she finally finds true love in the arms of a lathe-operator. Anna Lawton describes this film, which won the Academy Award for best foreign film in 1980, as having "all the features of a [Hollywood] blockbuster. Attractive characters and sets, linear narrative, sleek technical qualities, contemporary everyday life, a retro glimpse of 'the way we were,' and a Cinderella theme."[65]

The manner in which Golovskoy characterizes Menshov (whom he was assigned to interview to research a promotional booklet) is revealing of the structure of cultural prestige in the film world:

Menshov has directed only two films, but both have been successful at the box office because *he has a good feel for the Soviet movie-going public* . . . the man is interesting despite the fact that *his films are replete with exaggerated optimism.* . . . Menshov, formerly a popular actor, is now very proud of his accomplishments as a film director. *Not particularly intelligent, he tries to impress by using Latin words which he mispronounces.* Menshov explains that even President Leonid Brezhnev took notice of *Moscow Does Not Believe in Tears.* According to Menshov, Brezhnev telephoned Lev Kulidzhanov, First Secretary of the Union of Film Workers, to compliment the film. Brezhnev reportedly said that he was so moved he wept. Menshov goes on to say that this film will become the equivalent of *Chapayev* (1934), considered to be the most popular Soviet film ever made. . . . Although Menshov faithfully followed the scenario by Valentin Chernykh he as a director nevertheless takes full credit for the film.[66] (Emphasis added)

For Golovskoy, it seems, Menshov fails to meet any of the accepted criteria for occupying the status of authentic artist. His films are full of "exaggerated optimism" rather than the truth. He is presented as somewhat ridiculous for the naïveté with which he revels in his position as darling both of the leadership and of the popular audience. Golovskoy implies that Menshov's success stems not from his individual talent (for he was doing no more than "faithfully" following the screen play) but from his cultural proximity to the "Soviet movie-going public," which presumably, like Menshov himself, is "not particularly intelligent." In short, Golovskoy presents Menshov as displaying all the symptoms of artistic heteronomy.

Menshov was well aware of his unpopularity with much of the filmmaking elite. A recent press interview indicates that one of the charges against him was that in presenting such an optimistic picture of Soviet life, he implicitly betrayed the intelligentsia dissidents who were then languishing in jails and psychiatric wards. The manner in which he defends himself is interesting in that he does not argue that his film was "just entertainment" and had no political significance. Rather, he presents himself as, after all, a man (and artist) of principle, arguing that *Moscow* did no more than reflect the excellence of the society in which he lived.

Q: In your best known film you . . . glorified the "Soviet way of life." Did you really believe in its superiority?
M: You know, I believed, and I continue to believe. And I'm not fond of the word "fairy-tale" [*skazka*] being applied to the film.

I could well understand the reason for the hostility of filmmakers toward *Moscow*. But it's one of those cases where presupposition outweighs fact. I read how Ulyanov[67] got up somewhere and said: "How can anyone take this tawdry piece of hypocrisy seriously. Sakharov is imprisoned, dissidents are suffering and he can create this crude comic strip of a movie [*lubochnuyu kartinku*]." And this got me thinking: well let's take the example of your own life. A boy arrives from Omsk [in Siberia], gets into the Shchukin Institute, works, lives in a hostel, drinks—and heavily. Twenty years later he's a People's Artist of the Soviet Union. So what's this? A fairy tale? Or real life? It's a normal life-story. And I made it to the top in more or less the same way. I know many such life-stories. But it's as if there's some kind of agreement in our artistic circles: life here is very bad, there are no opportunities in this social order, you can only get anywhere through connections [*po blatu*], and so on. . . . I never used *blat*. [Yet] I rose up from total poverty. How could the people who hewed the coal beside me in Mine No. 32, imagine that, after twenty years, I, a hauler on the main tunnel, would receive an Oscar?[68]

Somewhat contradictorily, Menshov then switches the main thrust of his defense from the claim that his film is an accurate reflection of Soviet social mobility to the argument that the responsibility of filmmakers is to raise their "patients'" morale rather than accurately inform them about their life-problems: "There are different approaches when talking to a sick man, you can tell him he is sick with cancer or you can not tell him. Our tradition is not to tell him."[69]

The attacks on Menshov and the way in which he defended himself embody conflicting visions of a filmmaker's social role, visions that implied different stances toward the intelligentsia's status in Soviet society. While Golovskoy attempts to delegitimize Menshov by emphasizing his failure to belong to the intelligentsia or to represent its ideals, Menshov counters by presenting himself as (unlike the intelligentsia) an authentic representative of the common people. These conflicts find their reflection in the text of *Moscow Does Not Believe in Tears* itself, in which a major theme is the inversion of usual Soviet hierarchies of social prestige. In terms of occupational status Katya's seducer is clearly an intelligent (he works in television). However, through his exploitativeness and snobbery, he fails to embody the ideal of intelligentnost. Gosha, Katya's lover in her middle-age, is a decent, sincere, down-to-earth lathe-operator who proclaims the dignity of manual labor. The challenge the film posed to intelligentsia claims to moral superiority may help explain the ill-feeling it aroused among Menshov's peers.[70]

Intelligentsia filmmakers condemned Menshov as opportunistic for creating a film that directed the same accusation at the intelligentsia itself. The struggle was not an equal one, however, as the terms on which it was fought placed those, like Menshov, who basked in official favor at a systematic disadvantage in relation to those perceived as independent of the authorities. For all the tears of joy and sorrow his films put on the face of Brezhnev and (presumably) tens of millions of other Soviet filmgoers, the model of cinema represented by Menshov's work was compromised in the eyes of many of his peers, owing precisely to the official approbation it enjoyed. For the partisans of art during the late-Soviet period, pandering to mass taste meant political servility. When, following perestroika, they achieved a dominant position in the industry, commercial cinema was relegated to the margins.[71]

1. Pyotr Todorovsky, director of 1989's *Intergirl*, the last major box-office success of Soviet cinema. Active in the industry since the 1950s, he still recalls with bitterness his conflicts with the bureaucracy.

2. Veteran director Eldar Ryazanov hefting a prize for his 1996 film, *Hello Fools*. Best known in the Soviet period as a maker of "sad comedies," in 1980 he gave an outspoken speech before the Filmmakers' Union condemning artistic "opportunism," following the release of his controversial satire of Soviet bureaucracy, *Garage*.

3. Gleb Aleinikov, who with his brother Igor, is considered one of the pioneers of the "parallel cinema" movement of the 1980s. The son of civil engineers, he did not apply to film school, assuming that without family connections he stood no chance of gaining entry. (Photograph by Liza Faktor)

4. Sergei Solovyov, director of the 1988's youth-oriented film *Assa* and head of the Russian Filmmakers' Union in the 1990s. In a 1991 interview he criticized his fellow filmmakers for tailoring their products to the tastes of foreign audiences in the hope of winning hard currency profits.

5. The Pushkin Cinema in Moscow, once the city's largest, has like many other theaters turned over part of its premises to more profitable activities: in this case, a twenty-four-hour casino. (Photograph by Liza Faktor)

6. Videos on sale at a Moscow street kiosk. In the 1990s, American titles dominated both video and theatrical distribution. (Photograph by Liza Faktor)

7. Director Karen Shaknazarov shooting his 1991 film *Assassin of the Tsar*. Summing up the state of the post-Soviet film industry he declared, "Now there's no censorship. But, then again, we don't have any films to censor."

8. Still from *Assassin of the Tsar*. Starring Malcolm McDowell and made in partnership with a British company, the film was one of the many co-productions shot during the final years of perestroika.

9. Valery Todorovsky, director of *Love* and *Country of the Deaf*. One of the best-known of the post-perestroika generation of directors, he is a firm opponent to the belief that cinema should aim to morally educate its public.

10. Still from Valery Todorovsky's 1998 film *Country of the Deaf*. The director describes contemporary Russia as a "cinematic Klondike" of material.

11. Still from Alexei Balabanov's 1994 adaptation of Kafka's *The Castle*. Balabanov's aim was to "take intellectual material and make it a thriller." He went on to shoot the more conventional, and more widely distributed, thriller *Brother*.

12. Nikita Mikhalkov's daughter Anna, playing in his 1997 film *The Siberian Barber*. The children of established figures in the industry have strong advantages in gaining entry into the highly competitive world of Russian filmmaking.

13. Vladimir Khotinenko with his prizes for Best Picture and Best Director at the 1994 Nika Awards ceremony in Moscow. He advocates a cinema that explores the nature of the "Russian soul."

14. Director and actor Nikita Mikhalkov, shooting *The Siberian Barber*. Since the international success of his 1994 film *Burnt by the Sun*, which won the award for Best Foreign-Language Picture at the American Academy Awards, Mikhalkov has occupied a dominant position in the post-Soviet film world.

PART TWO

AFTER THE REVOLT

4

If there was ever a moment when the Soviet intelligentsia seemed likely to fulfill Konrad and Szelenyi's prediction that they would attain "class power," it was the years of perestroika. Gorbachev considered the intelligentsia his primary ally in his campaign to revivify Soviet society.[1] Unlike his predecessors, Gorbachev systematically favored people of intelligentsia social background in his appointments to high political office[2] and attempted to roll back the "leveling" trend of the Khrushchev and Brezhnev eras by raising salaries for intellectual occupations. As Alexander Yakovlev, his chief of ideology, put it, "Perestroika is impossible without the intelligentsia because perestroika is also the intellectualization of society."[3]

A central feature of this attempt to "intellectualize" society in the interests of reform was Gorbachev's liberation of most areas of cultural production from bureaucratic control. In 1986 the key posts responsible for overall supervision of culture and the media were granted to liberals, who proceeded to wield the "cadres weapon" with a will.[4] Between 1986 and 1987 a high proportion of Brezhnev-period appointees within the cultural administration were displaced. Their replacements were not only more sympathetic to reform but generally possessed backgrounds as professional cultural producers rather than Party administrators.[5] The other means by which the leadership sought to break the grip of the Brezhnev-ite establishment on cultural production was by encouraging the creative unions actually to function as the representative institutions they were theoretically supposed to have been. These policies offered heterodox cultural producers the chance to put the aspirations and resentments they had harbored since the 1960s into institutional and creative practice.

Although the extent of change varied markedly from one sector of cultural production to another, in each area the newly emboldened reformists expressed their dissatisfaction at bureaucratic interference in creative decisions and the privileged position occupied by the supposedly talentless hacks favored under Brezhnev in remarkably similar terms.[6] The following call to arms launched against the "old-guard" secretariat of the Russian Writers' Union exemplifies such rhetoric: "Why are we, whose duty is to preserve not only the sacred traditions of artistic freedom and civic-minded implacability toward evil, but also the indispensable ethical qualities of the Russian intelligentsia—dignity, decency and honor—being so tolerant of displays of bureaucratic arrogance and lordly, or rather, lackey-like boorishness in the leadership of the Russian Republican Writer's Union?"[7]

The reformers' central goal was not just to change the personnel and policies of the bureaucratic cultural establishment but to dismantle the centralized system of supervision and patronage that had made the abuses of the "era of stagnation" possible. They sought the dissolution of the socialist mode of cultural production itself. While their eagerness for "independence" from central institutions was in part motivated by the ideology of specifically *artistic* autonomy, it can also be seen as a particular manifestation of a more general political-economic dynamic that characterized state socialist societies in this period, as official ideological and coercive restraints loosened. Whereas under liberal capitalism the distribution of the social product is experienced as the unarguable outcome of the "natural," impersonal workings of the market, under state socialism the state, as Michael Burawoy puts it, was experienced as the "transparent appropriator and redistributor of surplus."[8] Thus workers and managers in all but the most blatantly unproductive areas of production had the perception that the fruits of their labor were being expropriated and squandered by the authorities. Once the leadership began to encourage "self-management" (and later full privatization) in the hope of restoring enterprise efficiency, production institutions reacted to the opportunity by seeking autonomy from central control in order to end the extraction of "their" surplus.[9] This logic encouraged an ever increasing degree of institutional and economic fragmentation, affecting not only production enterprises but also political structures (thus contributing toward the impulse toward national and regional separatism that has characterized postsocialist Eastern Europe and Eurasia).

While the perception of exploitation was not in itself inaccurate, we can argue that for a number of reasons it tended to be exaggerated, causing production institutions (and regional administrative units) to overestimate the material benefits that would flow to them from the dismantling of central control. For one thing, within official Soviet discourse regarding the purpose and value of productive activity, the category "surplus" was fundamentally different from "profit" as understood within a capitalist system, being tied not to exchange value but level of physical output.[10] (Physical production indicators were supposed to correlate with the creation of use-value, though in practice they rarely did so.) Participants in production institutions that would not have generated profits under a capitalist system might nevertheless believe that they were not being sufficiently rewarded for the tangible (if not usable) "surplus" they produced. Furthermore, the structural consumer shortage created by central planning meant that even those products that were in demand so long as the system persisted frequently lost their value once it was dismantled and market exchange and foreign trade liberalized. In other words, the state socialist political-economic system gave institutional and individual producers the immediate perception that they would be better off without it, even though their capacity to be "productive" was ultimately enabled by its continued existence. Few areas of Soviet life during the "period of transition" illustrate this dynamic better than the film industry.

Although pro-reform factions emerged within all sectors of Soviet cultural production during the perestroika period, their success in seizing control, or transforming the structures, of the central supervisory and representative institutions within each particular sector varied widely. Along with cinema, the other major area of cultural production where the majority of creative workers took the first available opportunity to elect leaders committed to institutional reform was theater.[11] The pioneering radicalism of the filmmakers' and theater workers' organizations is explicable in terms of the collective nature of creative activity within these sectors and their direct subordination under the Soviet system to a single monopoly institution (in the case of theater, the Ministry of Culture).[12] In literature the outcome of Gorbachev's summons to reform was very different. Unlike their equivalents within the fields of film and theater, liberals were blocked from taking control over the union structures by an alliance between the "russophile" faction and the old union leadership, leading to an increasingly vituperative standoff between the two sides that persisted until the end of perestroika. This did not prevent the large-scale expression of liberal views in print, however, because by comparison with film and theater, Soviet literary and newspaper publishing was already institutionally diversified, with a wide variety of public organizations producing publications. Once overall ideological supervision was relaxed under Gorbachev, and reformists appointed to the editorships of many key publications, this diversity allowed liberal writers and journalists to reach a public even in the absence of overall institutional transformation.

In institutional terms, one of the most conservative areas of cultural production under perestroika was television. Until the foundation of a second network under the authority of the Russian Federal Government in spring 1991, a single state agency, Gostelradio, administered production and transmission throughout the Soviet Union, allowing the political leadership to retain overall control over editorial decisions. Unlike workers in other sectors of cultural production, television employees had never been granted a representative body (although the journalists' and filmmakers' unions included many individuals working largely for television) and thus had no platform from which to demand creative or institutional autonomy.[13] The leadership's reluctance to loosen its direct institutional control over television is explicable in terms of the medium's central position in the overall order of cultural production. Television remained, therefore, the best barometer of official views regarding the reform process, even as other areas of cultural production spun increasingly out of official control.[14]

"MORAL AND TALENTED PEOPLE" TAKE CHARGE

Within cinema, the first public sign of this process of officially sponsored revivification was a series of uncharacteristically forthright attacks on the film industry's leadership published in the press during the winter of 1985–86. The technique of launching a preliminary press barrage to signal a change of policy and personnel had long been used by the Soviet leadership as a prelude to periods of liberalization and clampdown. In December 1985, the director Vladimir Motyl bemoaned the steady downward drift in attendance figures and the increasing share of the exhibition repertoire taken by foreign imports and reruns of Soviet classics. He saw these trends as the outcome of Goskino's preference for safe, "gray" productions over controversial pictures more capable, he maintained, of attracting audience interest.[15] Shortly thereafter, Grigory Chukhrai wrote in *Pravda* of the lessons that the Experimental Creative Film Studio, which he had headed until 1973, held for the industry's renewal.[16] Significantly, both commentators saw the economic inefficiency of the present system as the consequence of bureaucratic interference in artistic creativity; bureaucracy was painted as the common enemy of both entertainment and aesthetic values, an association that allowed filmmakers' "independence" to be presented as the solution to both ills.

These (orchestrated) rumblings of discontent were given their head at the Fifth Congress of the Filmmakers' Union in May 1986, which followed shortly after Gorbachev unveiled the policies of glasnost and perestroika at the historic Twenty-seventh Party Congress earlier that year. Yakovlev engineered the election of an entirely new union secretariat with Elem Klimov as first secretary.[17] According to the critic Yuri Gladilshchikov writing a few years later, the Congress was gripped by a utopian fervor characterized by:

> A revolutionary romantic illusion: Life would become good very quickly and change instantaneously if moral and talented people took the helm, destroying the former nasty system.
> The union saw its task as freeing the cinema from the diktat of functionaries and from lying, removing film production from state control and introducing the market. Down with the State Cinematography Committee! Long live independent cinema![18]

Despite the directed nature of this "revolution," the new leadership seems to have been genuinely popular with union members. The makeup of the new union secretariat exemplifies Verdery's observation that "moral capital" acquired by prior suffering at the hands of the state became an important criterion for achieving public influence in postsocialist society.[19] Most were drawn from the more nonconformist wing of the industry; and several, like Klimov himself and Gleb Panfilov, had had their work banned or obstructed by Goskino during the "era of stagnation."[20] Most also were "people of the 1960s" (*shestidesyatniki*) whose political and artistic aspirations had been shaped by that decade's move from liberalization to renewed repression. Conversely, all members of the former cinematic establishment were ejected from the union secretariat. Indeed, Sergei Bondarchuk, under Brezhnev the most officially favored director of all, narrowly avoided expulsion from the union itself. The terms in which Nikita Mikhalkov expressed his opposition to Bondarchuk's expulsion, "no one can deny that he is an artist,"[21] suggest strongly that this was precisely what was being denied; this was not because filmmakers were suddenly disgusted by Bondarchuk's aesthetic sensibilities, but because his long and distinguished record as the Soviet film industry's premiere "opportunist" was symbolically incompatible with the then dominant moral-political interpretation of what it meant to be an "artist." Mikhalkov was booed for his pains and sat out the rest of perestroika in haughty isolation from the affairs of the union.

Given the radical mood among filmmakers and the approval they enjoyed from on high, Yermash's days at Goskino were also numbered, and in August 1986 he was replaced by the less compromised figure, Alexander Kamshalov.[22] The net result of these upheavals was a profound shift in ultimate authority over the industry away from Goskino and toward the reformist leadership of the Filmmakers' Union.

For the rest of the perestroika period, the union continued to take a firmly "liberal" line both on issues affecting the film industry itself and the wider struggle for political democratization and economic destatization taking place within Soviet society as a whole. When in 1989, for instance, the union's members elected their delegates to the Supreme Soviet (this was the first national election in which a proportion of the representatives were chosen by free multicandidate voting), every candidate in contention espoused a strongly reformist platform. The consensus for reform within the union was such that one film journalist quipped at the time: "Our election is in the best traditions of socialist realism: there is a competition between fine candidates and even finer."[23] In strong contrast to the Writers' Union, where a powerful "patriotic" faction came out in virulent opposition to perestroika, whatever conservatives there were among filmmakers' ranks kept a low profile.

Initially the union's liberal mood placed it firmly in the Gorbachev camp but when, in the last years of perestroika, he appeared to be moving closer to the conservative faction within the Party leadership, filmmakers pushed strongly for more radical reform. Between 1989 and 1991, the union lobbied against the Party's attempt to exclude the "cultural sphere" from its legalization of private business activity and pressed for the end of state ideological controls over television. By transforming itself into a loose confederation of national unions at its Sixth Congress in 1990, it also led the way in recognizing the movements for national autonomy that shortly thereafter broke the USSR apart.[24]

THE NEW MODEL OF CINEMA AND THE NEW ORTHODOXY

The Fifth Congress resulted in more than just the replacement of the industry's leaders. The incoming secretariat also advocated the systematic reform of the industry's institutional structure through the promulgation of a "new model of cinema," aimed in Klimov's words, at transforming "the administrative model into a self-managing one."[25] The centrally imposed *templan* was to be abolished, and studio creative associations were to gain the right to set their own repertoires; their managers were no longer to be appointed from above but elected by the "employee collective." The concomitant of decision-making freedom was to be financial responsibility: all production units were to go over to a self-financing system (known as *khozraschet*) under which they would be expected to make a profit or face bankruptcy. The new model of cinema was in fact a specific application of Gorbachev's general attempt to improve efficiency in the economy at large by replacing administrative fiat with elements of worker control and financial accountability. Before examining the effects these reforms had in practice we should consider why Soviet filmmakers were so ready to embrace them.

For the union leadership, the new model's key attraction was that it promised to dismantle the system of bureaucratic control that for so long had frustrated their artistic aspirations and, it was claimed, systematically rewarded "conformism" over artistic endeavor. In a 1986 press interview for *Pravda*, Klimov declared that the new model would "facilitate a rise in the ideological and artistic level of all cinema, barring the path to the screen to hacks, timeservers and wheeler-dealers, and opening a wide road to talented people and artists who know how to hear and listen to the times and to create films that meet the criteria of genuine art."[26]

Not only did he argue that the new model would prevent the production of the "gray" films churned out during the Brezhnev years, he believed that a reformed cinema would no longer pander to the taste of the lowest common denominator in the manner of the recent "spate of films aiming at box-office success but oblivious of the educational mission of art, films that were often not above vulgarity and crude, primitive gimmicks."[27] Despite the new model's requirement that production units become self-financing, Klimov's goal in introducing it was not to satisfy "actually existing" audience taste, therefore. Rather, he hoped that the improved films whose production it would foster would in themselves raise the cultural level of the mass public to the point that it would be able to appreciate "genuine art." "It's a fact, unfortunately, that people are inclined toward bad mass culture. And it is not only the authorities who are responsible. Many filmmakers produced bad films that helped lower the viewer's level. As a result, many people go to movie houses just to relax and enjoy themselves—to stop thinking. *We have to enlighten them and make them want to think*" (my emphasis).[28]

Klimov's espousal of what he himself referred to as a "messianic" conception of film's contribution to glasnost seems to have been widely shared by other influential filmmakers of the period.[29] In 1988 the journal *Soviet Film* published a series of mission statements by the elected heads of the thirteen "creative associations" involved in feature filmmaking at Mosfilm and Lenfilm, the country's two largest studios. These individuals included many of the Soviet Union's most prominent film directors and screenwriters, such as Rolan Bykov, Georgy Danelia, and Sergei Solovyov. Under the reforms of 1986, their positions as creative association chiefs gave them a central role in deciding the character of the film industry's output. No fewer than nine of their statements explicitly stressed that their selection of projects would be based on artistic and/or ethical criteria, while only one (that of Menshov, head of the "Genre" association at Mosfilm) specifically prioritized the production of entertainment cinema.[30] Solovyov, for instance, stated that the members of his "Circle" association "have in common . . . ethical principles, that is, we try to be true to art in any social and economic conditions. . . . To us, Stalinism is not an abstract notion but a system of values which we fiercely oppose,"[31] while Yuli Raizman of the "Comrade" association declared, "Our main task is to raise psychological drama to a level where it will address social problems."[32]

The new model aimed, therefore, to better satisfy audience taste only insofar as this taste conformed to the artistic and ideological goals of reformist filmmakers. The parallel with early socialist realism is striking. Whereas the primary imagined public of the Party leaders who instituted socialist realism was an upwardly mobile, ideologically committed working-class audience, that of the most glasnost-era filmmakers was the educated, politically reformist intelligentsia. In neither case, however, was the socially delimited character of these intended audiences acknowledged. Rather than being understood as particular social groups existing among others with alternative but also legitimate tastes, their assumed needs were treated as the only ones that artists could legitimately address.

Under Western eyes, the ability of perestroika-era filmmakers to propound an ideal of cinema as a moral, educative art form while simultaneously agitating for the introduction of market relations appears puzzling. After all, seventy years of official Soviet propaganda had continuously, and not altogether inaccurately, rammed home the connection between the pursuit of profit and the debased character of Western mass culture. The simplest explanation might be that filmmakers had experienced the problems of the socialist mode of cultural production firsthand but had a merely theoretical awareness of the constraints that a market-based system would inevitably place on their work. They rejected the bureaucratic devil they knew for the capitalist devil they didn't.

Fears *were* expressed that the attempt to put the film industry on a commercial footing would jeopardize the production of art cinema, but this danger tended to be argued away on the grounds that there need be no contradiction between truly great art and popular appeal. In 1988, Alexei Gherman, the prominent Leningrad-based auteur director stated, for instance: "I am skeptical of all the talk about elitist, commercial, alternative and other kinds of cinema. . . . Klimov was sure that his film [*Come and See*] would never be released. But now it has been seen by more than 60 million people. Think of Tarkovsky, Yoselani, and the best of the 'Leningrad School' films."[33] As we have already seen, the partial accuracy of this perception depended on the existence of a cultural economy of shortage and was thus a poor guide to the new conditions created by perestroika.

Paradoxically, the Soviet filmmakers' faith that the new model of filmmaking posed less of a threat to their creative autonomy than the old command-administrative system turned out to be quite correct. This was not because no contradiction became apparent between filmmakers' creative aspirations and the tastes of the mass audience; the breakdown of the cultural economy of shortage not only exposed this contradiction but greatly sharpened it. Rather, the new conditions created no systematic incentive for filmmakers to answer to this taste: in the decade following the Fifth Congress Russian cinema did not in fact become subject to the dictates of the mass market and thus preserved its artistic freedom from the toils of capitalism. However, by escaping state control, while failing to become a capitalist culture industry, post-Soviet filmmaking ceased to function as an industry at all.

THE END OF CENSORSHIP

The most basic institutional change initiated by the Fifth Congress was that, de facto, Goskino lost its powers to supervise studio production and ban films from release.[34] A vital role in the process of rolling back Goskino's authority was played by the "Conflict Commission," established by the new union leadership to supervise the release of "shelved" films from the late-Soviet era and defend filmmakers from further instances of "bureaucratic arrogance."[35] In the next two years the commission was able to secure the release of around sixty previously banned films, including the auteurist works of Kira Muratova, Alexander Sokurov, and Alexei Gherman.[36] The directors' public reputations were rehabilitated along with their films.

Under Gorbachev's benign regard, the position of creative artists in relation to the film bureaucracy was not merely strengthened by the activities of the Conflict Commission, it became invincible, for the commission won every case it fought.[37] The apparatus of editorial control unraveled to the point that even studios were unable to prevent the release of films made under their auspices.[38] In 1989, for instance, when Mosfilm tried to block the distribution of Savva Kulish's *Tragedy in Rock Style* (*Tragediya v stile rok*) because, as Anna Lawton puts it, "its depiction of drug abuse and sex orgies was considered too crude," its managers were overruled by Goskino itself.[39] By mid-1989, union secretary Igor Lissakovsky was satisfied that "ideological" censorship no longer existed,[40] while in 1990 the Supreme Soviet accorded legal status to what had for some time been a *fait accompli* by drastically curtailing the grounds on which the state was allowed to censor the media.[41]

Naturally, the curtailment of censorship warmed the hearts of Soviet and Western liberals alike. However, an awareness of the extent to which Soviet censorship functioned in large part as the equivalent of the selection and editing processes typical of Western cultural corporations suggests that its abolition may have been less of a self-evidently good thing than it seemed to many at the time. Several Russian filmmakers I spoke to in 1995 clearly felt (with, as they themselves recognized, the benefit of more than a little hindsight) that the abolition of directly political forms of censorship contributed to the marked deterioration of both "artistic" and "professional" standards they perceived in post-Soviet filmmaking: "When censorship disappeared, the professional level went down everywhere—among screenwriters, film directors, actors."[42] Director Karen Shakhnazarov shares this view: "Now it's clear there were good things in the censorship system. On the one hand you had political censorship, but you also had censorship of taste and now people without education can make films. . . . And now it's clear that there are no times when artists don't have problems. In America too, a director can't make any films he wants. That's the way the world goes. You could live with this censorship."[43] The end of censorship meant that there was no institutionalized selection mechanism operating within Soviet film production—a unique situation for any culture industry. Meanwhile, as I will discuss in more detail below, market-based mechanisms of control either failed to develop or were distorting in their effects.

SELF-MANAGEMENT AND THE DECAY OF PRODUCTION DISCIPLINE

After January 1988 the studio creative associations were granted the right to retain the profits from their activities. Once full self-financing status was reached, they were also supposed to assume responsibility for financial losses.[44] In practice the transitional stage became indefinitely prolonged. *Khozraschet* did, however, have the immediate effect of allowing the associations to lobby for government funds and make production decisions independently of their parent studios. The associations also acquired the right to hire and fire workers, in place of the permanent labor contracts that film industry workers (like all Soviet workers) had previously enjoyed. According to Vladimir Portnov, the chief editor of the Gorky Studio in Moscow, the creative associations' newfound power was not accompanied by the assumption of real responsibility:

Artistic directors [of associations] used to say: I will answer for what is done. And when you shyly asked them: "How will you answer?"—they said that if they failed they would not be elected for a new term. . . . In fact there was no responsibility. This situation lasted till they were told: in that case if you are responsible then find money yourself. And then it turned out that many of them were like swimming coaches sitting on the side of the pool. As soon as they were asked to get in the water, they realized that they could drown and they began to demand money and ask for government protection.[45]

In the same interview, Gorky Studio's general director, Alexander Rybin, claimed that the general aspiration for independence led to the break-down of coordination between each association (vital given that they shared common production facilities), and even between workshops. Per-haps unsurprisingly, given his professional position, he also complained that the requirement that all occupants of managerial positions be elected by the staff undermined his managerial authority.[46]

The net result of these changes seems to have been a further weaken-ing of discipline within the production process itself, as the former com-mand-administrative system was dismantled without forms of work organization based on financial accountability emerging to take their place. According to Rybin: "At first sight in America, everything on the shoot is the same as it is over here. Someone is eating, someone is sleep-ing, someone is unloading a van, someone is waiting around. But it turns out that they get things done ten times faster. Because [their] system works. Even if we stood on our heads, we couldn't get things done that fast *because we have no system*" (emphasis added).[47] "Liza," a contemporary film critic, confirms this picture, arguing that the resulting decline in production discipline not only further slowed the pace of work (thereby increasing costs) but undermined the aesthetic and technical qualities of the final product.

[In the Russian film industry] if the director doesn't say, "You and you. Do this and this," no one will do it. Maybe in America it's different, but in the average Russian film that's the way it is. In an average *Soviet* film it was different, maybe because people were a little bit—well I'm not saying they were afraid, but they felt that it was their job to do this and to do that. And then after perestroika, when there was a period of complete freedom [laughs] in all areas of life not only in film industry, people stopped thinking that "I have to do my small job," because it seemed unimportant. And I think that [now] if you have an untrained director . . . and he doesn't tell someone to place the light so that the characters cast a shadow—Well if [the lighting operator] is a good guy he'll do it, but if he's average he'll think, "Oh just let it be."[48]

More concisely, one director who had shot a film at Mosfilm in 1991 described the studio to me as a *bordak* (lit. bordello, fig. shambles). Combined with the end of censorship, the result of this further decay in production discipline was a generally acknowledged deterioration in the capacity of Soviet filmmakers to produce "professional" appearing films, even as they were fully exposed to foreign competition.[49]

MONEY-LAUNDERING AND THE INDEPENDENTS

The partial legalization of private business activity following passage of the Law on Cooperatives of 1988 ended the state's claim to monopoly over cultural production and stimulated the rapid formation of "independent" film production companies.[50] Although the Party leadership had second thoughts about allowing cooperative activity "within the ideological sphere," the Filmmakers' Union successfully lobbied against this ban, and from 1989 on cooperative studios swiftly multiplied, to reach an estimated 160 in 1991.[51] By then, as Andrei Razumovsky, head of Fora-Film (the first film production cooperative) and president of the Independent Filmmakers' Association, put it, "Anyone can become a producer with enough money."[52] The independent sector was responsible for the short-lived boom in the Soviet film industry's output that took place in the last years of perestroika: in 1991 the number of feature films produced peaked at 375, over double the 1980s' average of 150.[53]

For a time, many of the industry's observers and participants looked to the cooperatives to renew the efficiency and dynamism of Russian cinema as a whole.[54] For a number of reasons this did not, in general, prove to be the case. Like their counterparts in other spheres of economic activity, the film co-ops rarely invested in new production facilities. Rather, they leased space and equipment from the state sector. Usually they were set up by former employees of a particular studio and remained closely associated with their parent organization. In practice, the line between the state and private, and between for-profit and not-for-profit sectors of film production was by no means clear. Take, for instance, the rather enigmatic description of the status and *modus operandi* of the Leningrad independent production company, Panorama, offered by its head, Ada

Stavitskaya, in 1989, "We aren't a private company and we aren't a state company. We're independent of Lenfilm, although it helped a lot on our first pictures. It is not a money-oriented company. Sponsors fund its projects, Western-style. Then we sell the films and pay our sponsors a percentage."[55] The film co-ops existed in a symbiotic rather than competitive relationship with the state sector, therefore; state studio managers were willing to work with them because they enhanced their ability to grasp new opportunities for revenue generation that circumvented regular administrative (and following Gorbachev's workplace reforms, democratic) structures.

Whatever the juridical status of the independents, they could perhaps have played a constructive role in reforming the film industry if they had been systematically oriented toward creating films that domestic audiences would pay to see. That they were not stemmed not from a lack of healthy interest in financial gain but from the proliferation of non-usevalue creating possibilities for revenue generation that took place as the Soviet command-administrative economy unraveled between 1989 and 1991. Chief among these was the use of film production to launder illegally acquired money and evade state taxation.

Owing to the large but variable expenditures and complex production processes inherent in filmmaking, world film industries have at various historical moments proved an apt medium for money-laundering. A significant black economy existed in the Soviet Union before perestroika, but there was little possibility for transforming profits from illegal business activity into legitimate capital because there was no legal form in which significant concentrations of private capital could be held. The legalization of cooperatives transformed the situation—in the economy at large by creating institutions authorized to seek profit but subjected to punitive levels of taxation, and within the film industry itself by allowing the foundation of filmmaking companies that operated outside direct state supervision. The two parties were not slow to realize the possibilities for cooperation.

Many participants within the film world believe that this trend caused the industry lasting damage:

> VZ: I didn't want to work during that period—there was an unpleasant "cooperative period," when dirty money came into cinema, and we made about 400 films in a year. . . . It was a completely unprofessional, damaging time.

LZ: Everyone with money decided to shoot films—these people were not professionals.

(GF: Why was film a good place to launder money?)

VZ: Because there was no supervision, you couldn't control this money. Filmmaking was rather cheap. They would shoot a film for a million and say they'd made ten million profit.

AC: No, they didn't declare their profit because then they'd have to pay taxes. Rather they declared higher expenses than their real ones.

(GF: Why did that period end?)

AC: Because filming became too expensive.[56]

The effect of the influx of dirty money into late-perestroika cinema industry was to further undermine the incentive to orient production toward the satisfaction of audience demand. Films fulfilled their economic purpose in the mere act of being produced. In a sense, therefore, the poorly made, use-valueless films made in this period were the (dys)-functional equivalent of the gray cinema of the late-Soviet period. As an introduction to the market, the money-laundering period was an unhelpful training for the rigors that lay ahead. Most serious perhaps were the effects it had not on the neophyte filmmakers who jumped on the money-laundering bandwagon but on more talented directors like Vasily Pichul, who were encouraged to believe that there was no necessary contradiction between artistic self-expression and commercial independence: "To find money for filming right now is not a problem, there's plenty of money. *It's even possible to find the kind of sponsor who will give help without getting anything in return*, if the director doesn't want to get involved in film distribution" (emphasis added).[57] Pichul concluded from this miraculous availability of obligation-free finance that Russian directors could throw off the shackles of state control without having to become dependent on producers and studios in the manner of their American counterparts: "And so, I am for independent cinema, in which each director will be boss of his own film. I am sure that only this route can save us."[58]

Unfortunately for such uncompromising visions of directorial autonomy, the attractiveness of film production as a medium for money-laundering vanished in the early 1990s. Privatization created more lucrative possibilities for the investment of illegally acquired capital, while in real terms, the cost of filmmaking rapidly escalated.[59] As the dirty money dried up from 1991 onward, the numbers of films produced slumped and the number of independent studios in operation dwindled to almost nothing.

THE IMPACT OF WESTERN MARKETS

Even before perestroika, relations with the West had a vital impact on both the economic and symbolic dynamics of Soviet film production. Because of its technical shortcomings, the Soviet industry depended on the Western imports for decent quality film stock and equipment, while distribution deals for Soviet films in the West were a useful source of scarce hard currency (which could in turn be used to finance imports of equipment and films for exhibition). Access to foreign film and equipment and the chance to take part in foreign coproductions were keenly sought prizes within the Soviet film world; the authorities' tendency to award these privileges to a small circle of establishment filmmakers was a major source of resentment among their less favored peers.

In the late-Soviet period, both the authorities and filmmakers had a vital interest in Soviet cinema's critical reception in the West. The authorities regarded any successes won by Soviet films at Western film festivals as welcome recognition of the country's artistic prowess, while those films released abroad that challenged Western stereotypes regarding Soviet ideological conformity served as useful evidence of the Party's benevolent treatment of artists (although the domestic public might nevertheless have to be protected from such works).[60] Meanwhile, for the unofficial artistic reputation of filmmakers, recognition in the West functioned as the symbolic equivalent of hard currency. Before perestroika, therefore, the Soviet film industry could be said to be in a state of latent dependency on the West; both symbolically and economically, the West was a great deal more important to the Soviet film industry than the Soviet film industry was to the West.

The Law on State Enterprises of 1987 ended the monopoly of Goskino agencies over international film trade by enabling studios to deal directly with foreign partners.[61] Although the state continued to restrict trade by imposing punitive rates of taxation on hard currency earnings and forbidding the expatriation of ruble profits, Russian studios and production units responded swiftly to the chance they were now offered to tap into the West's material and symbolic resources directly. By 1988 not only were almost a third of Soviet films made as coproductions with largely Western partners,[62] providing production services for Western projects had become a central source of revenue for Soviet studios. While this trend provided immediate material advantages to Soviet film production in terms of hard currency earnings and access to improved technology, it weakened its incentive to satisfy the domestic audience. Owing to the rapid decline in the ruble's purchasing power, revenues from foreign deals became far more attractive, and far more easily won, than the non-convertible and rapidly depreciating "wooden" rubles (as they were derisively known at the time) produced by domestic ticket sales.[63] In a 1991 interview Solovyov commented when asked if he sold his films abroad: "At the present exchange rate, if you sell a film for say 100 thousand dollars, in the USSR you'll get two million rubles. With this kind of money you can shoot one ballet film after another and live high off the hog."[64]

The influx of easy money from foreign sales and domestic money-laundering operations fueled the rapid escalation in the film industry's production costs and salary levels. At the beginning of perestroika, prices of production services in the Soviet Union were a good deal cheaper than those typical of the West. By the mid-1990s they had equaled or exceeded them, despite the continuing inferiority of technical standards. Not only did this inflation eventually reduce Russia's attractiveness as a shooting location to foreign partners, it made it increasingly difficult for those producers who were still oriented toward the national audience to return their budget from domestic distribution. A studio that spurned the foreign market would swiftly find its most talented staff quitting to seek higher salaries at studios that embraced it. In sum, foreign money and "dirty" money created an intense but short-lived economic boom for the production side of the industry at precisely the moment when the bottom was dropping out of the domestic box office.

The growing importance of the Western market also had a profound influence on the nature of the industry's creative output during this period. Its effect was to encourage Russian filmmakers either to reproduce nostalgic clichés about "Mother Russia" or to create grim exposés of the seamy side of the Soviet Union's traumatic past and troubled present. In the same interview quoted above, Solovyov expressed his disdain for both strategies: "But generally, I don't like the 'sell-Russian-souvenirs-for-dollars' level of relations with foreign partners, when they say, 'Make us a picture about the Volga' or, 'Make us a picture about perestroika.' To make culture for export and coin pots of money by selling balalaikas is not my style."[65] Any Russian filmmaker who achieved critical or commercial success in the West, therefore, ran the (almost certain) risk of being attacked either for selling a chocolate-box (*kliukva*, lit. "cranberry") version of Russian culture or, as one of my informants put it, "showing our reality as something terrible so they feel sorry for us."[66] While these criticisms betray the continuing influence of traditional Soviet sensitivities about hard currency profits and denigrating the country to foreigners, they also exhibited a reasonably accurate perception of the main directions that Western tastes in Soviet cultural output took during this period. Indeed, they typify the grounds on which the cultural products of any poor, troubled, and "exotic" country are likely to appeal to the culturally privileged audiences of economically privileged countries.

However demeaning and artistically uninteresting the chocolate-box strategy, it was the trend toward social exposé for export that had the most negative impact on Russian cinema's capacity to appeal to a broad domestic audience. The interest of highbrow Western publics such as film festival juries and buyers for public television stations in the dark side of Soviet life, combined with the disproportionate economic influence even such relatively meager markets wielded in the Soviet context, to a great extent reversed the balance of costs and benefits usually associated with the decision to make "serious" rather than "popular" cinema. The price offered for a single showing of a Russian movie on a European television station, for instance, could easily match its entire net return from domestic theater distribution. One result of this perverse structure of economic incentives was the concentration of many studios on documentary rather than feature films production, because of the greater ease with which the former could be sold to foreign television.

If Western audiences had proven more interested in Soviet popular cinema, the effects of the West's disproportionate influence on the incentive structure for film production might have been less distorting. However, even the Soviet films most widely distributed in the West during the period of perestroika, like *Repentance* (*Pokayanie*, 1986) and *Little Vera* (*Malenkaya Vera*, 1988), never broke out of the restricted confines of the "art cinema" distribution circuit. Not only did Soviet cinema's export prospects suffer from the popular Western audience's usual refusal to watch films in anything other than its native tongue (or English), Soviet films were generally too "unprofessional" in technique and emotionally demanding in theme to have broad appeal abroad. As Oleg Rudnev, director of Sovexportfilm, commented: "The press has more than once written about the wretched visual quality and sound in Soviet films, the lack of professionalism among many screenwriters, directors and actors. But the reasons why our films are unpopular [with foreign mass audiences] go much deeper. Our foreign partners believe it is not only a question of our films being long drawn-out, boring and indeterminate genrewise. It is also a question of philosophy. Audiences are put off by the intransigent and ruthless mode of thinking they promote."[67]

These tendencies were further exacerbated by the manner in which the Soviet Union's opening to the West intensified filmmakers' quest for international recognition of their artistic prestige. In the late-1980s, Soviet productions (including many of works that had been shelved under Brezhnev) flooded Western film festival programs and, owing in part, we can assume, to their novelty value, and interest in the USSR's political transformation, garnered a good number of prizes.[68] Festival juries were likely—at any rate, relative to popular audiences—to reward formally challenging or "socially significant" work over the merely entertaining and technically competent.[69] Even after the novelty value of Soviet cinema faded in the early 1990s, the international festival circuit continued to give symbolic sustenance to Russia's auteurs whether a domestic market for their work existed or not. Take for instance the following description given by a Russian film critic of the reception of Russian entries at the 1994 Berlin Film Festival: "Kira Muratova, whose whimsical, refined and very strange *Passions* will hardly be shown extensively in Russia, and Alexander Sokurov, whose *Whispering Pages* [*Tikhie stranitsy*] no distributor will work with at home, [had their films] screened in the large festival hall. . . . [T]hese were happy days for our filmmakers, who regained confidence seeing the hall packed with serious and well-disposed audiences watching their films."[70] As Dondurei commented, "We seem to have settled on a festival-centered model of Russian filmmaking, in which a onetime showing in Locarno, Nantes or Rotterdam takes the place of runs in Chelyabinsk or Syzran."[71]

While doubtless welcome in its own right, the symbolic capital won at international film festivals also played a vital role in enabling art-oriented directors to find financial backing for their work. As revenues from the domestic box office dwindled in the early 1990s, foreign film foundations became an important source of finance for those Russian directors who enjoyed an international reputation. A particularly important role was played by the fund established by the French government in 1990 under the auspices of the Centre National de Cinématographie (CNC) for the support of East European filmmaking. A CNC representative described the fund's purpose in a speech in Moscow as "not charity but strategy on our part. By helping East European cinema industries to survive we are solving a number of common problems, one of which is the need to stand up to American expansion."[72] By mid-1994 the CNC had helped finance the production of twenty-five films in the former Soviet republics. Although the CNC did not confine its support to art cinema, it devoted a substantial proportion of its resources to the work of auteur directors such as Kira Muratova, Alexei Gherman, Vitaly Kanevsky, and Alexander Kaidanovsky. If the fund's purpose was indeed to encourage East European audiences to watch European rather than American films, it is not clear how subsidizing such directors was likely to further this goal.[73]

The close correlation between success at international film festivals and the capacity to obtain noncommercial funding gave those we might call the "world-class auteurs" of post-perestroika cinema a degree of immunity from the economic decline of the domestic industry. Festival prizes meant funding for further art films, which (all being well) garnered further prizes; the audience back home never had to enter the circuit. We see, therefore, that the tendency of many post-Soviet filmmakers "to make films for themselves" rather than for mass audiences made sense as a strategy for the maximization of not only symbolic but also strictly economic capital. Although the number of positions at the top of the world art cinema hierarchy was inevitably small, to their Russian occupants they offered not only internationally recognized prestige but also material insulation from the decay of the domestic industry. Unlike their Western counterparts, therefore, Russia's filmmakers did not experience a trade-off between competing within what Bourdieu calls the "inverted economy" of artistic prestige and participating within the "normal" economy of mass market success, for the simple reason that, whereas the former continued to operate smoothly, the latter had broken down.

THE BREAKDOWN OF DISTRIBUTION

Perhaps the greatest mistake the artistic revolutionaries of the Fifth Congress made was to prioritize the reform of production over that of distribution. This failure was by no means coincidental: it grew out of the long-standing inattention of late-Soviet cultural producers to the problem of winning a popular audience. Distribution was initially left in the monopolistic hands of Goskino and then subjected to a chaotic and unplanned process of commercialization after the implementation of the Law on State Enterprises. In the commercially oriented film industries of the West, distribution is the main generator of profit, and distributors tend to determine the activities of film producers by, for instance, setting the terms on which they are willing to provide preproduction finance for new projects.[74] The Filmmakers' Union leadership (which significantly included no one working in distribution) seems to have been either unaware of or unwilling to recognize this home truth of commercially dominated filmmaking. As a result, the post-perestroika film industry was crippled by an almost complete breakdown of coordination between distributors and producers. The head of a video distribution company summed up the resulting situation to me thus: "Somehow the process of production has got divorced from the process of distribution. Someone gives money for the film, and he never gets it back. Another person gets this money and makes the film but cannot sell it. Then people distribute the film and they don't make money. Somebody gets the money but it doesn't go back to where it started. Even a very good film can't make any money if you don't know what's happened to it."[75]

Under the terms of khozraschet the Soviet distribution network was broken up into regional "Cinema-Video Organizations" (KVOs), each of which was free to buy rights to whatever films it liked, and obligated to make a profit.[76] Faced with the absence of a reliable supply of popularly appealing, domestically made production, they swiftly turned to importing the cheapest possible (in every sense of the word) foreign-made films, favoring in particular American "B" action movies and European pornography. Frequently they purchased pirated copies. Their shortsighted pursuit of profit was at least as destructive of the industry's viability as the filmmakers' drive for creative independence. According to a study by Russian film sociologist Daniil Dondurei, the narrowness of the post-perestroika exhibition repertoire had the effect of driving away all sections of the traditional filmgoing public other than poorly educated male youth.[77]

Some commentators within the industry alleged that the distributors' rejection of post-perestroika Soviet cinema was not motivated by commercial factors alone. In 1990, the KVOs were brought together into a single organization through the formation of the Association of Video and Film Employees (AVKIN) under the leadership of Ismail Tagi-Zade.

AVKIN sought to restore Goskino's old monopoly on film distribution and importation with the significant difference that now *only* foreign films were to be distributed. The Filmmakers' Union (many of whose members had gone into the distribution business on their own account) vociferously condemned AVKIN's activities and accused it of acting as a front organization for the recently deposed leaders of pre-perestroika Goskino, including Yermash and Nikolai Sizov. Oleg Rudnev, for example, posed the rhetorical question:

> Who do you think is so zealously hammering nails into the coffin of Soviet filmmaking and farming out movie theaters to wheeler-dealers? You won't believe it—the former leaders of Soviet cinema. The film generals of the era of stagnation. All those who were so concerned about the "ideological conviction and Party spirit" of Soviet cinema, who couldn't bear "pernicious bourgeois" cinema. . . . [Their] requests/demands are passed along to the "higher-ups" with uncommon ease, while the film community's super-urgent proposals on measures to protect multinational Soviet cinema and adopt a law on the cinema get nowhere.[78]

Following the end of AVKIN's attempts to reestablish monopoly in 1991, it was, by contrast, the extreme fragmentation of the local distribution network that had the most negative effects on the ability of film producers to reach domestic audiences. The KVOs were too small and undercapitalized to pay anything more than rock-bottom prices for foreign imports. Furthermore, the major distributors usually had to rely on the KVOs to distribute the films they had bought national rights to at a local level and had no reliable means to prevent the latter from underreporting their ticket sales.[79] In Moscow and large provincial cities the majors, in fact, preferred to deal directly with theaters. However, according to the press officer of one major distribution firm, by 1995 there were only fifty theaters in the whole country that regularly drew large enough audiences for his company to consider it worthwhile working with them in this way. The overall effect was to further reduce the price the major distributors could pay to producers. Combined with the general slump in theater attendance, the result was to create a situation in the early 1990s where, in Valery Todorovsky's words: "If we estimate the average budget of a movie today at $500,000, then not even a genius producer can return that money from distribution in Russia."[80]

The problem that fragmentation and marginal profitability in film distribution posed to the economic viability of domestic film production was exacerbated by the complete absence of reform in the exhibition sector. Cinemas were undercapitalized and run down and frequently leased their premises to more profitable businesses such as nightclubs and car dealerships. By law, however, they remained off-limits to privatization on the grounds that as "cultural institutions," they were too sacred to be left to the vagaries of the market. In 1994, for instance, Yuri Luzhkov, the mayor of Moscow, decreed that the city's 120 film theaters be returned to city district management (some had previously been turned over to their workers' collectives), cease to rent their space out for non-film-related commercial purposes, and show only domestic films. His spokesman justified this move on the grounds, "They refuse to show domestic, artistic films; they just do it to make money. . . . We want them to be just theaters and not to concern themselves with commerce."[81] Judging by the film repertoire while I was in Moscow in the year succeeding the decree, its positive goals went unrealized; it was, however, successful in preventing the major distribution firms from carrying out their plans to buy and renovate old theaters (and perhaps not coincidentally, allowed the city government to continue to profit from the theaters' continuing "noncultural" commercial activities). The effect such policies had on retarding the reintegration of the industry along commercial lines is suggested by the following lament by the head of a Moscow-based distribution firm I interviewed in mid-1995:

(GF: What kinds of efforts are there being made to improve cinemas around the country?)
I think unfortunately [under present conditions] only the government can do this work. Although I would with pleasure buy theaters, they are not for sale, or even for rent. They are municipal property. It's forbidden to sell cultural institutions. They are afraid they will be turned into casinos, et cetera—though they are anyway. I think they should be sold but with conditions attached. . . . For instance what does it mean to be a distribution company which has no chain of theaters? No one does [in Russia]. So we in our turn depend not only on the government but also on the theater bosses and the KVOs. For instance with *What a Wonderful Game* [*Kakaya chudnaya igra*, a film directed by Pyotr Todorovsky, which she was currently

distributing], the director of one of the biggest theaters in Petersburg personally didn't like it and refused to show it.

My idea is that the theaters should be turned into multiplexes with good concession stands. A place could be rented that would give a good profit. This would allow you to show commercial and art movies in the same theater. So movies wouldn't be the main source of profit for the film theater even though they would make money.[82]

Some basic observations of the situation in Moscow during the period of my fieldwork illustrate the desuetude into which cinema distribution and exhibition had fallen by the mid-1990s. No domestic productions had a general release date or advance advertising through the media; there were no cinema previews of forthcoming showings; film posters were shoddily hand-painted; film theaters were dingy and dirty—the odor of their rarely cleaned toilets often penetrated the auditorium; their projection equipment was outdated and functioned erratically; no refreshments were on sale; prints were overused; foreign-language films were not dubbed or subtitled but given a Russian language voice-over by a single, generally bored sounding, invariably male, actor. Given such conditions, which were by all accounts considerably worse outside Moscow (many provincial theaters were not even heated), the audience's desertion of the theaters was unsurprising.

By the last years of perestroika, almost all areas of cultural production, whether or not their key decision makers had resisted reform, were being impacted by the general transformation of the basic political economic and institutional structures of the Soviet order. Following the political breakup of the Soviet Union and the liberalization of prices decreed by Yeltsin's government in January 1992, a general crisis in domestic cultural production set in. Costs spiraled upward with inflation, effective demand plummeted with the general impoverishment of the population, and imports of Western cultural products flooded into the country. The socialist mode of cultural production had decisively broken down. Reviewing these developments, Condee and Padunov write: "Viewed from the distance of Russia's entire history, the geographic and economic displacement of the culture industry from the central place it traditionally occupied in Russo-Soviet daily life is an unprecedented development in Russian cultural politics, the wholesale displacement of the cult of high culture. This displacement has no parallel in post-eighteenth-century Russian social or cultural history."[83]

Nevertheless, the impact of these changes was not felt equally across all sectors of cultural production. The breakdown of the Soviet distribution system had a particularly adverse effect on those sectors of cultural production where a physical product must be manufactured, distributed, and sold—which include book publishing and recorded music as well as cinema. The distribution of books, for instance, was carried out by small-scale, regionally based wholesalers. With their limited expertise and financial resources, these firms, like the KVOs, dealt largely in the titles they found easiest to sell. Thus the startling preponderance of "lowbrow" fiction and self-help literature in Russian book stalls from around 1990 and the tiny print-runs of "serious" titles were caused not only by pent-up public demand for mass literary genres neglected under the old system but also the inability of publishing and distribution firms to promote minority taste literature on the nationwide scale necessary to make it profitable.[84] The fragmented and localized nature of distribution also contributed to the prevalence of intellectual piracy in all these sectors. Although piracy may well have increased the total scale of distribution by keeping prices down for consumers, it also ensured that little or none of gross revenues made their way back to producers. This further starved the production sector of finance, contributed to the undercapitalization of the cultural industries, and reduced the economic incentive of their managers and creative workers to tailor their products to the market.[85]

By contrast, such problems had a far less serious impact on cultural sectors where the relationship between production and consumption is less organizationally complex; that is, on the one hand, those based on physical copresence of artist and consumer, such as theater and live music, and at the other end of the technological spectrum, the broadcast media. Although Russian television suffered like the rest of post-Soviet cultural production from organizational confusion and undercapitalization, because it remained free-of-charge at the point of reception, it retained, or even (as consumption of most other media declined) increased, its public during this period.

Not all sectors of cultural production saw as dramatic a displacement of domestic works from distribution in the course of the early 1990s as cinema did. The overall trend toward the increased importation of Western commercial culture is partially explicable in terms of the Russian public's interest in fruit that, if not entirely forbidden, had certainly been hard to come by as long as the state maintained its institutional monopoly. However, there is a striking contrast between the overwhelming dominance that imported products achieved within cinema and television drama and the 85 percent market share maintained by locally produced music within the Russian market that cannot be explained in these terms alone.[86] Along with television drama, film is the most expensive of all types of cultural production. Thus national industries capable of amortizing initial production costs within a large domestic market can distribute their products abroad cheaply enough to undercut local producers forced to attempt to recover their costs within smaller or poorer markets. In historical practice, of course, American production has dominated the international trade in film and, to a lesser extent, television drama.[87] Within film especially, this tendency has been exacerbated by Hollywood's deliberate concentration on the creation of high-budget, technologically complex movies whose "production values" no local industry has the financial capacity to match. Since the opening of the Russian media market to foreign imports coincided with a period of undercapitalization and fragmentation of distribution structures, it was generally more economical for cash-starved Russian television programmers and film distributors to buy imports than to pay for, or commission, domestic production, even if (as was not always the case) the latter had more potential audience appeal.[88]

Conversely, foreign products posed far less of a competitive economic threat in areas of cultural production like music where the ratio of distribution costs to production costs is higher and where "high production values," no matter how generously financed, have less impact on the consumers' experience. Presumably, Russian consumers were less impressed by the technological superiority of, say, a Whitney Houston recording over one by Alla Pugacheva than they were by the production values of a James Cameron film as against one by Vladimir Menshov. The particular robustness that the much despised genre of popsa has shown in the face of foreign competition may also reflect the exceptional extent to which during even the late-Soviet period, the character of its output and the creative aspirations of its performers had been determined by "commercial" rather than ideological or artistic values. A rock producer quoted by Cushman states, for instance: "This music is very easily understood, and that's why our people, who are undeveloped in the cultural sense, are oriented to this easy music, to the simplest variety of it, with hackneyed rhymes, with the simplest images and symbols, with the monotonous re-frains. And these musicians are very easy to control. They are as replace-able, interchangeable, as in the past years."[89] That is, the extent to which Russia's pop music scene retained its national autonomy in the post-So-viet period depended on the high degree of creative heteronomy accepted by its artists.

STATE FINANCE AND STATE REGULATION

Given the post-Soviet film industry's failure to reconstitute itself on com-mercial lines in the early 1990s and the inability or unwillingness of for-eign funders to support more than a small minority of filmmakers, film production came to depend on two major sources of noncommercial fi-nancial support in this period, one traditional and one novel: the state and private sponsors.

Despite the dismantling of Soviet command-administrative structures within the film industry, the state continued to play a vital role in setting the parameters for the industry's operations. As an all-Union body, Goskino ceased to exist with the country's fragmentation in 1991. How-ever, at the request of the Russian Filmmakers' Union itself, it was reborn in early 1992 as the Russian Film Committee (Roskomkino).[90] Its new director, Armen Medvedev, former editor of *Iskusstvo Kino* and consid-ered a "liberal" figure within the late-Soviet film bureaucracy, was eager to reassure filmmakers that he had no wish to return to Goskino's old dictatorial ways. Indeed he scrapped several measures aimed at the strengthening state control over the industry that had been decreed by the Soviet government shortly before its demise (in particular a proposed quota on the importation of foreign films). Roskomkino's declared pur-pose was to establish a loose, nondirective framework of regulation and financial support for the industry, including the licensing of films for distribution, investment in commercially viable production, and the pro-vision of subsidies to noncommercial areas such as educational films for children. Medvedev himself seemed to be widely respected among film-makers, but the Roskomkino bureaucracy he headed enjoyed less confi-dence: As one distributor put it to me, "He's just one man and the people working for him are the same old nomenklatura."[91]

*   *   *

In the early 1990s, government expenditure on the industry totaled an equivalent of around $20 million dollars annually[92] with about three-quarters of this sum going to production (usually as partial subsidies) and the rest taking the form of subsidies aimed at encouraging distributors to buy Russian films.[93] The proportion of films benefiting from state subsidies rose in the 1990s as other sources of finance dried up. In 1991 only twenty-four features out of the year's total of 375 received state funds, but by 1995 the great majority of new productions were wholly or partially reliant on state money.[94] By then, every filmmaker I spoke to or read interviews with was convinced that without state subsidies domestic production would entirely cease.

Formally at least, the mechanism for allocating these subsidies was placed in the hands of industry personnel rather than state bureaucrats. The decision to approve production funding for a particular screenplay was made by Roskomkino's "expert jury," consisting of twenty prominent directors, scriptwriters, studio editors, and film critics (note the characteristic absence of distributors). First prize at certain domestic film festivals also carried with it a guarantee of government funding. As usual in post-perestroika Russia, however, theory and practice coincided rather little. A jury member I interviewed complained that although they made their decisions after a good deal of high-minded artistic debate, in reality, money was disbursed through what she called "fox tracks"—hidden, winding paths through the bureaucracy's tangled thickets.[95] Filmmakers had to make "daily" visits to Roskomkino's offices to plead for the money they had been promised.[96] Just as in the past, personal connections played a vital role in ensuring success.[97]

Perhaps not surprisingly, in interviews a number of filmmakers had complaints about the criteria used for allotting funds. One young director, for instance, was convinced that the jury favored artistically unchallenging and conservative work: "Mostly these people are very old and very traditional people. They don't know where film is moving now and they're totally disoriented."[98] A critic suggested that it was Roskomkino's officials, rather than the jury members themselves, who had a systematic tendency to favor older, less innovative directors, as the latter had established institutional clout and knowledge of the bureaucratic game:

(GF: Are there still "nomenklatura intrigues" in the government film funding process?)
Yes, there are bound to be because it's their [the bureaucrats'] way

of life. They fight for their own positions. They decide with whom it's better to work so as to be comfortable in their own positions. But it's not up to the talent of the director. So they will support the strongest figure. . . . Because sometimes talented people are not strong, . . . and they have bad relations with certain people so it's not easy for them. As always, nomenklatura people try to find people with whom it's easier to work.[99]

However, the chief complaint filmmakers had against the allocation process was not that it had any systematic bias but rather that overall funding policy appeared to lack any general and predictable direction. Shakhnazarov commented:

(GF: Are there any general preferences in the allocation of government funds . . . serious films versus comedies, and so on?)
I don't think they have any policy. This is a problem too. It would be better if they decided either to do only commercial Russian cinema to return the public to the theaters or said, "Let's only do serious films for festivals." But they don't have any [general] idea. They just read [the script] and say that's good, that's not. . . .
(GF: So if you submit a script you can't know in advance if this is the kind of thing they'll like?)
No. I don't have any idea. Nobody knows. I think they've given support to a lot of shit. On the other hand they've given support to directors and films I think are good.[100]

For Alexander Rybin, head of the Gorky Studio, the government's lack of repertoire policy prevented cinema from playing its full role in society. "National self-consciousness can be formed and improved by cinema above all else."[101] He cited the Hollywood Western as an example of the kind of myth-making cinema that he believed Russia stood sorely in need of. Such views as Rybin's and Shakhnazarov's suggest that the state's renewed role in keeping Russian cinema alive had awakened a certain "fear of freedom" among at least some sections of the filmmaking community; financial dependence restored the attractions of ideological dependence. So far—apart perhaps from its tendency to neglect the most avant-garde filmmakers—the state appears to have failed to respond to these desires, leaving filmmakers to chart the twisting fox tracks of artistic and bureaucratic patronage with no clear directions from on high.

*   *   *

The state's policies fostered Russian filmmakers' dependence on its financial largesse by failing to create or enforce a legal and fiscal framework capable of making domestic production commercially viable. In contrast to many West European countries, for instance, the state offered no tax incentives for filmmaking, despite the declared preference of studio heads for this kind of support over direct subsidies.[102] Perhaps the greatest obstacle to creating a commercial industry in which a share of sale and exhibition profits would reach producers was the prevalence of piracy throughout not only theater distribution but also the rapidly expanding sectors of video and cable television distribution.[103] Here the government's actions were often actively counterproductive. In 1993 it imposed a 70 percent tax on video sales and a registration fee on films going into video or theatrical distribution equivalent to $3000, measures which distributors argued provided an incentive for piracy, given the state's continued failure to enforce intellectual property rights.[104]

By offering the film industry direct subsidies while failing to provide it with impersonal forms of protection, the state—or to be more exact the film bureaucracy—created conditions in which the expenditure of a relatively meager sum of money gave it a disproportionate degree of influence. At the same time, this enforced dependence on the state lessened filmmakers' need to orient their work toward the mass domestic public. This situation does not appear to have been the result of deliberate strategy on the part of the government, since there is little indication that Yeltsin's regime *had* any overall policy for the film industry (let alone the capacity to enforce it). More likely it was simply the result of post-Soviet state institutions continuing to do what they knew best—that is, exercise bureaucratic patronage by handing out other people's money.

PRIVATE SPONSORSHIP AND THE RISE OF THE "NEW RUSSIANS"

The breakdown of the socialist mode of production was part of a general transformation of the Soviet sociocultural order that many educated Russians interpreted as marking the end of the intelligentsia as a distinct and dominant status group within postsocialist society. One of the most striking developments in society as a whole during this period was the catastrophic hollowing out of the state-funded technical and educational infrastructure upon which the livelihoods and social status of the "broad intelligentsia" depended. Between 1990 and 1997, as overall GDP halved, capital investment fell by 90 percent (to below the level needed to compensate for physical depreciation) and expenditure on science fifty-fold,[105] trends that Stephen Cohen has characterized as marking "the literal demodernization of a twentieth-century country."[106] As funding for the state education system dried up, indications of a rapid decline in educational standards began to appear, while the changing structure of economic opportunities resulted in a steep decrease in the numbers of applicants for university courses in the humanities, science, and technology.[107] In the absence of an economic miracle, which at the time of writing appears extremely unlikely, these trends portend a drastic decline in the numbers of engineers, scientists, doctors, and teachers—the professions that had composed the bulk of the Soviet-era mass intelligentsia—that Russia will be able to support. Of course, the mass intelligentsia has not yet physically disappeared (although many of its members have emigrated), but those of its members who clung to their old occupations experienced a drastic decline in their standard of living in both relative and absolute terms as the state salaries they depended on either fell in purchasing power or simply were not paid.[108] The following lament from the editor of a struggling literary journal was typical of the way in which many educated Russians reacted to these developments: "The intelligentsia has lost its prestige. In fact, it's become a dirty word. Before, I had a good job with a decent salary. In a sense you could say I was victim like my sister who was a research fellow and is now redundant. Of course we're all for the changes, but we're still victims of them."[109]

Not all Russians suffered from the collapse of the Soviet order, however. The same period saw the rise of privately wealthy social elite commonly termed the "New Russians" recruited from the small section of the population sufficiently enterprising, politically well-connected, or criminally ruthless to take advantage of the opportunities for economic accumulation created by the breakup of the socialist political economy. According to the relatively modest definition advanced by the business-oriented newspaper *Kommersant* in 1992, to be a "New Russian" required at least enough income to enjoy a standard of living comparable to that of the Western middle classes—and only the top 3 percent of the population qualified. (The cutoff line was an income twelve times that of the average Russian.)[110] As levels of income inequality leapt from Scandinavian to South American levels within the space of a few years, the most fortunate members of this class became wealthy by any country's standards. In striking contrast to the old Soviet political-administrative elite, New Russian material privilege was put on public display. The rich swiftly developed a taste for the most conspicuous possible forms of consumption such as luxury cars imported from Germany, while their tastes were given general exposure through the attentions of the post-Soviet media. By the mid-to-late 1990s a small inner circle of the new rich, the so-called "oligarchs," had secured ownership over much of the newly privatized economy, including important sections of the mass media, especially television and newspapers.

In the discourse of the contemporary Russian intelligentsia (the "old Russians" as they sometimes ironically refer to themselves) the decline they perceive in their material and cultural status is inseparably linked to the rise of the New Russians and the social order based on private economic accumulation and conspicuous consumption they represent. As one educated young Russian put it: "Most people now know the names of businessmen and bankers but not creative people. Now only money counts."[111]

For many *intelligenty* the emergence of the New Russians spells the marginalization of the cultural values they hold dear, not merely because of the latter's open pursuit of material self-interest (which as we have seen was anathema to Soviet and pre-Revolutionary interpretations of intelligentnost), but also because of their perceived tendencies toward criminality and cultural philistinism. The literal and stylistic criminality attributed to "New Russians" was captured by the widespread use of the slang term *krutoi*. From its original meaning of "hard" as in "hard-boiled egg," by late-perestroika the term had become a generalized term used to connote a fearless, hypermasculine, streetwise young man who knew how to make money and how to splash it about. The set of qualities denoted was roughly equivalent to those celebrated by U.S. gangster rappers. In the early 1990s the stereotypical *krutoi chelovek* could be recognized by his crew cut, Mercedes, and, most distinctively, his burgundy blazer: the expression *krasnyi pidzhak*, "red jacket" sometimes functioning as a convenient metonym for its wearer. The krutoi ideal can be seen, therefore, as blending Russia's long-established criminal subcultural traditions with a specific appropriation of Western consumerism.

The following jokes current in the mid-1990s play off perceptions regarding New Russians' low level of culture and learning:

A New Russian comes into a jewelry store and asks to see the biggest gold crucifix they have in stock. They get it out of the safe and show it to him. After examining it for some time he says finally, "Well, I guess I'll take it. Only you'll have to cut that gymnast off."

A New Russian meets one of his old classmates from high school. The guy is a miserably underpaid scientist in some crumbling research institute.

"It's weird that your life has ended up so lousy," the New Russian ponders. "You were so brilliant at school—you always got stuff straight away that left me completely clueless."

"And I wonder how you've become such a success," the schoolmate confides. "Back in school you didn't even know how to figure out a percentage."

"Well the way I make my money story is pretty simple really," says the New Russian. "I buy a ton of iron ore for a hundred bucks and then I sell it abroad for two hundred. The remaining one percent is my profit."

We should be wary of taking such perceptions at face value, however. The implication that only poorly educated and uncultured individuals are capable of succeeding within the post-Soviet business world is quite simply untrue. Empirical research suggests that the social origins of new rich are quite diverse; although many are drawn from the world of organized crime, and many more could in some sense be said to be involved in it, a significant proportion of the New Russians are well educated. The Russian sociologist Alexei Levinson writes, for instance, "We have a bourgeoisie that is enlightened right from the outset [of its existence]. In terms of numbers of years of education per person, this group leads all other social groups. A person who is very rich and completely uneducated—maybe one could meet such people in the provinces or in organized crime, but I never saw them."[112] The intelligentsia's anti-New Russian discourse should not be interpreted, therefore, as a perhaps stereotyped but broadly accurate description of the objective cultural characteristics of the economic elite, but more symptomatically: because intelligentsia discourse traditionally treated being cultured and being moral as inherently linked, the New Rich's drive for economic accumulation symbolically excludes them from ranks of the cultured, whatever their "objective" cultural attainments. Equally, those who wish to claim the status of being cultured have to distance themselves, at least publicly, from any interest in moneymaking. This analysis suggests that, as a signifier within contemporary intelligentsia discourse, the "New Russian" may be regarded as the functional equivalent of the Soviet nomenklaturshchik, that is, the Other against which the cultivated, morally upright ideal of the intelligent is defined. In other words the New Russian is the postsocialist avatar of the classic intelligentsia hate-figure—the meshchanin.

Significantly, during my period of fieldwork I found that even many young educated people who had entered the world of private commerce expressed antagonism toward New Russians and their supposed values. For instance, one economics graduate in his early twenties working at a major Moscow bank was keen to stress that despite his job he was not a New Russian: "To me that means someone who makes a lot of money quickly, without having any education."[113] Another young man employed in what he described as "finance" found his work "depressing" but hoped that once he had made enough money he would be able to pursue his real love—filmmaking. (His taste in film was uncompromisingly auteurist: the French New Wave and Peter Greenaway as well as Russian parallel cinema.) His ideas on the subject of art and commerce reflect the traditional opposition within intelligentsia discourse between culture and self-interest: "Money and art are opposites, because the mentality you need to make money is short-term and pragmatic whereas art is about expressing the harmony of a society. That's why in our present conditions where we have no harmony art has a small part to play. It's the same in the West, I think. [Gestures to a Coke can on the table in front of us] And now we're surrounded everywhere by this kind of shit. . . . It was different earlier in the century when the arts were really respected."[114] Vitaly, also in his early twenties, acted on his similar distaste for the world of business. He had been working in a stockbrokerage firm in St. Petersburg, where he told me he could make $5,000 a month in commissions. But he couldn't escape the feeling that he was "robbing people" (given the state of post-Soviet financial structures this probably was not so far from the literal truth), so he quit his job to enter a newly established program in "philosophical anthropology" as a graduate student.[115]

While these individuals may not have represented a typical cross section of educated Russian youth (I met them through casual social contacts, which doubtless imposed a systematic bias on the kinds of people I got to know), their involvement in private business made their continued allegiance to intelligentsia values of education, morality, and kultura particularly striking. They refused to identify themselves with the New Russians despite having the opportunity and even, it might seem, the incentive to do so. If intelligentsia ideology can still appeal to individuals with no apparent (material) interest in conforming to it, present rumors of its demise seem to be exaggerated. Anxieties regarding the "crisis" of Russian high culture are symptomatic of the real challenge that postsocialist transformations in Russian social structure and cultural economy are posing to intelligentsia status. Yet their prevalence also shows that, so far, the intelligentsia has lost neither its sense of identity nor its capacity to shape post-Soviet public discourse.

The survival of the intelligentsia as a distinct sociocultural grouping within post-Soviet society implies that its traditional values continue to have an impact on the aspirations of professional creative workers. At the same time, however, the economic livelihood of many members of the post-Soviet creative intelligentsia has come to depend in one way or another on the New Russians. The newly wealthy achieved influence over cultural production through three main mechanisms whose impact was felt to varying degrees across different sectors:

First, their economic prosperity, combined with the impoverishment of the mass of the Russian population, "old intelligentsia" included, meant that much commercially oriented cultural production became geared to their tastes. To take the print media, for instance: whereas the circulation of the traditionally influential literary journals declined a hundredfold between 1990 and 1997, newly founded glossy magazines instructing the wealthy in how to spend their money with taste, such as *Domovoi* and *Stolitsa*, proliferated.[116] The first signs that Russian filmmaking might be able to benefit from this trend emerged with the success of the upmarket Kinomir cinema built by foreign investors in 1997 (Russian-made films rarely formed part of its repertoire, however).

The second mechanism was through the establishment of direct ownership, a trend most dramatically illustrated by the concentration of broadcasting and print media in the hands of the so-called "oligarchs" during the mid-1990s. Highbrow newspapers like *Sevodnya* and the no-longer appropriately named *Nezavisimaya gazeta* (Independent Gazette), although in style and content still oriented toward an intelligentsia market, came to depend financially on subsidies from their wealthy owners, rather than the shallow pockets of their readers. The oligarchs' primary motivation in constructing these "media empires" seems to have been to acquire political influence and thereby persuade the Yeltsin regime to arrange for their acquisition of more "privatized" state property, rather than the direct pursuit of profit through commercially oriented cultural production.[117] Again, this trend little affected the film industry, since cinema, like other noninformational genres of cultural production, had comparatively little value for the pursuit of these restricted propaganda goals. Unlike their Communist forebears, post-Soviet elites had little interest in the wholesale reconstruction of popular subjectivity.

The third means was through nonprofit-oriented sponsorship. It was this that had the primary impact on Russian filmmaking during the early 1990s. A notable feature of the Russian media in this period was their celebration of the patronage of the arts by pre-Revolutionary industrialists, who were presented as examples for their contemporary New Russian successors to emulate.[118] In 1991 a number of banks and businesses founded the Metsenat ("Maecenas") society for the purpose of subsidizing cultural activity. As the president of the Russian Banking Association put it: "There are great similarities between the present and pre-Revolutionary times. Just like then, there is a new class of businessmen. Just like then, businessmen feel strong ties toward culture and the arts. Russia might be unique in that its business community realizes the role of art is important. It always has."[119] The new economic elite's tendency to engage in *metsenatsvo* (artistic patronage) is a further indication of high culture's continued status in post-Soviet society. Clearly the prestige offered by metsenatsvo is sometimes directly convertible into further material gain, as for instance when banks and investment funds use arts sponsorship to increase public confidence in their respectability. However, its appeal derives also from the newly wealthy's more general need to legitimate their position, not only in the eyes of society at large, but also perhaps in their own. One scriptwriter commented on this phenomenon sardonically: "It's for the vanity of the 'New Russians.'. . . They think they become members of a high class."[120]

As this comment suggests, many filmmakers are skeptical about the New Russians' motives and taste in patronizing the arts. Accounts of difficulties in dealing with sponsors frequently mention the supposed cultural otherness of the new rich. Take for instance the manner in which a professor of scriptwriting at VGIK described her reaction to being offered a job fund-raising for an organization similar to Metsenat:

> I think it's very difficult for me to speak to businessmen whether in Russian or in English. And I don't believe they really want to help

the cinema. They will give a large sum of money to help their girl-friend or for advertising. But I don't believe they'll give a lot if I ask them to do it. I don't think most of our businessmen are educated people—they don't know cinema or artists.

(GF: Do you think they would like to become educated?)

I think they'd like their children to be educated. Maybe we can speak to their children who will get a good education. But they don't know books or artists or music, and it's very difficult to communi-cate with them. And it's *very* disagreeable to have to talk with people about money. I don't want it to be my profession to speak about money every day, and to ask for money. It's not a very pleasant role.[121]

Such accounts reflect the post-Soviet intelligentsia's general belief that the New Russians are incapable of a "disinterested" appreciation of artis-tic values. Nevertheless, these scruples were not sufficiently compelling to prevent filmmakers from taking full advantage of private financial support whenever they found it available. Most seemed prepared to accept money from any source, whatever its likely origins. The scriptwriter of a criti-cally acclaimed film released in 1995 whose central theme was the moral degradation of contemporary Russia (not least its sordid materialism) told me that the movie's two major sources of finance were, first, a mysterious man who showed up at irregular intervals during the shoot with a cash-filled briefcase and, second, a prominent "investment fund" (which at the time were essentially speculative schemes for relieving ordinary people of their savings). He was well aware of the character of the latter sponsor, commenting: "It's a kind of company like Khapura Invest or MMM, which gathers money from a lot of people, so publicity is very important for them." At the film's premiere the fund's president sat next to the director and scriptwriter as they fielded questions from the press.

Almost entirely lacking in the Russian film industry during the early-to-mid-1990s was private investment made in the expectation of receiving a profit from mass distribution. As Valery Todorovsky put it: "It seems that Russian financial structures can be divided into two different groups. The first categorically don't want to participate in [filmmaking] as they think it can never be at all profitable. The second go crazy and practically give you money. I know several cases of such presents. There's no golden mean of reasonable people who participate with a rational expectation of getting their money back at a reasonable rate of return."[122] Todorovsky was rare among filmmakers in believing that such "rational" investment could even in principle play a positive role in film production. More commonly, filmmakers saw businesspeople not as potential partners with whom it might be possible to engage in mutually beneficial cooperation but as a kind of natural resource—albeit a scarce and capricious one—to be plundered in pursuit of their purely artistic objectives. It may be for his advocacy of real commercial investment that Todorovsky was known within film industry circles as one of the most prominent "New Russian" filmmakers.[123]

Private capital's relative lack of interest in using cinema as a means either for generating profit or for securing political influence allowed filmmakers to retain a greater degree of autonomy than their counterparts in many other areas of cultural production during the 1990s. Although, as we will see, the need to attract private sponsorship had a major impact on the character of filmmaking in this period, it did not conflict directly with the ideology of artistic independence itself because it was granted to those lauded at national or, better still, international film festivals. That is, its primary beneficiaries were those successful under the autonomous principle of hierarchization. This situation was not of course ideal from the filmmakers' point of view. Their sponsors' indifference to the nature of filmmakers' output meant that the generosity of their support was distinctly limited; its total level fell far short of the sum necessary to keep production at pre-perestroika levels. By the mid-1990s, therefore, the problem filmmakers faced if they were to continue to work was less that of defending their autonomy than of reestablishing the ideological relevance of cinema to external audiences and sources of financial support.

5

FROM MASOCHISM TO MYTHOLOGY

The upheavals brought about by perestroika transformed the structure of challenges and opportunities within which Russia's filmmakers operated. The breakdown of the Soviet command-administrative structure of film production and the dissolution of Soviet ideology as a whole initially inverted and then rendered irrelevant the opposition between creative orthodoxy and heterodoxy that had characterized the field during the late-Soviet period.

In the five years between the Fifth Congress and the Soviet Union's political dissolution in 1991, filmmaking was dominated by attempts to violate both the thematic and formal orthodoxies of Soviet-era cinema. Previously taboo subjects such as prostitution, youth violence, and drug abuse were presented in styles that ranged from the brutally naturalistic to the brutally grotesque. In the early 1990s, however, something of a reaction to the "dark cinema" (*chernukha*) of perestroika set in, resulting in a move toward what I term *national popular* cinema, in which the dominant theme was the reaffirmation of national identity rather than the deconstruction of official Soviet representations of society. Both these stages of development arose out of filmmakers' attempts to devise new position-taking strategies capable of winning them symbolic capital in the radically transformed context of post-perestroika cinema. Before examining them in more detail, therefore, let us consider the forces at work within the cinematic field as a whole in the decade following 1986.

CREATIVE DISORIENTATION

As we saw in Part One, the position-taking strategies of late-Soviet filmmakers were defined in relation to an officially imposed conception of aesthetic and ideological orthodoxy. Official requirements might be embraced, maneuvered around, or resisted, but they could scarcely be ignored. Although few post-Soviet filmmakers advocated a return to the old order, many, including even those who had suffered under the old system, felt that the unfettered expressive freedom they now enjoyed deprived them of the foil against which their creative practice had once been opposed. As Valery Zalotukha put it: "Art is the kind of thing which is created against something, especially in the case of our country." As early as 1988, Alexei Gherman, a prominent late-Soviet auteur director whose work had frequently been blocked by the film bureaucracy, had complained: "Perhaps in our time we spent so much effort gaining permission to tell little truths that we have lost the ability to see the bigger truth. . . . I'm judging by myself. I offered the studio several ideas for films that until recently I wouldn't dream of making and they were approved in no time. And then a strange thing happened: unchallenged, the ideas faded away."[1] In his own case, at least, Gherman's fears appear to have been well founded. After *My Friend Ivan Lapshin* (1982), he produced no new films until *The Car Khrustalyev!* in 1998, which despite seven years of effort and high expectations from critics, bombed embarrassingly at the Cannes Festival that year.

Of course, the imposition of orthodoxy by the state is not the only means by which an aesthetic mainstream can come into being against which less conventional work may define itself. In the West (at any rate in the "pre-postmodern" era), the capitalist culture industries have clearly played this role for autonomy-claiming culture producers. Contrary to many predictions, however, for the reasons we considered in Chapter 4, the market principle did not become hegemonic within post-perestroika cinema. Although the post-Soviet cinematic field was as much characterized by a competitive struggle for symbolic capital and material resources as its late-Soviet and Western counterparts, by comparison to these fields, clear and stable criteria for both popular and artistic success were only weakly present.

The absence of any hegemonic orthodoxy in the film world of the mid-1990s is illustrated by the contrast between a young post-Soviet director's interpretation of her marginalized status at this time and the dualistic account offered by Zorkaya of the unequal distribution of privilege in the late-Soviet period.

Those who become favorites of the cinema world can always find money. Unfortunately it isn't always in accordance with creativity, because there are a lot of very talented people who don't have the strength to find money. . . . And now for them [sponsors] to give you money you have to be, I don't know, Valery Todorovsky. You need that kind of loud name. And there's also some kind of politics, earlier we had the Filmmakers' Union, at the time of stagnation, there was also a politics of favorite and "out" directors, those who were loyal and those who fought with the government. And now that's all forgotten and we have a new politics. . . . *It's like official Hollywood and the underground. I don't mean that the in-crowd are "official" in the sense that they make commercial films* but it's a similar situation. . . . And they monopolize access to the media. And they arrange *"prezentatsiia"* [premieres and release parties] and press coverage. And naturally when someone is famous, when he has a name, he can get money. . . . [M]y film was at around eight or nine festivals in America and in Iran. So it has some general human appeal, but they don't like it.

I don't like this tendency for the formation of clans . . . by nature I don't want to answer to any organization; I'm a free artist [laughs]. My mother always said that I'd always be alone and never achieve anything. . . . It's probably like that everywhere: everyone tangles together like snakes. I don't want that. *We say that talented people are always apart but untalented people always unite.* And they make a concerted effort to make sure they get what they want. . . .

It's very hard to speak of a "general line," we can only talk of concrete people. . . . [Describes how the goodwill of bureaucrats made or broke directors in Soviet times.] And now it's completely different. It's young, good-looking, well-dressed people and they watch the film and then have cocktails and the director whose film everyone has come to see can already tell as they leave the hall what they think.[2] (Emphasis added)

She appears to feel that by comparison with the dominant clique she herself is a "searching and genuine artist" (to use Zorkaya's characterization of the directors marginalized within the late-Soviet system). Presumably, it would be tempting for someone in her position to see herself as the victim of a coherent conception of cinematic orthodoxy on the part of the "in-crowd," yet she explicitly rejects this possibility. Rather, she presents talent as in-itself incompatible with success under present— indeed, she implies, any—conditions. According to her, the new establishment does not repress "out" directors, it simply ignores them.

The distribution of festival prizes, private sponsorship, and government funding appears to bear out her perception that while privileged positions within the cinematic field existed in the post-Soviet period, they were not monopolized by any group pursuing a specific conception of filmmaking. "Elite" and popularly oriented filmmakers competed with one another on approximately equal terms.[3]

The conditions fostered by perestroika hampered the ability of Russian filmmakers to define their creative goals in a further crucial respect. During the late-Soviet period the existence of a relatively stable system of homologies between various sections of the public and filmmakers had allowed many of the latter to believe, with some justice, that their work had relevance for and appealed to at least some sections of the audience. The profound transformation undergone by both the film world and Soviet society in this period effectively broke up the former system of homologies, leaving many filmmakers feeling unclear about who their potential audience was or what it might care about. One scriptwriter commented: "In the Soviet period I used to have an idea of whom I was writing for. I wrote about the problems in everyday life of unusual women characters, and the audience I imagined was what you could call the broad intelligentsia, not so much an elite, but more generally educated people like doctors and teachers. But Moscow has changed since then, and I don't know where these people are or what they care about these days."[4]

Given the unfamiliar and rapidly evolving context in which they were now operating, post-Soviet filmmakers interested in winning an external audience faced the problem of identifying new correspondences between their creative goals and the tastes and concerns of their public. By the mid-1990s, this already difficult task was further complicated by the collapse of the Soviet distribution system. Rather than allowing actual public demand to make itself felt, distribution decayed to the point that even films that potentially could have attracted large numbers of viewers, or at least an enthusiastic minority audience, were unable to do so. This created a barrier between artist and public higher than any existing during the late-Soviet period. As the cinema-going public dwindled in total size and deserted domestic cinema for foreign productions, the question "With What Shall We Lure the Viewer?" was asked by filmmakers with ever more urgency. Its answer, however, remained elusive.[5]

Combined with the absence of a hegemonic Other against which to struggle, the difficulties of imagining and reaching the post-Soviet audience may explain the "artistic decline" (judged in terms of critical reception) suffered by many of the most prominent directors who had been active in the late-Soviet period. Many directors of this generation entered a long period of creative silence following the inception of perestroika, and some ceased to make films altogether.[6]

MESSIANIC ELITISM AND ITS DISCONTENTS

Although the old opposition between "art" and "opportunism" lost its force following perestroika, we can continue to classify the position-taking strategies of Russian filmmakers in this period according to the type of public they sought to address. We can distinguish therefore between an *elite* filmmaking strategy, oriented toward a minority intellectual audience (or even, no audience at all), and a *populist* filmmaking strategy aimed at the broader public.[7] The following account of the 1989 Filmmakers' Union plenum, published in *Soviet Film* captures, if in a somewhat caricatured fashion, the division between these camps during the perestroika period:

The "commercialists" seem to be speaking on behalf of the people and the government. Their credo is exciting, entertaining, money-spinning cinema that is within the mental range of any viewer from an intellectual to a semi-literate granny. They look up to the model of the American cinema which has the secret of universal appeal.

The "aesthetes" wave the banner with the picture of Tarkovsky, frequently mention Sokurov and Parajanov, predict the spiritual death of our cinema as a result of self-financing and excessive pragmatism in the approach of the film studios.[8]

Contrary to the apprehensions voiced by the "aesthetes," the model of filmmaking they advocated retained a central position within the post-perestroika cinematic field. Indeed in some respects the structural conditions of post-perestroika cinema proved to be more hospitable to at least the most prominent elite-oriented filmmakers than to their "commercial" rivals.

One of the best-known and most uncompromising advocates of elite cinema in the period since perestroika was the Leningrad-based director Alexander Sokurov, described by Ian Christie as "a commanding influence on artistically ambitious younger filmmakers."[9] Sokurov owed his entry into film direction to Tarkovsky's support and, like his patron, as Johnson and Petrie put it, "makes considerable demands on the patience and visual acuity of his audience" in his films.[10] Sokurov shared Tarkovsky's aspiration to develop an ideal of filmmaking free from either commercial or political pressures and like him drew inspiration from Russia's nineteenth-century literary tradition. In a published interview given in 1987, he stated: "Russian cinema thought it had to make the same choices as in other countries: commercial sentimentality, narrative, representation. . . . Our cinema has for too long suffered from the paradox of politics overshadowing aesthetics, which has greatly damaged Soviet culture. The rights of aesthetics must be recognized."[11]

A generally favorable review published in Russia of his 1993 film *Whispering Pages* (*Tikhie stranitsy*) gives some idea of how Sokurov put this manifesto into practice. The review describes the film as

> another of Sokurov's elegies, a keenly emotional meditation on the subject of life and death—sooner death than life, sooner decay than well-being. . . . [I]t is based on Russian literature of the nineteenth century and paintings from private collections, it completes the mournful trilogy [of his earlier films] . . . there's no sense in adding up these familiar images into a connected plot. It is the atmosphere that is important, the overall emotional sensation, the state of the soul which suffers from depression on account of such a gloomy life, on account of crass ignorance, filth and poverty and the eternal hardships of Russian life and the endless road to God.[12]

In Bourdieuian terms, Sokurov's model of filmmaking is firmly oriented toward the autonomous principle of hierarchization. Through this strategy, he has achieved considerable success at international film festivals and been able to attract production finance from Western Europe.[13] Not altogether unsurprisingly, however, Russian distributors have failed to snap up his work.[14] Nevertheless he has been able to sustain a prodigious output in the period since perestroika: including shorts and documentaries, he made twenty-two films between 1986 and 1998.

The high degree of respect accorded Tarkovsky's artistic and moral legacy can be seen as both cause and symptom of the continued prominence of elite-oriented filmmaking in this period. Although as we saw earlier, scriptwriter Valery Zalotukha himself acknowledged Tarkovsky's influence, he also saw it as contributing toward the tendency of much contemporary Russian cinema toward intellectual pretension and formal obscurity.[15]

> (GF: Does Tarkovsky still have a wide influence in Russia today?)
> He had a big influence on us but maybe he damaged us. . . . A director doesn't think of himself as a professional who can make a drama, a comedy, a thriller, et cetera. He thinks he's a true artist, a true philosopher, but he has no basis for this. Especially Lenfilm has this disease; it's called *Tarkovshchina* [the Tarkovsky syndrome]—to be great philosophers and make unwatchable films. The same thing happened with Yesenin. Poets started drinking and committing suicide to imitate him, but it wasn't his fault.[16]

The continuing influence of Tarkovsky's ideals on many of the younger generation of filmmakers is exemplified by the manner in which Marina Tsurtsumia, who began her career during the perestroika period, conceives of her relationship to her audience. At the time I interviewed her, her 1993 feature film, *Only Death Comes for Sure*, an adaptation of Gabriel Garcia Marquez's novel *No One Writes to the Colonel*, had been shown at a number of international film festivals but had not been offered a domestic distribution deal.

> (GF: Who do you want to see your films?)
> That's a very difficult question. My viewer as I imagine him is someone *intelligentnyi* and educated who is emotionally sensitive. I don't shoot very difficult films, but they're not commercial [*kassovye*] pictures. They're not the kind you can go to, have a laugh, and leave.

They're not genre cinema—not Westerns or comedies. It's psychological cinema [laughs]. I've seen my viewers at the Kinocenter.[17] *But I don't do cinema for the viewers, I do it for myself.* It's a very selfish point of view but I know there are an awful lot of people who think the way I do. Of course it's not a wide audience. It's not for everyone. Of course every director wants to have a bigger audience.

You know NTV [a major private television network] shows films under the rubric "Cinema Not for Everyone" (*Kino ne dlya vsekh*). I don't like the term "elite cinema" because I don't think of it as only for an elite. . . . It's just that not all people are prepared. And now art has a particular mission to prepare people to understand such things, such big things.

(GF: So you think that cinema has an educational role?)

No, not educational, or moral, but it's a source of emotional—if we speak of art cinema—influence on the human brain, and the more subtle this influence is the stronger it is. That's when we can speak of art cinema. . . . It's a kind of magic. (Emphasis added)[18]

Although she refused to label herself an elite-oriented filmmaker, she nevertheless maintained that she made films primarily for herself. Like Tarkovsky, her awareness that in practice her potential audience was not a large one as "not all people are prepared" for such work only increased her faith in the importance of her artistic mission.[19]

However, not all directors in the post-perestroika period maintained this faith in the elevated social mission of art. In the event, the chief threat to the perpetuation of the messianic-elitist ideal of cinema turned out to be less economic than—to use the terminology favored by its advocates—"spiritual." A skeptical stance toward artistic messianism had become current among many members of the post-1960s generation of creative intelligentsia even before the final collapse of the Soviet order in the late 1980s. For this generation, all grand claims to moral leadership were suspect, including not only those of the Party but also those of the earlier generation of liberal intellectuals who came of age during the 1960s (known as the *shestidesyatniki*).[20] Within the late-Soviet unauthorized sphere of cultural production, this preference for the deconstruction of all ideology over the reconstruction of moral absolutes can be seen as the central distinguishing characteristic of the "postmodern" current in literature and visual art (as it was subsequently labeled by Western and

Soviet critics).[21] Once state controls over the film industry relaxed with perestroika, this trend began to find expression within cinema also, as many emerging and some established directors distanced themselves from the overt moralizing of the past.

Among the older generation of filmmakers, one of the most prominent of such apostates was Kira Muratova. Questioned in a 1990 press interview about whether any moral purpose informed the unrelenting pessimism of her 1989 film *Asthenic Syndrome* (*Astenicheskii sindrom*), she explicitly rejected the traditional expectation that because she was an artist she could or should feel "humanistic" concern for her public:

> Sometimes people ask: does the author love people? Does the director love people? I find such questions strange. I'm a human being myself, how can I love or not love people in general . . . cats and dogs may love man. As for me, I love some people and hate others. . . . I've developed an aversion for people, including myself. I'm not suggesting they must change. They can only change if they die. I sound gloomy, don't I? So you'd better not interview me. I don't think my words will help my film. On the contrary, some people may say: we used to think that you cared about us, that you wanted to make our society better.[22]

Striking as Muratova's disavowal of messianism in this interview was, she does not reject the doctrine of artistic autonomy itself; indeed, her refusal to take responsibility for her audience could be taken as implying its further refinement. She stated flatly, for instance, that she worked in cinema because "I simply like to make films. And you have to make a film about something. I simply make films about what is in me."[23] Similarly, at press conferences given during the Kinotavr Film Festival in 1995, a number of directors asked what audience might want or need to see their latest work declared themselves indifferent to the question, a public stance that would have been inconceivable in the late-Soviet period.[24] The conception of art this implies may be described as one of *amoral elitism*. Filmmakers working according to this principle continued to spurn conformity to the vulgar tastes of the mass audience but no longer attempted to justify this decision in terms of the mass audiences' own (imputed) best interests.

Not all filmmakers who rejected the morally didactic cinema of the Soviet period were as single-mindedly indifferent to public taste. Three of the younger directors I interviewed, Alexei Balabanov, Alexander Chernykh, and Valery Todorovsky, enthusiastically maintained that contemporary cinema was (or ought to be) characterized by the exploration of cinematic form rather than the exposition of moralizing "content." This, they believed, rendered the old dichotomy between art and mass cinema obsolete, enabling them to create films that were at once artistically sophisticated and popularly entertaining. All three presented themselves as iconoclastic rebels against Soviet-period artistic ideology; however, in certain features of their artistic discourse and practice the influence of this ideology is still apparent. While they have clearly abandoned the creative intelligentsia's traditional aspiration to morally legislate for society, they continue to conceive of themselves as free artists rather than entertainers of the masses. Unequivocal "amoralists" though they are, they seem unprepared to relinquish the status of artist altogether to embrace what we may term an *amoral-populist* conception of filmmaking.

A continued allegiance to artistic autonomy was most evident in the discourse of St. Petersburg director Alexei Balabanov. On the one hand, he seemed keen to succeed according to the changed rules of the game he saw at work within the contemporary international film world:

> (GF: Which direction do you see filmmaking as moving in?)
> Mostly emotional and energetic. It's not intellectual anymore. The time of Bergman and Fellini and Tarkovsky is over: they're very boring now. People want to see real feelings and energy. They don't want to think. Filmmaking is a mass industry and people want to see films that are stimulating and interesting. That's why we have Tarantino and Luc Besson's *Leon*.[25]

At the time I interviewed him he had directed two features, an adaptation of Beckett's *Happy Days* (*Schastlivye dni*, 1991) and another of Kafka's *The Castle* (*Zamok*, 1994). While both had received prizes at national and international film festivals, their subjects would seem out of step with his expressed admiration for filmmaking with "real feelings and energy." In fact, in making *The Castle*, he attempted the ambitious task of, as he put it, "tak[ing] intellectual material and mak[ing] a thriller." As it turned out, *The Castle* was not bought by a domestic distributor. Although disappointed by this rejection, Balabanov interpreted it as predictable in the light of the Russian audience's desertion of movie theaters and did not express any willingness to alter the character of his creative output to match public demand:

(GF: Could changing the kind of films you make improve the situation?)
No, I shoot films that I feel. I'm not a professional film director, I don't shoot stories. . . . I can do it because I know the profession but I wouldn't be able to put something personal in this film so it would be cold. Maybe five years later when I get older and lose this energy I have now I will make professional films and maybe successful ones but now I want to make art. I want to make art films. . . .
(GF: What counts as success for your films?)
It's when I see that people like it. *Not all people, people whose opinion I respect.* And that's very important for me. Of course it's good when people applaud and say it's good but when you know it's not, it's not a success. . . . [Y]ou [can] get a lot of prizes but you know it's shit and you know you've deceived people. *Of course I know how to deceive, how to make something with happy endings.* I like to watch these films but I can't make films like *Forrest Gump*.[26] (Emphasis added)

Despite his admiration for such notoriously "amoral" directors as Tarantino, the manner in which Balabanov justified his wish to make "art" rather than "professional" films betrayed his continuing allegiance to the conception of moral integrity propagated by traditional Russian artistic ideology.[27]

More thoroughgoing than Balabanov in his rejection of traditional conceptions of filmmaker as morally inspired artist was another young director, Alexander Chernykh. One of the writers for Kira Muratova's *Asthenic Syndrome*, he made his directorial debut with *I Love* (*Ya Lublyu*, 1994), a deadpan parody of classic Hollywood melodrama in which, he claimed, there was something to appeal to both intellectuals and "sentimental old ladies." When I spoke to him he was, like many contemporary filmmakers, engaged in a frustrating search to secure funding for his next project while working in television "just to eat," as he put it. He was an admirer of the American model of independent filmmaking and professed certainty that by keeping his costs low he could make films capable of turning a profit for their financial backers.

(GF: Do you see yourself as an "art" or as a "commercial" film-maker?)
Look at David Lynch, this is the way filmmaking is going. The time of the avant-garde is past and now artists must create for a mass audience. No more of that deliberately boring stuff. So I don't really see a problem with what people call "commercialism." Films should subordinate content to form. [He describes how the new generation of Russian filmmakers do this.] . . . This attitude is completely different from that of the old Soviet generation like Mikhalkov and Abdrashitov. They have messianic delusions. They think they can save the world by giving us some startling moral message like nineteenth-century writers. Mikhalkov thinks people are going to listen to him when they can watch *Larry King Live* on CNN! He doesn't understand how the world works now. . . . Art shouldn't have any politics.
(GF: Did you always think this way about art?)
Well, I hated the Soviet regime when I was growing up, and because our art was against Soviet power I was for art. When I was younger, I thought art should stand for truth against lies, et cetera, et cetera, but now I understand otherwise. We're living in an era of pure form.[28]

Even Chernykh does not appear to have completely abandoned the aspiration to artistic autonomy, however. Despite his recognition that in contemporary Russia, cinema had become a difficult and (financially) unrewarding enterprise, he remained keen to continue to work in this sphere and viewed his work for television as an irksome and temporary necessity—a stance that suggests a certain allegiance to artistic self-expression.

Equally, his contention that filmmakers should create genre cinema aimed at mass audiences seemed to be informed more by an intellectual enthusiasm for what he saw as the dominant contemporary aesthetic of "pure form" than by a practical willingness to subordinate his creative aspirations to external economic pressures. His argument that his creative aspirations spontaneously coincide with popular taste thus resembles the late-Soviet populists' assumption that "the people" hungered for the moral messages they wished to express. In both, autonomy is seen as compatible with popularity.

In practice, however, we may question whether making an intellectually sophisticated *parody* of a melodrama as an exercise in pure form is necessarily equivalent to producing a popularly accessible melodrama "straight." (And audiences, even sentimental old ladies, may well be capable of discerning the difference in the final product. Unlike the artistic purists discussed above, Chernykh devoted considerable efforts to getting *I Love* exhibited but was not able to secure a deal with a major distributor.)

Valery Todorovsky has figured already in this study as an advocate of "rational investment" in filmmaking and for Tsurtsumia the archetypal "young wolf." Following the national and international critical success of his 1992 film *Love* (*Lyubov'*), he became one of the best known among the generation of filmmakers to emerge after perestroika. His next film *Katya Ismailova* (*Podmoskovskie vechera*, 1994) was made as a coproduction with a French producer and backed by a theatrical distribution deal in France.

Like Chernykh—a friend from high school—Todorovsky is adamant that Russian directors must emphasize aesthetic form over ideological content and seek to please rather than preach to their audience.

> (GF: Do you think your films have any political or educational role for the country?)
> [Much laughter] One of the first things I understood about cinema, even as a student, was that cinema like every art has no educational role. Cinema can't change anyone or anything. So I understand it would be naive and stupid to try. And it's a very serious disease of our cinema to think that they should make films to educate and direct people in some way. And I think it's a feature of the new generation of Russian filmmakers that they don't try to educate anyone. They understand that cinema should entertain people and give them pleasure, and, if it can, create some original, new world.[29]

One of the central themes of *Love* is the problem of anti-Semitism: the Jewish heroine has been raped by thugs and, at the end of the film, abandons her ethnic Russian lover and emigrates to Israel in order to escape further persecution. The exposure of anti-Semitism was a common theme in Russian cinema of the time, being one more of the negative aspects of Soviet society that post-perestroika directors sought to bring into the open. Todorovsky admitted that the problem of anti-Semitism had a more than purely formal significance for him (and, one might add, given the real threat it poses in Russia today, more than purely formal significance for his domestic audience also). Yet he was anxious to disavow any moral intention in placing this theme within the film. The clear line he drew between his personal feelings and his artistic intentions is further indication of the distance he tried to put between himself and the traditional tendency of the Russian intelligentsia to identify artists with their works.

> (GF: What about the attack on anti-Semitism in your film *Love*—was it just there for formal reasons?)
> To make a picture about love you need some very strong levers to turn the action, to give the story dramatic tension. So when Shakespeare wrote about the Capulets, et cetera, it wasn't about the hostility between different clans, it was about love. You can't express love without hostility. So for me anti-Semitism was a serious enough obstacle to their feelings for each other to power the story. As well as that, it was a theme that at the time troubled me personally. So I consider the film to be about love and not about anti-Semitism. It would be naive to make a film to tell people that anti-Semitism is bad.
> (GF: What if praising anti-Semitism could make a film work?)
> Why not? I might protest against the film inwardly but it all depends on how it is made.[30]

Todorovsky shared with Balabanov and Chernykh a keen awareness of the state of play in the international cinematic field and, like them, tended to refer to foreign rather than Russian directors as models for emulation. Describing himself as a "hungry shark," whose hunger grew the more he devoured, he said that his experiences in the West had played a vital role in freeing him "from a kind of provincialism that without a doubt has made its mark on all of us."

> [I]t happened that my movies went out of the country so I had the opportunity to see a lot of Western movies and also see their technical methods. *So I came to think about cinema as a kind of production in the market which either has a chance to survive or no chance at all.* . . . So for example today, when I go to a film festival here in Moscow I see no difference between my work and that of German, or French, or English, or Belgian film directors. I think of myself as belonging to a community that in fact is divided only from Hollywood, which is really another world.[31] (Emphasis added)

In his eagerness to escape the provincialism he saw afflicting Russian cinema Todorovsky was prepared to abandon such traditions as the tendency of Soviet directors to depart from the shooting script (which he described as "a major disease for us"). He even accepted the necessity of placing his work under the supervision of a professional producer. On the other hand, his approach to filmmaking could only be said to be "commercial" insofar as it contrasted with the indifference of many of his peers to the problem of appealing to a public. His model was European art cinema rather than the Hollywood mainstream:

> When I speak about making entertaining movies, I don't mean that I want to go into competition with Steven Spielberg. I just mean that I want my movies to be shown in movie theaters. Because in fact not all pictures [in Russia today] are being made for the theaters. I want to make films that will pull in people who'll pay money for the chance to see them. They must be made in such a way that a regular kind of person [*normalnyi chelovek*] will find something interesting in them. Because I know that a huge number of Russian movies are made in a way and on subjects that make sure that no one will find them interesting. I want to make films like, for example, Kieslovsky [the recently deceased, émigré Polish director of the *Three Colors* trilogy], who's quite a serious artist but people want to pay and see his films. He made films of a kind that were intelligible to people.[32]

Unlike the messianic elitists, Todorovsky aspired to make films that an audience would pay to watch and was prepared to accept a degree of heteronomy in relation to the market to do so. But with Kieslovsky rather than Spielberg as his model, Todorovsky remained oriented toward the tastes of an educated international audience. Despite the clear contrast between Todorovsky's artistic ideology and that of, say, Tarkovsky or Sokurov, ultimately his work remained subject to the autonomous principle of hierarchization. The extent to which his films reached a paying public depended on their prior success in garnering film festival prizes: that is, they could only function as commodities if they were first recognized as art objects. Given the realities of film distribution in Russia during the mid-1990s where as he put it "not even a genius producer" could return a budget from domestic distribution, Todorovsky's concentration on making entertaining art cinema may well have been the most commercially viable strategy available.

* * *

The different artistic ideologies and creative strategies developed by these post-perestroika filmmakers reflect the existence of two fundamental choices available to them as participants in the post-perestroika cinematic field: that between the creation of elite versus popularly oriented cinema on the one hand and that between messianic "message" cinema versus an amoral cinema of "pure form" on the other. These choices may be thought of as defining two axes, one of ideological mission and one of breadth of intended audience, structuring a two-dimensional "space of possibles" (to use Bourdieu's term) within which in principle, at least, four opposing positions were available: (1) messianic elitism; (2) amoral elitism; (3) messianic populism; and (4) amoral populism. In both their artistic discourse and their creative practice Sokurov and Tsurtsumia appear firmly committed to the messianic-elitist position, Muratova to that of amoral elitism. The last three filmmakers were clear in their rejection of messianism but seemed ambivalent as to where on the axis of audience breadth they wished (or given the industry's economic situation, they were able) to position themselves. Indeed we may argue that, regardless of the extent to which they hoped to make popularly appealing films, their refusal to preach forced them to gravitate toward an elite-oriented creative practice. By refusing to foreground an ideological message in their work, they gave up the most promising strategy available to them to compete with Hollywood. That is, given the practical context in which post-perestroika filmmaking operated, a purely commercial cinema of amoral populism was the least tenable of any of the four positions theoretically available.

In the remainder of this chapter I wish to examine two major trends in filmmaking after the Fifth Congress which functioned, in part at least, as attempts to occupy the lower, mass-audience-oriented, half of this space: first, the cinema of social exposure that dominated filmmaking during the perestroika period, and second, a *national popular* trend that rose to prominence in the early 1990s following the dissolution of the Soviet Union.

PAINTING IT BLACK

In the later years of perestroika an impulse to expose the seamy side of Soviet life and history became a pervasive feature of most sectors of cultural production. Some of the individual works this movement produced were praised as bold attempts to tell the long-suppressed truth about such issues as Stalinist repression, youth alienation, and contemporary moral degradation. As a general trend, however, it was greeted by critics with almost universal disdain and came to be labeled using the generally pejorative slang term *chernukha* (literally, "dark stuff").[33]

Andrew Horton and Leonid Brashinsky characterize the stereotypical chernukha film as possessing the following elements:

1. The family, agonizing or already collapsed.
2. Average Soviet citizens unmasking their animalistic natures, ultimate immorality, and unmotivated cruelty.
3. The death of all former ideals, leaving no hope for the future after the closing credits.
4. Packed everyday conditions in "communal apartments" where several families live sharing all utilities, with the cockroaches being thrown in the neighbor's soup, naked light bulbs and torn wallpaper in the hallways, dirty graffiti on the staircases.
5. Senseless hysterics and fights arising from nowhere and dying down in the middle of a scream.
6. Usually a few "adult" scenes.[34]

While, as Horton and Brashinsky's account of the formula suggests, chernukha cinema tended frequently to dwell upon the most drearily mundane aspects of Soviet life, the genre could also incorporate more sensational themes such as insanity, murder, and drug abuse. Within Russian critical polemics the term chernukha could be applied to films that ranged from the grimmer elite-oriented works of the period, such as Muratova's *Asthenic Syndrome* and Vitaly Kanevsky's *Freeze, Die, Come to Life* (*Zamri, umri, voskreseni!* 1990), to the generally inept attempts to emulate Hollywood-style crime thrillers turned out by many of the cooperative studios. The key characteristic that united the works of the chernukha genre was the unrelentingly hopeless picture of Soviet life they presented.

With the significant exception of socialist realism, Russian culture—even Russian popular culture—has long shown a greater tolerance for the possibility that good may lose out to evil than that of the West (and America in particular); its heroes have been more likely to die as martyrs than win through to the kind of *kheppi ending* that Soviet critics of the

1920s found so exotic a feature of Hollywood cinema.[35] Even in the context of this cultural tradition, however, the depths of chernukha's pessimism were unique: Not only did virtue rarely triumph, its presence was scarcely detectable in the first place.

It is tempting to see the prevalence of chernukha as an understandable reaction to the troubled state of Soviet society in this period. However, despite the material difficulties and political-ideological uncertainties of the perestroika era, we can argue that most Russians had more cause for hope—if not perhaps, for contentment—than they had enjoyed either before or after. Democracy had for the first time emerged as a real possibility, while the full-scale socioeconomic collapse that turned out to be its price had not yet set in. More particularly, for cultural producers, the years of perestroika (as many in retrospect recognized) constituted something of a golden age. They more than any other sector of Soviet society benefited directly from the new freedoms of expression, while their economic position was buoyed by continuing state subsidies for culture, a financially lucrative wave of Western interest in their work, and a boom in most sectors of domestic cultural consumption. Why were the beneficiaries of this boom so intent upon propagating despair?

The answer must be sought in the actual or perceived advantages that "painting it black" offered cultural producers during this period. Three major forces were at work here. First, as we considered in the previous chapter, the "serious" Western public's appetite for grim revelations about the horrors of Soviet existence had considerable impact on the incentive structure of sectors of cultural production—such as cinema—that could be easily geared to foreign export.

A second factor was the legacy of late-Soviet patterns of artistic prestige. Critics of the trend toward chernukha commonly accused it of merely inverting the precepts of socialist realism, rather than escaping them.[36] A 1989 editorial in *Soviet Film* declared, for instance,

> Judging by films, only yesterday our country was inhabited by people who might have stepped off the Mukhina sculpture [the Stalin-era emblem of Mosfilm studios]—simple, democratic, brawny, confident and ready for great deeds. Today, if our films are anything to go by, we are a country of rock fans, drug addicts, teenage gangs, mafiosi, whores, a land of disenchanted cynical young people who have lost their will and interest in life and in doing anything useful. . . . Socialist realism con-

tinues to produce its crop of canned "educating" art. It is just as stilted, only in reverse . . . syrup has been replaced by mustard.[37]

This interpretation of chernukha as inverted socialist realism points to the continuing influence of the pattern established during the late-Soviet period whereby those who produced consolatory entertainment were liable to be viewed as cowardly or opportunistic conformists by their peers. Conversely, high status under the autonomous principle of hierarchization was most likely to be accorded to those whose work challenged the rosy picture of Soviet reality propagated by the authorities. So long as the Soviet system of cultural controls remained in place these impulses were restrained by the need to evade censorship. Following the dissolution of this system during perestroika, however, they could operate unchecked. As many pointed out, because exposing the negative side of Soviet experience no longer entailed the risk of official disapproval, it also became an easy means for former "opportunists" to establish their artistic credentials in the new ideological climate. Tsurtsumia remarked, for instance: "I find it amusing when people . . . who at that time made completely awful films which were lies . . . or people who shot films about Lenin, now make films which say he was like this, he shot these people. This I don't understand."[38]

Third, chernukha can be seen as a response to the dramatic increase in public demand for "the truth" about the society they lived in, a demand that although long present could only now be fully expressed. This upsurge was particularly evident in the case of the print and broadcast media, which lent themselves best to politically charged social reportage. Thus subscriptions to the "thick journals," especially those that fell under liberal control during perestroika, increased several fold between 1986 and 1988.[39] Perhaps the most dramatic evidence of popular interest in directly political forms of cultural production in this period were the massive viewing figures for unedited live television coverage of the meetings of the first democratically elected Supreme Soviet in 1990.[40]

In this climate, the fiction-based areas of the arts and media once valued by the (intelligentsia) public for their relative freedom from official ideological control risked marginalization by the news media. Creative workers and managers in these areas of cultural production who wished to maintain or expand their public sought to compete with the informational media by turning out increasingly "sensational" social revelations in fictional form.[41] In cinema, for instance, the biggest popular successes of the perestroika period were Yuri Kara's *Kings of Crime* (*Vory v Zakone*, 1988), which dealt with the "mafiosi" of the Brezhnev era, Pichul's *Little Vera*, which exposed working-class youth anomie, and Pyotr Todorovsky's *Intergirl* (*Interdevochka*, 1989), which featured a hard-currency prostitute.

We see, therefore, that the secret of chernukha's appeal to cultural producers in this period lay in the genre's capacity to attract mass audiences (and foreign buyers) yet avoid the stigma attached to escapist, consolatory entertainment by intelligentsia ideology. That is, chernukha promised its makers success under both autonomous and heteronomous principles of hierarchization. The editorial from *Soviet Film* quoted above captured this dual motivation thus: "[Chernukha] happens under the banner of the truth, under the banner of glasnost (indeed every new film makes a brave foray into a previously taboo area) and under the banner of making the film a paying concern (indeed every new film is a sensation)."[42]

The general move away from chernukha in the film industry during the early 1990s is explicable in terms of the disappearance of the three factors described above. By the time the Soviet Union fell in August 1991, both Western and post-Soviet audiences had lost their appetite for further revelations as to the decayed state of Russian society. Indeed, in the case of cinema, the slump in the domestic filmgoing audience predated the collapse of the Union by at least two years, suggesting that despite the large audiences won in this period by the handful of "publicistic" pictures mentioned above, most viewers were little interested in cinema as a medium for the exploration of social ills.[43] As early as 1989, industry commentators were warning that filmmakers' concentration on the seamier side of Soviet life was alienating the mass audience. In the summer of that year, Vladimir Dostal told *Variety*, for instance: "Films now are very hard to ban. There is an attempt to show the negative side of Soviet life in films, but that has meant fewer adventure films are being shot. . . . There is a high level of critical awareness but the audience is not very interested because they have it on television and in newspapers. The people want to go to the cinema to be entertained. Our directors have to learn to combine intelligence with commercial qualities."[44] By the early 1990s, therefore, Russia's filmmakers, like her cultural producers generally, faced a public with as little hunger for, and as many distractions from, what Bill Nichols has termed "the discourses of sobriety" as that of the West.[45]

Equally, the overtly politicized, message-based conception of culture's public role that stimulated the social problem cinema of the perestroika period, lost its attraction for the creative intelligentsia following the definitive collapse of the Soviet political order.[46]

As Zalotukha put it: "There were a lot of films which seemed good to us at the time [of perestroika] but they weren't from an artistic point of view. They only seemed good because they were against life under socialism. . . . They seemed interesting ideas for us but they weren't art. They were a social act, a political act. . . . Now we can't watch these films. They seem awful to us but about ten years ago we thought they were wonderful."[47] In many cases, as we have already seen, the reaction against cinema as "a political act" informed a rejection of all forms of message-focused cinema. In others, however, including Zalotukha himself, it stimulated a quest for an alternative conception of cinema that would take a different approach to the problem of combining social relevance with artistic and entertainment qualities.

NATIONAL POPULAR CINEMA

Despite the waning viability of social problem cinema, those filmmakers who remained interested in winning a popular domestic audience could not afford to give up the search for an ideological message specifically attuned to the concerns of the post-Soviet public. Given Soviet cinema's relative technical backwardness and lack of financial resources, this, it can be argued, was the only potential advantage its products had over the glossier imports of Hollywood. The trend in the Soviet cinema of the 1990s toward the production of films focused on issues of national identity can be seen as an attempt to answer this need. Daniil Dondurei, chief editor of the film journal *Iskusstvo Kino*, explicitly appealed for the creation of what he called a "national mythology" in order to win back a public he believed had been alienated by chernukha cinema: "There is no such thing as a national hero and nobody cares to create him. . . . What must be done is to create national mythology instead of wasting time on creating films which are not even mentioned, let alone attended. . . . The Soviet masters of culture depict their own society as one of criminals and in a masochistic way reopen its wounds. And at the same time these cinema experts consider such great hits as *Dallas* something disgusting."[48] In terms of the fourfold division of positions within the post-perestroika cinematic field outlined above, the films this trend produced generally fell under the category of *messianic populist* in that they offered their audience a moral message in popularly accessible form.

The issue of Russia's identity as a nation has occupied a central place in cultural and political discourse at least as far back as the debates between the Slavophiles and Westernizers of the 1840s. In the last decades of tsarist rule the autocracy attempted to co-opt the appeal of Russian ethnic nationalism in its own support; its attempts at forced cultural and linguistic russification of the imperial periphery ultimately backfired, however, by provoking national separatist movements that played an important role in the empire's collapse during the Revolution. As inheritors of the bulk of this Russian-dominated empire, yet guardians of a theoretically internationalist ideology, the Soviet Communist leadership's attitude toward Russian nationalism was ambivalent. On the one hand, it could prove useful in mobilizing the support of the USSR's ethnic Russian majority behind their rule in the face of real or perceived foreign threats; on the other, excessive reliance on Russian nationalist ideology risked jeopardizing both their claim to hegemony over the world revolutionary movement and their capacity to rule the (theoretically sovereign) non-Russian national republics with minimum resort to open force. In the late-Soviet period, the leadership's central response to this ideological quandary was to propagate a cult of allegiance to the multiethnic "Soviet motherland" that accorded minority nationalities a respected yet subordinate place under the benevolent tutelage of the "most progressive" of Soviet ethnic groups, that is, the Russians. While Russian culture clearly dominated within this compromise, its full expression—at least in the opinion of russophile dissidents—was partially submerged within the Soviet cultural ecumene.

When, following the Thaw, the intelligentsia began once more to express alternatives to official Soviet ideology and practice, the tsarist-era opposition between Westernizers and russophiles reemerged as a prominent feature of public (or underground) discourse.[49] When Westernizers criticized the regime for its failure to practice the authentic ideals of Marxist-Leninism or its deviation from the norms of liberal democracy, they drew upon universal rather than culturally specific values. Russophiles, by contrast, saw Marxism as an alien ideology whose introduction had resulted in the destruction of the country's unique cultural and historical traditions. In general, under Brezhnev, the regime seems to have regarded russophilism, at least in certain of its expressions, as less of a threat to its rule than Westernism, tolerating, for instance, the tendency of the Village Prose writers to wax nostalgic for a rural past untouched by industrial modernity.[50]

The attempted reform and subsequent collapse of the Soviet system ushered in a new phase in the history of Russia in which the redefinition of national identity emerged as a ubiquitous theme within political, intellectual, and cultural discourse. Political democratization and the legalization of market exchange vastly increased the scale on which information and commodities flowed into the country. Westernization ceased to be a theoretical possibility and became a practical and inescapable reality. At the same time, Russia's status in the world underwent a radical transformation: from being the dominant component of a multiethnic superpower capable of vying on relatively equal terms with the United States for global military, ideological, and technological hegemony, the country became a sovereign but impoverished nation-state. The introduction of Western models within the cultural, political, and economic spheres coincided, therefore, with a sudden and traumatic reduction of the country to subaltern status of which no Russian could be unaware.[51]

One reaction to this combination of Westernization and postimperial decline was the virulent ethnic chauvinism and anti-Semitism characteristic of the far right. During the perestroika period, the extreme russophile wing of the creative intelligentsia played an important role in formulating the ideologies upon which the "red-brown" (i.e., the Communist-fascist) political opposition based their appeal in the post-Soviet period. Most notably, during the late-1980s, the Writers' Union of the Russian Republic became the power base for a faction whose members included many of the most prominent representatives of the late-Soviet Village Prose school, including Andrei Belov and Valentin Rasputin. Under the patronage of "conservative" figures in the Politburo such as Yegor Ligachev, this group launched virulent attacks on the reform process in general and the allegedly "russophobe" character of glasnost cultural production in particular. Behind the russophiles' nationalist and anti-Western rhetoric lay a thinly veiled anti-Semitism, which was later expressed more openly. According to most commentators, the russophiles acted in alliance with the "gray" writers who continued to dominate the structures of the Writers' Union of the USSR, enabling the latter to fight off demands for institutional reform until the fall of the Soviet Union itself.[52]

Another cultural producer who played a prominent role in propagating national chauvinism during and after perestroika was the painter Ilya Glazunov. Since the 1960s he had become known as portraitist to the Politburo and a prominent advocate of art based on national cultural tradition rather than "Western" avant-gardist experiments. His 1994 exhibition at the Manezh gallery in Moscow attracted not only large crowds but also public appearances from Boris Yeltsin, Vladimir Zhirinovsky, and Gennady Zyuganov. The paintings on exhibit depicted villainous-looking caricatures of Africans abducting white maidens and Hasidim quaffing goblets of (presumably Russian) blood; the forces of good were represented by blond-haired, bare-chested warriors toting Kalashnikovs and Orthodox priests bedecked in swastika-emblazoned robes. Perhaps inspired by these scenes, Yeltsin took the opportunity of his visit to issue a statement refusing to withdraw Russian troops from the Baltic republics.[53]

Although influential, such forms of nationalism represented only the most extreme current within in a much broader trend toward the reaffirmation of national identity, which became a pervasive feature in Russian cultural life in the early 1990s. This movement manifested itself in fields as far apart as rock music, in which a number of bands introduced themes and instruments drawn from folk tradition[54] and the appropriation of Russian literature by television commercials. (In one campaign, for instance, Dostoyevsky's famous dictum: "Only beauty can save the world" was used to sell kitchen tiles.)[55] Interestingly, the more extreme forms of russophilism found no public expression within Russian filmmaking—the conception of national identity reaffirmed by national popular cinema was based on shared cultural tradition, rather than common descent. Indeed, nonethnic Russians made up a significant proportion of its practitioners. Why this should have been so is not clear: one possible explanation, offered by Turovskaya, lies in the manner in which working relationships within literature differ from those typical of filmmaking. Literary works are created and judged primarily as the product of discrete individuals. Authors tend to see each other as competitors for material and symbolic resources, and given the right circumstances this competition may take on ethnic overtones. Filmmaking, however, is an inherently collective enterprise whose participants cannot afford to be too fussy about their selection of colleagues. Since people of non-Russian descent were strongly represented in the Soviet industry, filmmakers of different ethnic backgrounds frequently worked together on a day-to-day basis. As Turovskaya points out, public expressions of ethnic chauvinism would jeopardize the maintenance of essential working relationships.[56] We may also suggest that by giving individuals from different groups practical experience of relating to one another as collaborators rather than competitors, these circumstances may have lessened the inherent appeal of chauvinist belief-systems.

One indication of the renewed affirmation of national cultural tradition within the cinema of the early 1990s was a wave of costume adaptations of Russian literary classics.[57] Along with *First Love*, such chestnuts as *Anna Karenina*, *Three Sisters*, and *The Government Inspector (Revizor)* all received reworkings in this period. In a 1994 interview with Vladimir Dostal, the general director of Mosfilm, the film journalist Viktor Matizen commented somewhat skeptically on this trend, "It seems you're concentrating on historical pictures—an escape from the present day—and new screen adaptations . . . [of old classics]. After all Grigory Melekhov, Prince Myshkin, and Anna Karenina are characters that have already appeared on the screen, moreover in your productions."[58] Dostal replied that these films formed a welcome contrast to the cinema of the immediate past: "In the past few years there have been practically no such movies. There was a somewhat delirious obsession with freedom, everyone rushing to tackle new subjects. But this is now over, and as you see, a leaning towards the classics regaining ground. There's another factor that has to be taken into account. All the pictures I listed . . . have been commissioned by the state."[59]

Period pieces and literary adaptations were not the only type of nationally oriented cinema to emerge in this period. Among films set in the present, a frequently occurring trope during the early 1990s was what we might call that of *exile rejected*. Examples included Yuri Mamin's *A Window on Paris (Okno v Parizh*, 1993), Vladimir Khotinenko's *A Patriotic Comedy (Patrioticheskaya komediya*, 1992), Dmitri Astrakhan's *You Are My Only One (Ty u menya odna*, 1993), and Shakhnazarov's *American Daughter (Amerikanskaya doch'*, 1995). In each of these films the protagonists are offered the possibility of leaving Russia to lead a "normal, civilized" life in the West—often by magical means—and refuse it, realizing that, for all the country's problems, their connection to Russia is organic and indissoluble.

This formula allowed filmmakers to acknowledge the difficulties of existence in contemporary Russia while simultaneously offering their domestic audience the consolation that by patriotically sticking it out back home they are doing the right thing. In Mamin's comedy *A Window on*

Paris, the hero Kolya, who teaches "aesthetics and music" at a St. Petersburg high school, stumbles across a magical portal that allows instant travel between Russia and Paris. Toward the end of the film he brings his teenage pupils with him to Paris. They give him the slip, planning to stay on permanently and support themselves by begging on the street or working at McDonald's; one girl implies that she can survive as a prostitute. When he catches up with his charges, Kolya tries to persuade them to return for their families' sake, but they argue back saying that their families will be better off without them. The words of his final appeal to them encapsulate the message of the exile-rejected formula: "You're right. You were born at the wrong time in a miserable bankrupt country. But it's still your country. Can't you make it a better place?"

Another feature of *A Window on Paris* worth noting is its reproduction of the opposition between authentic Russian intelligentnost (personified by Kolya) and the meshchantsvo portrayed as rampant within both Western society and that of Russia as it undergoes the "transition to the market." Bedecked with such slogans as "Money Doesn't Stink!" the school Kolya teaches in is now dedicated to the inculcation of capitalist values. In a confrontation with its principal (whose New Russian philistinism is symbolized by her gold lamé jacket) he inveighs against this policy: "You used to train the builders of communism. Now you train the builders of capitalism. And the results are the same: cruelty, ignorance, and thievery." Things are no better in Paris, where Kolya is offered a job playing the violin in a restaurant only to find that he is required to play with no trousers on. As an old Russian friend he meets in Paris who had emigrated some years ago tells him: "No one here needs Mozart with pants." The friend goes on: "Nobody here wants art. Nobody. . . . See those people there . . . they're talking about the food they're stuffing in their mouths. Remember us in the communal apartment on Lenin Square, at my kitchen table with a hundred bottles of vodka and one pickle. How we talked about art, the fate of Russia, about God." We see here Mamin using the popular medium of cinematic comedy to propagate the cult of high culture.

Considering the desuetude into which distribution and exhibition had fallen by the time of its release, *Window on Paris* enjoyed considerable popular success. Although not in itself capable of regaining the popular audience, the cinema of national reaffirmation possessed the additional and perhaps more immediately useful advantage for its makers of allowing them to offer post-Soviet economic and political elites opportunities for ideological legitimation in return for their financial support.

An example of such a mutual beneficial relationship is offered by Vladimir Khotinenko's decision to shoot a film based on the memoir *We Are Your Children, Moscow* by Yuri Luzhkov, the mayor of Moscow. In the course of the 1990s, in collaboration with his scriptwriter Valery Zalotukha, Khotinenko established a reputation as one of the leaders of the "new generation" of Russian filmmakers. His films such as *Makarov* (1994) and *The Muslim* (*Musul'manin*, 1995), which drew heavily upon the conventions of the Hollywood thriller to explore the dilemmas of the post-Soviet "Russian soul," were recognized at international film festivals and laden with prizes within Russia. Zalotukha saw their work as part of a new movement toward the creation of a distinctively Russian (as opposed to Soviet) cinema: "As a term, 'Russian Cinema' didn't exist until recently. When Khotinenko and I shot *Roi* [*The Swarm*] at the beginning of perestroika I said, 'Let's make a Russian film' and we both felt uncomfortable hearing those words. Now the term exists. I've tried to understand what it means and I formulate it as cinema that investigates the Russian national character and soul."[60]

Over the same period, Luzhkov emerged as one of the most powerful political figures in Russia. He too has based his ideological appeal on what might be called a national popular strategy. As mayor, one of his main priorities has been a prestige-oriented construction and restoration program aimed at restoring the glories of capital's tsarist and Orthodox past, presumably in order to co-opt their prestige. The centerpiece of this program was the rebuilding of the huge Cathedral of Christ the Savior by the Moskva River, demolished under Stalin's orders in 1936. In his autobiography Luzhkov claimed that restoring the cathedral had been his lifelong dream.

The demolition and restoration of the cathedral features prominently in the film pilot Khotinenko presented at *Dom Kino* in August 1997, which portrays the mayor's childhood as a poor but lovable urchin on the streets of 1930s Moscow.[61] At its premiere a number of filmmakers pointedly compared the film to the notorious screen adaptations of Brezhnev's World War II memoirs produced during the 1970s. The response of Khotinenko and his key collaborators on this project, scriptwriter Pavel Finn and producer Rolan Bykov, was both disingenuous and unrepentant: Bykov claimed, for instance, that Luzhkov was not even aware of their activities and had certainly not provided them with any financial support. A second line in Bykov's defense was that it was time for Russian cinema to abandon the compulsive negativity it had wallowed in since perestroika: "We just have to learn to make movies about normal people again, not crooks, not bandits."[62] Few of the members of the film community present seem to have swallowed Bykov's claim that the possibility that Luzhkov might be gratified by *We Are Your Children* had never crossed his mind. Nevertheless, for some at least, its making was justified by the dire material straits in which Russian cinema now found itself. As Yuli Gusman, head of Dom Kino, commented: "I just saw some of the best shots in years, and I'm glad that my colleagues here can make a movie in which they will be able to use a helicopter, maybe even for free, instead of filming each other in a dark yard on a half-a-million ruble budget."[63]

THE CREATOR CULT OF NIKITA MIKHALKOV

By far the most successful practitioner of the national popular strategy in the cinema of the 1990s was actor and director, Nikita Mikhalkov. His 1994 film *Burnt by the Sun* (*Utomlennye solntsem*, 1994) not only appealed to theater audiences and domestic and foreign critics but consolidated his public reputation as advocate and personification of Russian national ideals. His example was not typical, for his status as Russia's most prominent post-Soviet filmmaker owed much to his reputation as a film actor. It is, however, indicative of forces more widely at work within the post-Soviet cultural economy.

Typical of the kind of acclaim *Burnt by the Sun* received in Russia was one film critic's declaration that in it Mikhalkov had created "a landmark in our national culture."[64] In the last twenty years, as an actor, director, and latterly political figure, Mikhalkov the person had himself become something of a landmark of Russian national culture. He got off to a good start: his father Sergei was head of the Soviet Writers' Union and author of the national anthem, while through his mother's line he is descended from a line of eminent writers and artists of the nineteenth century.

This dual inheritance of Soviet and pre-Revolutionary privilege made Mikhalkov, in a sense, a personification of the tensions inherent in post-Soviet Russia's search for a usable past. In the 1970s he established his reputation as an actor and director with a string of popular and critically acclaimed films. Owing perhaps to his father's elevated status in the official cultural establishment, he was able to pursue his work without being identified as either an artistic nonconformist or an opportunistic nomenklaturshchik. He claimed: "I was not a dissident but I never joined the party. People used to ask me how I could work. I worked, but I never made deals. I managed to make my films the way I wanted."[65] Perhaps again owing to his protected status, he was known for his Hollywood-style work methods—he shot films quickly according to a precise shooting script. Although (perhaps in part because) he did not play a prominent role in the upheavals of the perestroika-era film industry, he has since emerged as the most powerful and respected figure in the Russian film world.[66]

Even in the Soviet period many of his films had a russophile tinge; for instance, in his 1979 release *Oblomov* the innocence and spirituality of the eponymous hero is counterposed to the "un-Russian" rationalism and worldliness of his German-descended friend Stoltz. Following the breakup of the Soviet Union, Mikhalkov became a vocal advocate for the need both to restore pre-Revolutionary Russian culture and institutions (including the monarchy) and to preserve the positive aspects of the Soviet past against what he has termed the "New Bolshevism" of Yeltsin.[67] In interviews he claimed that, being lawless yet God-fearing by nature, Russians can only be governed by a strong, divinely legitimated autocrat:[68]

> In Russia we have never respected laws and always have tried to break or avoid them. . . . If in France the law can become God so they can live without God's truth, in Russia the laws were obeyed only because of God. That's how the Russian person is made. . . . The thing is that Lenin and Stalin were educated people, a good deal better educated than the rulers who succeeded them. They knew history; they knew what kind of religious mentality our people have, a monarchical mentality. And because of that they were able to deceive such huge numbers of people.[69]

Once an associate of Vice-President Rutskoi, he has since moved closer to the government, running successfully for the State Duma as a candidate for the pro-Yeltsin, "Our Home is Russia" party in 1995.[70] Whether this was because he decided that even he could not do without friends in high places, or because he considered that Yeltsin had embraced nationalism sufficiently to be worthy of his support is unclear. One of his associates suggested to me that his belief in Russia's need for a firm government (perhaps ultimately with himself at its head) was more fundamental to him than nationalism as such: "He's not really a nationalist, it's just necessary to seem one. Maybe he wants to run for president, not this time but next. Basically he's a *derzhavik*, that's someone who wants a strong state."[71]

The following description of his office suggests that he was fully aware of the publicity value of his inherited cultural capital and keen to emphasize its distinctively national character: "The director has also rediscovered his aristocratic roots. A giant framed genealogical chart tracing his lineage back to Tolstoy and Catherine the Great hangs over the couch in his office in Moscow. Gregorian chants played softly in his office as he spoke."[72]

Despite the hostility toward the westernization of Russian culture which Mikhalkov demonstrated both in films such as *Urga* and *Anna from Six to Eighteen*, and in his public pronouncements (for instance, he described contemporary Moscow as resembling the exaggeratedly bleak depictions of capitalist decadence in Soviet films of the Cold War era), he proved highly effective in working with foreign producers both in his own work and by providing services for foreign film crews through his Tri-Te production company (including *Police Academy VII: Mission to Moscow*).[73] One of his production managers claimed that the secret to his success was that, unlike most of his competitors in Russia, he charged international producers local market prices rather than whatever he thought rich foreigners could afford, while guaranteeing an exceptionally swift work-pace. (Apparently the only occasion he ever canceled shooting was during the Yeltsin putsch of October 1993.) As he put it himself in a recent interview, referring to archetypal opposition in *Oblomov* between the soulful, lethargic hero and the dynamic, "Western" energy of Stolz, "I want to be like Oblomov but it turns out that I live like Stolz."[74]

However, the ability of his production company to work effectively in contemporary Russian conditions was not purely the result of its "un-Russian" efficiency. According to two former employees, Tri-Te provided the best "roof" (*krysha*), as they put it, in the film business, which offered its staff immunity from the chaotic lawlessness all around them.[75] Within his fiefdom, I was told, Mikhalkov practiced the paternalism that he preached, assuming the affectionate yet bullying manner of a feudal squire (*barin*). He was given for instance to pinching his employees' cheeks. Apparently this management technique works. Several filmmakers I spoke to commented enviously on the Mikhalkov's unique ability to keep his production team together. Evidently he wields considerable personal charisma off screen as well as on:

> Some people are fanatical about him and would work for free. He's so powerful. When you're with his organization you feel like there's a wall around you and you're free of the government and the mafia. . . . He'll be famous forever because of his work. He's a genius. Who's going to remember Chernomyrdin in fifty years time? And his father was the famous Sergei Mikhalkov. He was never with the government. All the women of Russia love him and he's a model to many of the men of Russia. He's clean. He's a moral authority. (An employee at Tri-Te)

In *Burnt by the Sun*, Mikhalkov took on perhaps the most traumatic theme in Soviet history to make a movie that, rather than doing anything so masochistic as to examine the historical forces that made Stalinism possible, manages to celebrate the eternal essences of Russian culture. In so doing he at once exploited and consolidated a potent *mythological* that is, to follow Barthes, dehistoricized, concept of Russian national identity.[76] This dehistoricization allowed the film to function effectively in two fields: abroad, the film worked as a moderately saleable cultural commodity, offering foreign audiences an experience at once enticingly exotic and acceptably familiar; within Russia, it presented an ideology that offered to rebuild the severed links between the intelligentsia, the political-economic elite, and the mass public around the eternal truths of homeland and autocracy.

Such mythologizing interpretations of history are a common enough feature of postsocialist Europe. What made Mikhalkov's strategy distinctive was the manner in which he presented *himself* as the personal embodiment of the kind of mystically ordained authority that he claimed to be the only force capable guiding the Russian people.

Within the film-text, the distinction between artist and artwork is systematically elided. Mikhalkov directed and produced the movie and co-wrote the script. He took the central role of the Soviet general and Civil War hero Colonel Kotov, while Mikhalkov's own child, Nadya, played the colonel's daughter. Even the country house in which the bulk of the movie was filmed was located in the same village as Mikhalkov's own family dacha. Given these multiple identifications between the real Mikhalkov and his fictional alter-ego, it is unsurprising that Mikhalkov personalized the russophile message of the film in terms of the opposition between the loyal, patriotic, and self-sacrificing Kotov and Mitya, the hard-done-by but morally bankrupt, cosmopolitan intellectual who destroys him.

Condee and Padunov have argued that the sudden influx of global commercial mass culture since perestroika has spelled the end of the "creator cults," which had formed such a prominent feature of Soviet cultural life.[77] While many of the *specific* creator cults of the late-Soviet period have fallen into abeyance, the example of Mikhalkov's multiple and mutually reinforcing successes as director, actor, ideologue of monarchism, and paternalistic manager suggests that as a general phenomenon creator cults may still have a future in post-Soviet cultural life. His success may indeed have stemmed from his exploitation of a shortage in the supply of national artistic heroes.

Set in August 1936, at the height of the Great Purge, *Burnt by the Sun* opens with Mitya receiving orders to supervise Kotov's arrest at the dacha where the colonel now lives with Marusya (Mitya's former lover) and her pre-Revolutionary intelligentsia family. He arrives at the dacha and tells Kotov that he is to be arrested but the colonel courageously refuses to alarm his family by passing on the news and, once the black NKVD car comes to take him away, goes stoically to his doom. In the last scene, a presumably remorseful Mitya slashes his wrists and lies dying in the bath of his Moscow apartment. Clearly, Purging People Is Wrong and No Good Comes of It—a message that evidently warmed the hearts of both the American Motion Picture Academy and the Cannes festival jury.

Evidently Yeltsin's election campaign staff considered *Burnt by the Sun*'s depiction of the evils of Stalinism—and by extension Zyuganov's Communist Party—sufficiently compelling to have the movie shown on national television on the eve of the 1996 presidential election. However, both within the film text and in his public political pronouncements Mikhalkov indicated that, while he condemned Stalinist terror, he had no problems with the concept of charismatic dictatorship as such. In a crucial scene near the start of the film, when an army training exercise threatens to flatten the local peasants' crops, they send a messenger to Kotov's house to ask for his protection. Tugging on his military mustache (whether by accident or design he has the appearance of a rather idealized version of Stalin), Kotov mounts his horse and gallops to the fields, where he browbeats the young officer in charge into pulling back his tanks. Thus in a film set at the height of the purges and four years after the collectivization of the peasantry, Mikhalkov contrived to portray himself/ Kotov—supposedly a Red Army general of proletarian descent—as the model of a pre-Revolutionary country noble, protecting his loyal serfs against the intrusion of technological modernity.

Given the grim times in which it is set, the film is also remarkable for its sheer visual *attractiveness*—a quality that radically distinguishes it from the films of chernukha. The woods and fields are dappled by the summer sun, the characters dressed in rather stylishly cut linen suits. In fact the film presents a world stylistically identical to Mikhalkov's portrayals of turn-of-the-century gentry life in his previous adaptations of Chekhov. As the director of Moscow's Kinocenter suggested, the film combined apparent anti-Stalinism with an implicit appeal to a distinctively post-Soviet version of the "nostalgia for empire" theme of the Merchant-Ivory / *Out of Africa* / *Indochine* genre in recent Western cinema. The stylistic similarity between post-Soviet and postcolonial retro may have been a further factor behind Mikhalkov's ability to garner prizes and, as a review of *Burnt by the Sun* in *Variety* put it, "solid specialty release dollars," in the West.

If Russia's film distribution system had not collapsed, *Burnt by the Sun* might have been guaranteed a sizable domestic audience. As it was, Mikhalkov was forced to market it by employing what one might call a "feudal" rather than a capitalist commercial strategy: he toured the country in person and urged, some say instructed, local government and business leaders to exhibit his movie.[78] He described the process thus:

Look at *Urga* [his previous film which also won a prize at Cannes] for instance, which made it around the whole world but was virtually unshown in Russia. Now we are pursuing a different route, having chosen you could call a rather crude method: we are carrying out the distribution of our film ourselves. I am personally going to this or that region, I meet the chief administrators and bankers and talk to them . . . the question was put thus: do you want people to watch our film in your area? Will you help us? Don't demand that the money you put in be returned immediately, wait. You will lose something. . . . We are prepared to add to the film credits the logo of your bank, your firm, your company if you need that. But understand: by helping us you are doing something important and needed. . . . And already we've enjoyed a major response.[79]

That is, to ensure an audience for his film Mikhalkov had to enlist the support of the emerging class of New Russians. He claimed that their responsiveness to his appeals derived from their shared interest in constructing a new moral order in post-Soviet Russia:

I don't ask my Russian sponsors where their money comes from, for me it's important that they spend it on a worthy cause.

Today in Russia there is no clean money, but among the "new rich" people have already appeared who understand that you can't wear more than one pair of shoes at a time, people have appeared who want to live *here*, and not to spirit money away *there*. People have appeared who want to build here. And these people already need a legal order, specifically a *moral* legal order.[80] (Emphasis in original)

Mikhalkov's rise to preeminence within the post-Soviet cinematic field indicates the powerful advantages the national popular strategy offered cultural producers bent on escape from the honorable but cramped confines of autonomy. By celebrating Russia's national distinctiveness he was able simultaneously to appeal to a domestic audience searching for consolation in troubled times, elite groups eager to establish their legitimacy in the eyes of the general population, and even foreign audiences with an interest in thought-provoking but intelligible exotica. Better still, he was able to reach out to these external sources of financial and symbolic support while at the same time underlining his claim to the status of authentic artist, preoccupied not by fame or profits but by the fate of the Russian people.

So striking has been the contrast between Mikhalkov's ever-snowballing power and prestige and the degeneration of the film industry as a whole that in December 1997, the Russian Filmmakers' Union reenacted the oldest script in Russian history: At the Union's Third Congress he was offered the union presidency in the hope that his personal leadership could restore the industry to order and prosperity.[81] Mikhalkov accepted the crown proffered him on condition that he be allowed to replace the union secretariat with his own team and that he receive complete authority to overhaul the union's financial affairs.[82] His election was confirmed at an extraordinary congress in May 1998 at which he unveiled proposals aimed at rebuilding the industry's economically and organizationally fractured institutional structure. Key elements of his plan included the recentralization of the Filmmakers' Union and the establishment of a "Russian Extra-Budgetary State Fund for the Development of Cinematography" with the authority to collect distribution revenues and license production for all studios operating on government property.[83] The plan would seem to represent an attempt to reestablish many features of Goskino's old monopoly control over the industry. If accepted (and more to the point) realized, it would signal filmmakers' voluntary relinquishment of the institutional autonomy for which they had recently fought so hard.

The aspiration of Russian filmmakers for artistic autonomy grew out of the distinctive ideological, sociocultural, and political-economic context within which Soviet cinema was placed. This aspiration influenced both the modes of creative practice characteristic of the late- and post-Soviet periods and the radical institutional transformation that the industry underwent during perestroika.

The types of creative practice and discursive self-presentations adopted by late-Soviet filmmakers suggest striking parallels between the dynamics of this field and that of high cultural production in the West (or at any rate France) as theorized by Bourdieu. Most centrally, both can be seen as structured around a fundamental contradiction between achieving high status in the eyes of other participants and satisfying externally imposed expectations. Bourdieu's theoretical model works particularly well in illuminating the dynamics of the late-Soviet film industry because it stresses the *relational* nature of artistic identity; that is, the manner in which cultural producers define (or justify) their work in relation to that of their peers. For this reason I have found Bourdieu's approach more suggestive of Soviet conditions than the tendency characteristic of the largely U.S.-based "production of culture" perspective to treat different social milieus of cultural production as separate "art worlds" (to use Becker's phrase), each governed by their own criteria of success.[1]

The greater relevance of Bourdieu's relational mode of analysis to the case of late-Soviet filmmaking does not necessarily indicate its general theoretical superiority to the production perspective. Its applicability results from the high degree to which cultural life in both France and the Soviet Union was centralized by comparison to that of the United States. Put crudely, cultural producers will only define their projects in relation to those with whom they compete for recognition or material resources. The geographical concentration of Soviet filmmaking (and other forms of cultural production) in Moscow, and more fundamentally, its institutional monopolization by Goskino and the Filmmakers' Union, created a highly unified social milieu that threw together, and fostered competitive relations between, individuals who in other circumstances might have had the luxury of ignoring one another's existence. Setting aside for one moment the particular influence of the state socialist mode of cultural production, French cultural life has historically resembled that of Russia in its centripetal character, owing ultimately to the centralized character of the French state and its peculiarly prominent (by comparison with most other Western countries) role in cultural patronage.

At the same time, however, the parallel I have identified between late-Soviet filmmaking and Bourdieu's account of the field of cultural production raises questions that cannot be resolved within the bounds of an exclusively Bourdieuian perspective. For one thing, the wider socioeconomic conditions that Bourdieu sees as essential for the formation of an autonomous sphere of cultural production were effectively absent under the socialist mode of cultural production. The process of autonomization, he writes, "is correlated with the constant growth of a public of potential consumers of increasing social diversity, which guarantee the producers of symbolic goods minimal conditions of economic independence and also, a competing system of legitimacy. It is . . . [also] correlated with the multiplication and diversification of agencies of consecration placed in a situation of competition for cultural legitimacy."[2] Late-Soviet (and indeed late-tsarist) society may well have been sufficiently differentiated to have had the potential to support an autonomous sphere of cultural production—it was certainly more urbanized and educated than that of early-nineteenth-century France. However, in the case of cinema, at least, this potential was blocked by the Soviet state's successful maintenance of institutional monopoly. (Although the emergence of the "unauthorized sphere" within other sectors of cultural production may have indeed been fostered by increasing sociocultural diversification over the late-Soviet period.)

Second, Bourdieu argues that autonomization does not characterize the sphere of "large-scale" cultural production. He makes the traditional assumption of commentators working within the "mass culture" perspective that, as he puts it, "the emergence of large collective production units in the fields of radio, television, cinema and journalism, . . . entail(s) a transformation of the relationship between the producers and their works . . . and, consequently of the political and the aesthetic ideologies they profess. Intellectual labor carried out collectively, within technically and socially differentiated production units, can no longer surround itself with the charismatic aura attaching to traditional independent production."[3] As elsewhere in his sociology, Bourdieu is too ready to assume that subjectivity necessarily harmonizes with, and thus tends to reproduce, the "objective" social conditions within which it operates. The "aesthetic ideologies" characteristic of late-Soviet filmmakers clearly did not harmonize with cinema's institutional structures. Ultimately indeed they played a central role in their destruction. Thus, a Bourdieuian perspective on cultural production offers us a useful analytical vocabulary for understanding the dynamics of the field of late-Soviet filmmaking. It does not, however, offer an effective explanation of either what motivated many of its participants to resist the authorities' conception of their role or what allowed them to put their aspirations into creative practice in the face of a pervasive, officially imposed system of sanctions and rewards.

The aspiration for artistic autonomy was a specific expression of a wider conception of intelligentnost that played a vital role in defining the class (or more precisely status-group) identity of the mostly highly educated section of the Russian population. By emphasizing the role played by the unequal distribution of cultural rather than economic capital in structuring Soviet social hierarchy and influencing collective perceptions of social status, this argument departs from the orthodox Marxist approach to "class consciousness." The value of this analytical move is not confined to socialist societies. It is also a promising strategy for understanding the influence that the (typically highly educated) social background of creative workers has on the character of mass-cultural production in capitalist societies. Even under capitalism, the social positioning and ideological consciousness of both cultural producers and high-cultural consumers depend more upon their privileged possession of cultural capital than their *economic* class status. In economic terms nothing clearly distinguishes cultural elites from other elements of the educated middle class.

Surprisingly, Bourdieu himself, from whom I drew the concept of cultural capital, appears reluctant to make this move in his analysis of cultural production. Instead he emphasizes the "coincidental" character of the affinity evident between the works of autonomy-claiming cultural producers and the cultural-ideological sympathies of the culturally privileged, economically marginalized, "dominated fraction of the dominant class."[4] However, in the more general account he develops in *Distinction* of the role played by cultural capital in shaping the class structure of French society, he sees the oppositional ideological tendencies typical of "artists" as stemming from the "particular interest in disinterestedness" they share with other members of the general cultural elite.[5] These two currents within Bourdieu's thought need not be taken as contradicting each other—the tendency of artists to distance themselves from, or actively oppose, the dominant social order is doubtless overdetermined. However, a class approach assumes particular significance when we attempt to account for the resilience the aspiration for artistic autonomy shows in even such inhospitable institutional contexts as the culture industries of Western capitalism and the authorized sphere of socialist cultural production. We must recognize that cultural producers' creative aspirations and sense of identity are not simply determined by the particular conditions within which they work (although these must always be taken into account) but also by their sense of status within society at large.

As we have seen, late-Soviet filmmakers were, on occasion, able to put their aspiration for autonomy into creative practice through the production of "auteurist" cinema. Despite the range of control mechanisms at the disposal of the film industry's leadership, it was relatively unsuccessful, by comparison with its counterparts in the capitalist culture industries of the West, in securing creative workers' compliance. The root causes of this incapacity can be traced to the distinctive institutional, ideological, and economic characteristics of what I term the socialist mode of cultural production. While this mode of cultural production shared certain features with its corporate capitalist counterpart, it decisively failed to achieve a comparable degree of disciplinary power over its creative workers. This in turn implies that forms of bureaucratic control legitimated and motivated by the "law of profit" wield a degree of disciplinary force that socialist culture industries, for all their elaborate and intrusive machinery of censorship and patronage, were not able to match.

This contrast suggests that we should be wary of the tendency prevalent in recent historical studies of Hollywood to emphasize that even where cultural production is organized along "industrial" lines considerable scope for creative independence remains, owing to cultural production's inherently unpredictable and highly skilled nature.[6] Although a useful corrective to the simplistic "assembly line" paradigm of Hollywood that many commentators on mass culture (including Bourdieu) continue to adhere to, such qualifications risk losing sight of the big picture the contrast with the Soviet experience offers us. That is, from a comparative perspective, the Hollywood production system (along with those of other Western commercial culture industries) has—for better or worse—been remarkably successful in normalizing creative activity in the interests of capitalist accumulation.

* * *

If the comparison between the Soviet film industry and the culture industries of the West allows us to appreciate the disciplinary strength of the latter, the experience of post-Soviet filmmaking demonstrates that there is nothing either natural or inevitable about the emergence of mass market–oriented capitalist forms of cultural production. The process depends on the existence of a particular set of political-economic conditions that in the case of Russian filmmaking have generally not yet fallen into place. In particular, the post-Soviet state has not provided a regulatory environment capable of supporting the reconstruction of a mass-market oriented, commercially financed national film industry.

On the other hand, developments in the cultural economy since perestroika indicate that the market exchange of cultural commodities is a far more robust and in a sense "natural" phenomenon than their capitalist *production*; the growth in the commercial exchange (and piracy) of cultural goods was one of the earliest and most visible consequences of the lifting of state controls over the cultural economy that took place during perestroika.[7] Moreover, unlike the first attempts at commercial film production during the "cooperative period," the market in cultural goods survived the economic crisis of the early 1990s in remarkably good health. It appears, therefore, that a mass market in cultural goods will come into being wherever it is not actively suppressed by the state. The essential problem faced by the post-Soviet culture industries (and this argument seems equally applicable to material production generally) is that they have largely failed to tap into this market. Instead it has been dominated by legally or illegally acquired imports originating in the mass culture industries of the West.

During the relative economic stabilization of 1995–98, the first signs emerged of a revival in the prospects for commercial filmmaking. Most crucial, given that by then almost a third of Russian households owned videocassette players, was the increasing concentration of ownership that took place in the video production and distribution business. As larger and better-capitalized firms emerged, they abandoned piracy, finding it more profitable to pay production companies for exclusive distribution rights and to cooperate with the government in suppressing their smaller competitors still working outside the law.[8] As a result, video distribution became an increasingly important source of revenue for film production. Meanwhile, the startling success of the newly built Kodak Kinomir cinema opened in Moscow in 1997 showed that, if offered luxurious enough viewing conditions, the new Russian rich might add filmgoing to their repertoire of conspicuous consumption strategies. Plans were soon in the works to build similar theaters in Moscow and other major cities.[9] Fees for television broadcast rights also rose in this period, tracking the growth in television advertising revenues. In 1998, Igor Tolstunov, head of the newly founded NTV-Profit company estimated that a "good film in the commercial sense" could return approaching $500,000 to its producers, that is, given current production costs, just enough to break even.[10]

The formation of this uncompromisingly titled production firm was an outgrowth of the startling concentration of mass media ownership in the hands of the so-called "oligarchs" that took place during this period. In the long term, these "media empires" may possess sufficient financial resources and market dominance to rebuild Russia's capacity to produce visual entertainment.[11] So far, however, with the partial exception of Vladimir Gusinsky's Most-Media group, the chief focus of their activities has been the exertion of political influence through the news media in order to enable the further accumulation of property, rather than commercially oriented investment in cultural production. In any case, the primary market for commercial cultural production during this period was not the bulk of the Russian population, which remained excluded from the benefits of "stabilization," but the New Russians. The collapse of the ruble in August 1998 hit the pockets of this class with particular severity, throwing the already limited prospects for the development of nationally based commercial cultural production into renewed doubt.

Finally, this account of filmmaking in the post-perestroika period suggests that to understand the dynamics of particular national sites for cultural production we must consider how their internal prestige structures interact with transnational cultural "flows" (to use Appadurai's expression).[12] The case of the post-Soviet film industry throws this relationship into particular relief, in part because of the tendency toward globalization generally inherent (where not actively suppressed by state controls) in both art and mass-oriented cinema, and in part because of the suddenness of the transition from partial autarky to full integration which the national cultural economy as a whole underwent in this period.

We have seen that cultural globalization affected Russian filmmaking practice in two major respects: first, through the export of Russian auteur cinema to highbrow Western audiences, and second, through the inflow of Western commercial cinema to the Russian mass public. The Western art cinema market had the most immediate effect of encouraging the trend toward chernukha dominant in Soviet cinema during perestroika. In the longer term it offered material and symbolic sustenance to a small but influential group of auteur directors. (We may expect the latter trend to continue.) We may suggest, therefore, that the imbalance that all peripheral cinema industries experience between the export potential of their art cinema and the lack of interest international audiences show in their popular cinema helps concentrate prestige on the proponents of "elite"-oriented film. More generally, we may say that the greater international marketability of socially critical and/or aesthetically challenging cultural products stimulates autonomizing processes in national fields of cultural production where, owing either to the weakness of local audience demand (as in post-Soviet Russia) or to the rigor of state interference (as in the Soviet Union), their existence would otherwise be problematic. Artistic globalization fosters national artistic autonomization.

Once the Western fashion for all things Soviet faded from around 1990 onward, it was the *importation* of popular Western cinema that had the most powerful impact on the dynamics of Russian cinema production. Russia's filmmakers found both the economic viability of their profession and their authority as arbiters of national culture undermined by the influx of Western commercial film. They were economically and technically unable to compete with these imports' "entertainment values" and, owing to their continued adherence to the ideal of cinema as a medium for moral instruction and artistic self-expression, many of them were unwilling to try. Instead, they turned to the creation of what I term a *national popular* genre of cinema. In celebrating national cultural distinctiveness, this cinematic strategy simultaneously reaffirmed its makers' role as guardians of national cultural identity.

This move enabled a rapprochement between filmmakers and the post-Soviet political-economic elite that may signal a profound shift in the criteria by which status is accorded within the industry. In the late-Soviet period, it was those who refused to compromise with authority who dominated the unofficial hierarchy of prestige; today it is filmmakers like Mikhalkov and Khotinenko, prepared to attune their work to the ideological needs of Russia's political-economic elite, who enjoy hegemonic status. In its embattled post-Soviet circumstances Russian filmmaking has been forced to find a resolution to the old conflict between autonomy and heteronomy. In the name of Russian national culture, art and opportunism have been reconciled.

The key creative and decision-making personnel of the Russian film industry make up a relatively small community perhaps several hundred
strong, concentrated largely in Moscow. They are generally known to
one another; either personally or by reputation. This allowed me to re-
construct the patterns of prestige that structure their social world.

During my fieldwork, I gathered data from twenty-six people directly
involved in Russia's film world, in most cases conducting tape-recorded
interviews but occasionally noting the contents of informal conversations
as soon as possible after they took place. I also interviewed a similar number of people from both the "broad" and "creative" Russian intelligentsia. My interviewees in the film world itself included ten directors, four
scriptwriters, four critics, as well as distributors, promoters, and video
pirates (five total). I sought information on the organizational and economic structure of the contemporary industry, recollections of past conditions, creative goals, and attitudes toward the audience.

Most of my informants had some knowledge of English, and some
were extremely fluent. Around half my interviews were conducted in English, the other half in Russian; the language we used depended on the
relative balance of our linguistic abilities. In quoting the interviews given
in Russian, I have tried to render my informants' discourse into idiomatic
English; in the case of those in English, I have occasionally emended my
informants' grammar and vocabulary where I judged a literal transcrip-
tion might mislead an English-speaking reader. At points in my interviews where I was uncertain what Russian concept my informants'
English was meant to convey, I asked them to state it in Russian and
checked the correct translation later.[1]

Because one of my aims was to identify the discursive and ideological
structures that are *practically operative* in the social and creative practice
of Russian filmmakers (for instance, the criteria by which a director might
be praised or damned by his or her fellows), I tried as far as possible to
elicit the kinds of discourse that might take place in day-to-day conversation, as opposed to responses stimulated specifically by the pragmatic
context of the interview situation. Naturally, given my outsider status
(and the presence of a tape recorder), this goal can only have been approximated. It seemed worth making the attempt, however.

One of the major problems that I faced in conducting this research was persuading people active in the film world to grant me interviews. Despite the hard times on which the Russian film industry has recently fallen, filmmakers still occupy a relatively high status in society and tend socially and professionally to be busy people who were not especially flattered by or interested in the prospect of being interviewed by an unknown, foreign graduate student. The response I received from cold-calling people whose phone numbers I had found in trade publications and so forth (Russia has no private telephone directories) was only occasionally positive. (Usually I would be told to call back in a few weeks rather than refused an interview outright; a few weeks later I would receive the same answer.)

To overcome this problem I adopted two main methods of approaching potential informants. The first was to operate through social networking. I told my existing circle of acquaintances about my research project and asked for their help in finding interview subjects. Such interviews were generally granted as a favor to the friend who had introduced us. I may have lost something in representativeness by using this strategy, but I gained a good deal in goodwill and time given. In many cases I was invited to the interviewee's home, and the "interview" took the form of a discussion over dinner and drinks, sometimes with other friends and family present. I steered these discussions toward the topics in which I was particularly interested, but left them flexible enough to give my subjects a chance to express their own concerns.

The second means by which I arranged interviews was through my work as a freelance writer on film for the English language daily the *Moscow Times*. Under the auspices of the newspaper, I was able to obtain interviews with better known (and therefore otherwise less accessible) directors. I made it clear to subjects contacted in this way that I might use our conversations for my dissertation research also. These interviews tended to be shorter and more formal than those secured through personal contacts, and I worked from a predetermined list of questions. The interview took place at either my informant's office or a public place. With the exception of my final query, "Tell me something funny that happened during the shooting of your last movie," these interviews covered the same themes as those of the first group. Occasionally my interviewees requested that certain of their statements be kept "off the record" in my press articles but agreed to let me use them as data for my research. In my *Moscow Times* articles I was without exception positive about my interviewees and their work, which I hope fulfilled any expectations they may have had about receiving favorable publicity from agreeing to talk to me and also struck me as a (doubtless minor) service I could do for the Russian industry as a whole. In the present study, my analysis of Russian filmmakers' discourse and practice is rather less uncritical.

Although the means I used to select informants can hardly have produced a statistically representative sample of the Russian filmmaking community, I believe I was successful in interviewing people spanning a good range of the different groups from which it is composed. For instance, I spoke to some of the most prominent directors working in Russia today (Pyotr and Valery Todorovsky and Karen Shakhnazarov) as well as more marginal figures like Marina Tsurtsumia and Alexander Chernykh; my interviewees also professed a wide range of positions on the question of artistic autonomy. Surprisingly perhaps, I found that even individuals contacted through the same intermediary could express extremely diverse views on the nature of their creative activity. Ten of my twenty-six informants were women, which if anything overstates their representation in the industry as a whole.[2] To my knowledge, eight were wholly or partly of non-Russian ethnic background.[3]

One respect in which my interview sample did not reflect the social makeup of the filmmaking community as a whole was in the typical ages of my informants. The oldest person I interviewed was in his sixties and the youngest around thirty, but the great majority were between their early thirties and early forties (as of 1995), that is, old enough to have begun their professional careers (usually just a little) before perestroika. This is the age group from which what is sometimes referred to as the "new generation" of Russian filmmakers is drawn. This bias is, I assume, a consequence of my reliance on social networking (on the assumption that filmmakers tend to socialize within their own age cohort). My interviews tend therefore to underrepresent the older generation of directors who were already established by the 1970s, at least some of whom, such as Nikita Mikhalkov, Vladimir Menshov, Sergei Solovyov, and Alexei Gherman, continue to work and wield considerable influence within the industry today. I sought to remedy this shortcoming through my examination of documentary material.

A second limitation of my interview research, this one self-imposed, was its concentration on the Moscow filmmaking community at the expense of those of St. Petersburg and the Newly Independent States of the former Soviet Union.[4] While the Soviet film industry was concentrated overwhelmingly on Moscow, many of the most critically acclaimed films of the Soviet era came out of "provincial" studios, which were often less closely supervised than those of the center. Equally, some significant developments within the post-1986 industry, including the Tarkovskian art cinema of Lenfilm and the crime thrillers of the Catharsis production company in Kazakhstan, have taken place outside Moscow. Furthermore, despite the Soviet Union's political breakup, the film industries of the Newly Independent States remain closely intertwined. Nevertheless, the Moscow industry was and is large and complex enough to monopolize my attention during the period I had available for research. Comparing developments within the industries of the other former Soviet republics would clearly be a fruitful subject for future work.

In addition to my fieldwork interviews, my chief source of data for the post-1986 Russian film industry are press articles. I used this source in three major ways. First, they provided me quantitative data on such issues as production figures, audience attendance, and filming budgets; second, they permitted me to gauge the critical reception of particular films and follow discussions of major cinematic trends; third, they enabled me to supplement the interviews I collected during my fieldwork. Very often these published interviews dealt with many of the issues I concentrated on in my own fieldwork. By making use of the film press, I was able to check my fieldwork interviews against the larger picture and thus to gauge the general applicability of my conclusions. (I conducted the documentary research during and after my period of fieldwork.)

With the exception of my attendance at film festivals ("Kinotavr" at the Black Sea resort of Sochi in May 1995, and the Moscow International Film Festival in July of that year) and a number of film premieres and *prezentatsiya* (launch parties), I was not able to engage in direct "participant observation" of the Russian filmmaking as an area of professional activity. I never personally witnessed the process of film production, for instance. Because I have no training in filmmaking I could not do this as a salaried worker and because I had to support myself financially during my period of fieldwork by working in Moscow, I could not afford to do so as a volunteer. (I can claim, however, to have been a participant-observer in the role of film journalist.) As a result, my knowledge of film production and business is necessarily based on the accounts of others—any claim I can make to "ethnographic authority" must be as an auditor and reader rather than as an eyewitness. (This would inevitably be the case in the part of the study that deals with the Soviet period.) The validity of my conclusions must depend on my ability to judge the significance of my written and oral sources. From the point of view of methodology, therefore, the major part of this study—that which concerns the film industry itself—is more historical than ethnographic in the classic sense.

In one respect, however, this study has a more clearly ethnographic basis. In Moscow I rented a room in the apartment of a young "underground" artist through whom I met on a social basis a wide variety of people involved in different sectors of Russian cultural life. This, more than anything else, gave me a sense of the daily life and concerns of the creative intelligentsia. I also had the opportunity to discuss the ideas I was developing from my research with an informed and involved audience. This does not imply that the people I talked to always, or even often, agreed with my perspectives, but it does mean that they were developed through actual dialogue, in some cases fairly heated argument, with members of the contemporary Russian intelligentsia.

My experience as a teacher of English at "School No. 57"—one of Moscow's most famous special mathematical schools—as a private tutor, and at a private language school, where I taught one class of teenagers and one of adults, further broadened my range of social contacts. Whenever possible, I encouraged my students to talk and write about topics relevant to my research, such as their sense of national identity, their attitudes toward business, and their cultural tastes. (I sincerely hope that this somewhat selfish scheme did nothing to hinder their progress in English.) I also interviewed some of the students from my class of adults. This experience gave me some firsthand knowledge of the outlook of educated Russians outside the creative intelligentsia circles within which I was otherwise immersed.[5]

ATTRIBUTION OF INTERVIEW SUBJECTS

All interviews took place in Moscow except where otherwise indicated. Brief biographical and professional details of informants are given, followed by the language used in the interview and the month and year in which the interview took place.

In the case of directors and scriptwriters, I have attributed interviews giving real names, on the assumption that this enhances their significance to the reader, except where I judged, or they requested, that their statements be kept "off the record," in which case they are attributed as "Anonymous source, personal interview." Otherwise, I have given my informants the pseudonyms indicated in quotation marks at the beginning of the reference. In cases where informants requested anonymity only for certain statements but where I judged they could be identified from being mentioned elsewhere in the text, I have preserved their anonymity throughout.

Named Interview Subjects

Gleb Aleinikov. Film director, pioneer of "parallel" cinema, e.g., *Tractorists II* (1992), early 30s; taped interview in Russian, June 1995.

Natalya Andreichenko. Film director, Russian-Ukrainian, *Shamara* (1994), c. 30; conversations in Russian, Sochi, May 1995; Moscow, July 1995.

Alexei Balabanov. Film director, *Happy Days* (1991), *The Castle* (1994), late 30s; interview in English, St. Petersburg, March 1995.

Alexander Chernykh. Film director, *Uncensored Expressions, I Love* (1994), early 30s; taped interview in English, February 1995; conversations in English and Russian, February–July 1995.

Ivan Maximov. Director of animated films, late 30s; taped interview in Russian, March 1995.

Natalya Ryazantseva. Scriptwriter, frequent collaborator with Kira Muratova, early 60s; taped interview in Russian, June 1995.

Karen Shakhnazarov. Film director, e.g., *Dreams* (1992), *American Daughter* (1995); early 40s; taped interview in Russian and English, March 1995.

Vyacheslav Shmyrov. Artistic director of the Kinocenter, festival organizer, mid-30s; taped interview in Russian, April 1995.

Mark Slater. American director and producer working in Russia, c. 40; taped interview, April 1995.

Pyotr Todorovsky. Film director, father of Valery, e.g., *Encore, Again, Encore* (1993), *What a Wonderful Game* (1995), early 60s; taped interview in Russian, April 1995.

Valery Todorovsky. Film director, early 30s, *Catafalque, Love* (1992), *Moscow Country Nights* (1994); taped interview in Russian, March 1995.

Marina Tsurtsumia. Film director, *Only Death Comes for Sure* (1993), early 30s; taped interview in Russian, April 1995.

Maya Turovskaya. Film historian and theorist; interview in English, Durham, N.C., November 1997.

Valery Zalotukha. Scriptwriter for, e.g., Vladimir Khotinenko's *Makarov* (1993), *The Muslim* (1995), c. 40; taped discussion in Russian, March 1995.

Interview Subjects Given Pseudonyms

"Anastasia." Scriptwriter, professor at VGIK, late 30s; taped discussion in Russian, March 1995.

"Andrei." Banker, aspiring filmmaker, early 20s; conversation in English, April 1995.

"Basil." Film critic, early 40s; taped interview in English, May 1995.

"Boris." President of video distribution firm, c. 40; taped interview in English, July 1995.

"Dmitri." Press agent for major film distribution firm, late 30s, taped interview in English, June 1995.

"Ksenya." President of film distribution firm, c. 40; taped interview in Russian, July 1995.

"Lena." Film critic, 30s; conversations in English, October–December 1994.

"Liza." Freelance film critic, early 30s; taped interview in English, March 1995.
"Maria." Film and TV production assistant, late 20s; taped interview in English, April 1995.
"Marina." Retired sculptor, c. 60; taped interview in Russian, February 1995.
"Max." Economist for Moscow bank, mid 20s; conversation in Russian, November 1994.
"Natalya." Editor of literary magazine, c. 40; interview in English, August 1994.
"Olga." Literature graduate student, late 20s; conversation in English, August 1994.
"Tatyana." Film promoter and producer, c. 40; taped interview in English, April 1995.

Anonymous Sources

1. Production manager at Nikita Mikhalkov's production company, Tri-Te, early 40s; taped interview in English, June 1995.
2. Former production assistant at Tri-Te, early 20s; conversation in English, June 1995.
3. Roskomkino funding panel member and scriptwriter, c. 60; taped interview in Russian, June 1995.

NOTES

Introduction

1. Mark Rudinstein, "Ostrov 'Kinotavr,' " interviewed by Elena Koroleva, *Nika Press*, June 12–18, 1995, 7.
2. Figures on film production from Condee, "Dream of Well-Being." Condee states that Russian-made films currently occupy 10 percent of screen time. Given that their distribution is partially subsidized by the state, if anything, this figure overstates their share of the audience. The estimate of the share taken by domestically made films in the late-Soviet period is given by Golovskoy, *Behind the Soviet Screen*, 137.
3. "Boris," personal interview. For a list of personal interviews and method of attribution, see the List of Informants.
4. Yevgeny Miropolsky, head of *Yekaterinburg-Art* distribution company, "Yevgenii Miropol'-skii: Zarabatyvat. Ne ostanavlivatsia chtob firmu znali," interviewed in *KG*, no. 1 (1995): 26.
5. Havel, "Six Asides about Culture," 132–33.
6. Slater, "The Soviet Union," 1.
7. Lawton, *Kinoglasnost*, 2.
8. Ibid., 3; cf. Graffy, "Cinema."
9. Solomon, *Irony Tower*, xxii.
10. Of course, many of the latter, notably the military dictatorships of 1970s Latin America, resorted to extreme and arbitrary forms of state violence (i.e., torture and execution) more frequently than did most late-socialist regimes. However, the latter's control over the arts and mass media was largely confined to "negative" forms of censorship, rather than the imposition of a "positive" conception of aesthetic-ideological orthodoxy.
11. Azhgikhina, "High Culture Meets Trash TV," 43.
12. In *Hiding in the Light*, Dick Hebdige, for instance, argues that the "Americanization" of popular culture in postwar Britain helped challenge the country's traditional class hierarchy.
13. See, for instance, Fitzpatrick, *Cultural Front*, and Kenez and Shepherd, " 'Revolutionary' Models for High Literature."
14. See, for instance, Stites, *Russian Popular Culture* and *Culture and Entertainment in Wartime Russia*; Cushman, *Notes from Underground*; Riordan, *Soviet Youth Culture*; and Smith, *Songs to Seven Strings*.
15. See, for instance, Youngblood, *Movies for the Masses*; Horton and Brashinsky, *Zero Hour*; Horton, *Inside Soviet Film Satire*; Kenez, *Cinema and Soviet Society*; and Turovskaya, "Tastes of Soviet Moviegoers."
16. Condee and Padunov, "Not by *Bred* Alone."
17. Bogomolov, "The Revitalization of the Soviet Film Industry," 41. Cf. Dondurei, "Artistic Culture."
18. Marshall, *Masters of the Soviet Cinema*.
19. Valery Zalotukha, personal interview.
20. "Maria," personal interview.
21. Pre-Revolutionary apartments, subdivided under Soviet rule for cramped occupation by multiple families sharing facilities: notoriously the least desirable form of housing in Moscow and Leningrad.
22. Valery Zalotukha, personal interview.
23. Vyacheslav Shmyrov, personal interview.
24. Verdery, *National Ideology*.

25. See, for instance, Verdery's argument that the competition between cultural producers cannot be understood "in terms of [Bourdieu's theory of] competing capitals." Verdery, *National Ideology*, 80–81.

26. Bürger, "Literary Institution and Modernization."

27. Bourdieu, *Field of Cultural Production*, 115.

28. On the "cultic" nature of state socialist art, see Groys, *The Total Art of Stalinism*.

29. Klinka, "Writing from the Empire," xix–xxiv, xxii–xxiii.

30. For general statements of the production perspective, see, for instance, Peterson, "Culture Studies," and Crane, *Production of Culture*.

31. Becker, "Art as Collective Action."

32. Bourdieu, *Field of Cultural Production*, 115; cf. Crane, "Reward Systems," and Williams, *Sociology of Culture*, 112–15.

33. Speaking of a medium's "inherent" technological characteristics is of course something of an oversimplification. In historical practice the development of cultural technologies has been shaped by the dominant interests in society—in the case of the West, this has meant private capital primarily, and in the socialist world, the political leadership. In the event, both culture-producing corporations and the Communist leadership seem to have shared an interest in prioritizing the development of forms of cultural technology (such as television) that encourage a high degree of separation between the moments of cultural production and consumption. In the West this allowed the concentration of profit, in the socialist world the centralization of ideological production.

34. For general theoretical accounts of the capitalist cultural industries from a political-economic perspective, see Garnham, *Capitalism and Communication*; Horkheimer and Adorno, *Dialectic of Enlightenment*; and Ryan, *Making Capital from Culture*.

35. On the scope for individual creativity within Hollywood, see Staiger, *Studio System*; on the culture industries generally, see Chanan, *The Dream That Kicks*, and Ryan, *Making Capital from Culture*.

36. See the discussion in Wolff, *Social Production of Art*, 60–70.

37. "John Ford's *Young Mr. Lincoln*." See the discussion in Lapsley and Westlake, *Film Theory*, 116.

38. Verdery interprets the prevalence of such value claims in Romanian intellectual life as stemming from the instrumental advantages they offered its participants as they struggled against one another for cultural authority and political status. While she admits that intellectuals may have a "genuine attachment" to such values, she does not offer an account of why they become prevalent in society at large (*National Ideology*, 19). I believe a class-based approach enables us to attempt this task.

39. Liehm, "Author's Foreword," in *Politics of Culture*, 78–79.

Chapter 1

1. From *prisposoblyat'*—"to adjust to, accommodate to." The root is as neutral as the English equivalents. The term originated in official Soviet discourse to denote Party workers who pretend enthusiasm in order to curry favor with their superiors.

2. Eldar Ryazanov, speech at the plenary session of the Filmworkers' Union, Moscow, December 2, 1980; quoted in Golovskoy, *Behind the Soviet Screen*, 117.

3. Berlin, *Russian Thinkers*, 181–82.

4. Bourdieu, *Field of Cultural Production*, 37–38.

5. Zorkaya, *Illustrated History of Soviet Cinema*, 270.

6. Anonymous source, personal interview.

7. "Marina," personal interview.

8. Cushman, *Notes from Underground*.
9. Ibid., 99.
10. Ibid., 127–30.
11. Verdery, *National Ideology*, 91.
12. Although derived from Latin, the word "intelligentsia" itself originated in Russia and was only later adopted in Western Europe—generally to describe radical intellectuals. It was coined by the otherwise little remembered novelist Pyotr Boborykin. Malia, "What Is the Intelligentsia?" 441.
13. Quoted in Nahirny, *Russian Intelligentsia*, 8.
14. Konrad and Szelenyi, *Intellectuals on the Road to Class Power*.
15. McClelland, *Autocrats and Academics*.
16. See also Shatz, *Soviet Dissent in Historical Perspective*.
17. Althusser, "Ideology and the Ideological State Apparatuses."
18. Quoted in Boym, "Paradoxes of a Unified Culture," 821–22.
19. See Dunham, *In Stalin's Time*, and Nahirny, *Russian Intelligentsia*, 8. The English translation is complicated by the fact that the Russian *meshchantsvo* functions as both abstract and collective noun. An individual member of the *meshchanstvo* estate, or exhibitor of the qualities figuratively associated with it is a *meshchanin*. The adjectival form is *meshchanskii*.
20. Quoted in Brown, "Trifonov," 115.
21. A. I. Volodin, "On the Traditions of Our Country's Intelligentsia," *Pravda*, March 10, 1987, published interview reprinted in *CDSP* 38, no. 10 (1987): 23.
22. Trifonov, *Taking Stock*, 14.
23. Ibid., 108.
24. Ibid., 138.
25. Trifonov is satirizing here a widespread trend among the intelligentsia in the 1960s and 1970s; see Shlapentokh, *Soviet Intellectuals*, 203–23.
26. Trifonov, *Taking Stock*, 146.
27. Trifonov, *Obmen*, 47.
28. Ibid.
29. Ibid., 54; my translation.
30. Ibid., 92.
31. See, for instance, Shlapentokh, *Soviet Intellectuals*, 201, and Zinoviev, *The Yawning Heights*, 197.
32. Quoted in Mickewicz, *Media and the Soviet Public*, 79.
33. Cushman, *Notes from Underground*, 56.
34. Ibid., 61.
35. Quoted in Shlapentokh, *Soviet Intellectuals*, 22.
36. Tarkovsky, *Time within Time*, 53.
37. The Komsomol was the youth organization of the Communist Party. Activism within it was the usual first step for those with nomenklatura ambitions.
38. Klugman, *New Soviet Elite*, 63.
39. Bourdieu, *Distinction*, 283.
40. Ibid., 317.
41. According to some comparative studies it may be only marginally applicable to other countries, such as the contemporary United States, in which high cultural competence appears to play a less important role in defining social boundaries. On the limited role of cultural capital in American society, see Lamont, *Money, Morals and Manners*, and DiMaggio, "Social Structure, Institutions and Cultural Goods," 133–55.
42. Verdery, *National Ideology*, 92–93.
43. Humphrey, *Karl Marx Collective*, 111.

44. Kelly, Pilkington, Shepherd, and Volkov, "Introduction: Why Cultural Studies?" 7–8.

45. Brooks, "Russian Nationalism and Russian Literature."

46. Fitzpatrick, *Cultural Front*, 5. Although the Bolshevik *Proletkult* movement called for the fostering of an autonomous working-class culture, in practice this was a utopian construction conjured up by radical intellectuals that bore little relation to "actually existing" popular culture.

47. Quoted in Fitzpatrick, *Cultural Front*, 172. An indication of the Bolsheviks' respectful attitude to the past is the fact that the number of museums tripled within the first year of the Revolution. See Gleason, Kenez, and Stites, *Bolshevik Culture*, 17.

48. Sochor, *Revolution and Culture.*

49. See also Joravksy, "Cultural Revolution and the Fortress Mentality."

50. Quoted in Shalin, "Intellectual Culture," 67.

51. From Stalin's speech to the Eighteenth Party Congress, March 1939, quoted in Fitzpatrick, *Cultural Front*, 177.

52. Fitzpatrick, *Cultural Front*, 15.

53. Ibid., 256.

54. On the official Soviet policy of propagating classic literature, see, for instance, Friedburg, *Russian Classics in Soviet Jackets*; Lewitt, *Russian Literary Politics*; and O'Dell, "Socialisation in the Literature Lesson."

55. Shlapentokh, *Soviet Intellectuals*, 6.

56. Pipes, "Historical Evolution of the Russian Intelligentsia," 494. See also Friedburg, "Literary Culture," 249–45.

57. Marina Tsurtsumia, personal interview.

58. Quoted in Lewitt, *Russian Literary Politics*, 172.

59. Sakwa, *Russian Politics and Society*, 254.

60. Shlapentokh, *Soviet Intellectuals*, 64. On the expectation that socialist conditions would universalize high cultural appreciation, see Fisher and Volkov, "The Audience for Classical Music."

61. The figures come from a study published in the Soviet Union in 1971 by Yu. V. Arutinian, cited in Lipset and Dobson, "Social Stratification and Sociology in the USSR," 141.

62. Shlapentokh, *Soviet Intellectuals*, 64.

63. Humphrey, *Karl Marx Collective*, 364.

64. Quoted in Connor, *Accidental Proletariat*, 228.

65. In the 1970s, VGIK was supplemented by the "Higher Courses in Cinematography," a program geared toward mature and postgraduate students. Leningrad and some of the national republics also had their own institutions offering training in the technical filmmaking professions.

66. Karen Shakhnazarov, personal interview.

67. Bourdieu, "Forms of Capital," 243. Owing to the trend toward "leveling" in late-Soviet society, which narrowed and in some cases reversed income differentials between educated and uneducated occupations, the relationship of educational attainment to economic privilege was less clear. Connor, *Accidental Proletariat*, 101.

68. Bourdieu, *Forms of Capital*, 244.

69. Ibid., 246.

70. Lipset and Dobson, "Social Stratification and Sociology in the USSR," 166–67. Both Khrushchev and Brezhnev attempted to roll back this tendency toward educational/occupational hereditization. Under Brezhnev, class-based quotas for entry into higher education were introduced. These policies seem to have been relatively ineffective in reversing the overall trend.

71. Churchward, *Soviet Intelligentsia*, 37. For the privileged background of most entrants to musical conservatories, see Fisher and Volkov, "The Audience for Classical Music."

72. "Liza," personal interview.

73. Valery Todorovsky, personal interview.

74. Marina Tsurtsumia, personal interview.

75. We should note that with the exception of the period of the Cultural Revolution it appears that, as a class, the intelligentsia was not singled out for special persecution (Getty and Chase, "Patterns of Repression"). This does not imply that the intelligentsia did not suffer under the Terror, only that it does not appear to have been hit more severely than other elements of Soviet society, including workers, peasants, and Party officials.

76. By late 1980s Chinyaeva estimates that only 55–65 percent of those with a higher degree were from nonintelligentsia family backgrounds ("Soviet Mass Culture in Russia," 24).

77. Connor, *Accidental Proletariat*, 153; Matthews, *Privilege in the Soviet Union*, 20–21.

78. Fitzpatrick, *Cultural Revolution in Russia*.

79. Quoted in Shalin, "Intellectual Culture," 68.

80. Konrad and Szelenyi, *Intellectuals on the Road to Class Power*.

81. In his study of educational levels among Hungarian elites in the 1970s and 1980s, Ferenc Gazso finds that 11 percent of "cadre bureaucrats" were from intelligentsia or white-collar backgrounds, by comparison to 60 percent of "professional intellectuals," and concludes (contrary to the thesis set out by Konrad and Szelenyi in *Intellectuals on the Road to Class Power*) that "the attitude of the party-state towards this new generation of intellectuals was the same as towards the traditional intelligentsia: it was consistent in keeping the bearers of the intellectual culture and ethos far away from the really important positions" ("Cadre Bureaucracy and the Intelligentsia," 80). There seems no reason to suppose this pattern was any less characteristic of the Soviet Union.

82. Burg, "Observations on Soviet University Students," 528.

83. Klugman, *New Soviet Elite*, 23–24.

84. Farmer, *Soviet Administrative Elite*, 176; Klugman, *New Soviet Elite*, 63; Konrad and Szelenyi, *Intellectuals on the Road to Class Power*, 189.

85. Shlapentokh, *Soviet Intellectuals*, 123.

86. Bourdieu, *Forms of Capital*, 243–44.

Chapter 2

1. See Barber, "Working Class Culture and Political Culture," and Stites, *Russian Popular Culture*, 37–63.

2. On film, see Youngblood, "Americanitis" and *Movies for the Masses*.

3. Taylor and Christie, *Film Factory*, 207.

4. Taylor, *Film Propaganda*.

5. This model is adapted from Maya Turovskaya's characterization of the systemic characteristics of the Stalin-period film industry, which she implies was applicable across all sectors of cultural production. See Turovskaya, "The 1930s and 1940s," 52.

6. Herbert Gans argues this point in relation to the class composition of U.S. news journalists. Gans, *Deciding What's News*, 213.

7. In practice, even under Stalin, no film directors were imprisoned or executed (though a good number of ancillary and administrative personnel perished). In the late-Soviet period a single director, Sergei Parajanov, was imprisoned (for four years); although he was formally tried for alleged homosexual acts, the charges were motivated by the authorities' fear that his films incited ethnic nationalism. While outright repression was rarely used against film directors, it was well known to be a weapon that the authorities were prepared to employ if sufficiently provoked, or even (during Stalin's rule) if they were not.

8. Turovskaya, "The 1930s and 1940s," 49.

9. Kenez, *Cinema and Soviet Society*, 55.

10. Turovskaya, "The 1930s and 1940s," 49.

11. Quoted in Cohen, *Cultural-Political Traditions*, 224.

12. Cohen, *Cultural-Political Traditions*, 460.

13. Quoted in Christie, "Canons and Careers," 167.

14. The term was applied across different sectors of cultural production. Although it clearly expressed the evaluative prejudices of Soviet intellectuals, we do not have to share these to suggest an objective definition of the term: A work can be described as "gray" if it was neither well attended by the mass public nor regarded as interesting by critics.

15. Zassoursky, "Mass Culture as Market Culture," 14.

16. I adapt this term from the Hungarian economist Kornai's characterization of the socialist economy as a whole. See Kornai, *Economics of Shortage.*

17. They argue that consumer shortages endemic to state socialism were not merely a by-product of the inefficiencies inherent in the centralized system of economic planning but worked to uphold the rule of the political leadership, by making socialist subjects dependent on the state's redistributive largesse. Feher, Heller, and Markus, *Dictatorship over Needs.*

As an account of the material economy this thesis has the usual flaws of functionalism (things turned out this way, therefore they must have helped to preserve the status quo). With the benefit of hindsight we can say that material shortage played a vital role in undermining the legitimacy of socialist regimes. Applied to specifically *cultural* production, however, it is far more convincing, because here, shortage directly enhanced the state's ability to impose products embodying official ideology on its captive audience.

18. Turovskaya, "The 1930s and 1940s," 34–53.

19. Ibid., 43.

20. I do not wish to suggest that there is, in principle, such a thing as a "real" audience demand, distorted under state socialism but reigning supreme in capitalist market conditions. Rather I would argue that what becomes "popular" (or at any rate wins large audiences) depends on the institutional structures of the particular cultural economy in question; thus in capitalist societies, demand, particularly demand for cultural products, whose "use-value" depends on how they are perceived rather than on their physical characteristics, is influenced by advertising, publicity, control over distribution, and so forth. However, competition between private culture-producing corporations in the West places limits on their ability to ignore audience taste, limits that the socialist mode of cultural production did not face owing to its monopoly character.

21. Quoted in Turovskaya, "The 1930s and 1940s," 43.

22. Golovskoy, *Behind the Soviet Screen*, 59.

23. Mickiewicz, *Media and the Soviet Public*, 74–76.

24. Golovskoy, *Behind the Soviet Screen*, 61.

25. Christie, "The Cinema." See also Johnson and Petrie, *The Films of Andrei Tarkovsky*, 9.

26. "Tatyana," personal interview.

27. Johnson and Petrie, *The Films of Andrei Tarkovsky*, 11.

28. Golovskoy states that in 1980 Moscow distributors found half of new Soviet films unacceptable. *Behind the Soviet Screen*, 49.

29. The initial hope during the First Five-Year Plan was that revenues from cinema and radio would end the state's reliance on the duty on vodka. Taylor and Christie, *Film Factory*, 215 (document 83).

30. Kornai, "The Soft Budget Constraint."

31. Pyotr Todorovsky, personal interview.

32. Ibid.

33. "Liza," personal interview.

34. Golovskoy, *Behind the Soviet Screen*, 98.

35. Graffy, "Literary Press," 134.

36. Similarly, in visual art, the work of established artists was bought and exhibited (if often only briefly) by state museums, whether or not any members of the public actually viewed them. Oleg Grosse, "Toward the USSR Artists' Congress: Debts Must Be Paid," *Sovetskaya kul'tura*, January 16, 1988, reprinted in *CDSP* 40, no. 4 (1988): 12–13.

37. See Shlapentokh, *Soviet Intellectuals*, 66–68, on the intelligentsia's greater preference for critical and formally complex works as compared with the mass of population.

38. Such was the case with Tarkovsky's film *Andrei Rublev*, which was only released to the Soviet public five years after its completion.

39. Its full title was "Government Committee for Cinema Affairs under the Council of Ministers of the USSR" (*Gosudarstvenny komitet po delam kinemagratografii pri sovete ministrov SSSR*).

40. For a detailed account of the industry's institutional structure until the death of Stalin, see Babitsky and Rimberg, *Soviet Film Industry*, 1–66.

41. Humphrey, *Karl Marx Collective*, 106–8.

42. Ibid., 2.

43. Golovskoy, *Behind the Soviet Screen*, 8.

44. Pyotr Todorovsky, personal interview.

45. Golovskoy, *Behind the Soviet Screen*, 29–36.

46. Anonymous source, personal interview.

47. Ibid. This expression is rather commonly used in Russia. Presumably it originated in response to accounts in the official Soviet news media of the mistreatment of blacks in the United States and South Africa. As was often the case in the USSR, popular interpretations of official propaganda reversed the intended message. A theme that was meant to show the inhumanity of the capitalist West was adapted to express the perception that in the Soviet Union *everyone* was treated as a subhuman.

48. Johnson and Petrie, *The Films of Andrei Tarkovsky*, 9.

49. Valery Zalotukha, personal interview.

50. See Hough, *Soviet Prefects*, 283.

51. Golovskoy, *Behind the Soviet Screen*, 34.

52. Pyotr Todorovsky, personal interview.

53. The luxurious establishments occupied by Politburo members were fitted out with private film theaters.

54. Taped discussion with Valery Zalotukha, Lena Zalotukha, and Alexander Chernykh, Moscow, February 1995.

55. See Klimov, "Learning Democracy," 237.

56. Tarkovsky, *Time within Time*, 55; see also 24.

57. Bordwell, Staiger, and Thompson, *Classical Hollywood Cinema*.

58. Kawin, *How Movies Work*.

59. Of course, this account of Hollywood is somewhat idealized. The contemporary industry is notorious for huge budget overruns, inflated star salaries, and endless subsidies from financial backers, motivated as much by prestige as profit. Nevertheless, these well-publicized inefficiencies have rather little effect on the smooth running of the "below the line" realm of the production process, whose basic features evolved in the early twentieth century.

60. Pyotr Todorovsky, personal interview.

61. "Maria," personal interview.

62. Anonymous source, personal interview.

63. Ivan Maximov, personal interview.

64. Johnson and Petrie, *The Films of Andrei Tarkovsky*, 43.

65. Ibid., 9.

66. This lack of respect was not universal: in the 1970s and 1980s Nikita Mikhalkov was able to produce critically and popularly successful films at what, by Soviet standards, was an extremely high rate (averaging one each year), employing what Soviet filmmakers referred to as the Hollywood-style "iron scenario," that is one worked out with sufficient precision to keep improvisation during shooting to a minimum (Golovskoy, *Behind the Soviet Screen*, 94). However, he was the exception; his use of Hollywood production techniques was his own decision, not the result of his

adherence to a systemic requirement. It is likely that his lesser need for such defense strategies was enabled by his avoidance of dangerous themes and his highly placed connections within the Soviet cultural establishment: his father Sergei was an officially celebrated poet who wrote the Soviet national anthem (see Chapter 5).

67. Tarkovsky, *Time within Time*, 154.

68. Johnson and Petrie, *The Films of Andrei Tarkovsky*, 43.

69. Ibid., 59.

70. Tarkovsky, *Time within Time*, 342.

71. Ibid., 214.

72. Taylor, "Ideology as Mass Entertainment," 206.

73. See Stites, *Russian Popular Culture*, 147–58.

74. Stark, "Coexisting Forms in Hungary's Emerging Mixed Economy," 153.

75. I have in mind Michel Foucault's proposition that "power" should be thought of primarily as a creative rather than as a repressive force. See Foucault's *History of Sexuality*, Volume 1. The different modalities assumed by power in the West as opposed to state socialist societies suggest that the creation of modern forms of discipline, surveillance, and subjectivity formation is more closely related to the specific characteristics of the *capitalist* economic system than Foucault was willing to recognize.

76. Shlapentokh, *Soviet Intellectuals*, x, estimates the numbers of "educated people supposedly engaged in creative activity" in the mid-1980s at 700,000, of whom some 175,000 were members of creative unions, with the remainder consisting of academics and researchers working mostly within natural sciences.

77. Nepomnyashchy, "Perestroika and the Creative Unions."

78. On the institutional structure of literature and publishing, see Garrard and Garrard, *Inside the Soviet Writers' Union*; for classical music, see Rice, "Soviet Music"; for theater, see Glenny, "Soviet Theatre."

79. Shatz, *Soviet Dissent in Historical Perspective*, 118.

80. Golovskoy, *Behind the Soviet Screen*, 37–42.

81. Ibid., 73.

82. Ibid., 95; by "some countries" Golovskoy probably has in mind the United States—where he was living at the time of this interview.

83. A reference to an article I wrote for his journal in which I discussed the Soviet custom of "kitchen philosophy."

84. "Basil," personal interview.

85. The Russian idiom equivalent to "carrot and stick" in English.

86. Bourdieu, *Field of Cultural Production*, 115. We should note, however, that these institutions could only function this way given the absence of extensive state terror in the late-Soviet period. Under Stalinist conditions of mass denunciations and arrests, the collectivization of the cultural production must have further disabled the expression of nonofficial sentiments.

87. The lack of any necessary correspondence between "the 'ideological apparatus' of the bourgeois state" and the "actual profitable operations of the capitalist market" is argued, for instance, by Raymond Williams, in *Sociology of Culture*, 102.

88. On legitimating discourses within U.S. network television (and their contrast with those of Britain and the Netherlands), see Ang, *Desperately Seeking the Audience*.

89. Ryan, *Making Capital from Culture*, chap 5.

90. See Brooks, "Socialist Realism in Pravda," 975.

91. See Heller, "World of Prettiness," 695–99.

92. Bourdieu, *Field of Cultural Production*, 117.

93. Andrei Zhdanov, "Report to the Leningrad Branch of the Union of Soviet Writers and the Leningrad City committee of the Communist Party, August 21, 1946," in Daniels, *Documentary History of Communism*, 1:299.

94. In Lenin, *On Literature and Art*, 28. According to liberal Soviet commentators, Lenin intended his call for the creation of a Party-controlled literature to apply only to the pre-Revolutionary period. Certainly during his period in power he showed little interest in subjecting cultural production to the kind of orthodoxy demanded by Stalin.

95. Maxim Gorky's speech at the First All-Union Congress of Soviet Writers, August 1934, in Daniels, *Documentary History of Communism*, 246.

96. Fitzpatrick, *Cultural Front*, 250. On Soviet criticism's focus on issues of canonization and the assignment of aesthetic value, see Heller, "World of Prettiness," 692.

97. This applies to those artists like Tarkovsky whose Western reputation depended on their "purely artistic" achievements rather than those who had achieved renown as "dissidents." The authorities also took a dim view of any Soviet cultural producer whose works had reached the West outside official channels.

98. See Ryan, *Making Capital from Culture*, 37–41.

99. The major, if still only partial and temporary, exceptions to this rule are situations where autonomy-seeking artists turn out to be more attuned to public demand than the corporate apparatus of cultural production. An obvious example of this would be the transformation of popular music in the 1960s, which was spearheaded by performers (paradigmatically the Beatles), who successfully demanded far greater creative control over their work than any popular musicians had previously enjoyed.

100. Quoted in Cohen, *Cultural-Political Traditions*, 111.

101. Groys, *Total Art of Stalinism*, 6.

102. Brooks, "Socialist Realism in Pravda," 985.

103. Dobrenko, "Disaster of Middlebrow Taste," 784–93. Dobrenko distills these principles from Soviet research of the period into workers' responses to literature. We may assume that such research was not without its own political-aesthetic bias and may have been aimed precisely at using the supposed *vox populi* to authorize the imposition of what would shortly be labeled socialist realism. Nevertheless, it seems to indicate that socialist realism answered to the tastes of at least the "active Soviet public," that is, the workers in the process of becoming bureaucrats whom Jeffrey Brooks sees as the primary "imagined public" of Stalinist cultural production.

104. See, for instance, Bourdieu's account of petit-bourgeois taste in France in *Distinction*, chap. 6.

105. Quoted in Dobrenko, "Disaster of Middlebrow Taste," 773.

106. See Lahusen, "Thousand and One Nights," on the flood of fan letters written by readers of *Far from Moscow*, an archetypally turgid Stalinist "production novel."

107. Heller, "World of Prettiness," 697; Condee, "Introduction," ix.

108. Quoted in Cohen, *Cultural-Political Traditions*, 291.

109. Quoted in Taylor, "Ideology as Mass Entertainment," 204.

110. Sokurov, "History of the Artist's Soul," 23.

111. Tarkovsky, *Time within Time*, 49–50.

112. Downing, *Internationalizing Media Theory*, 73.

113. On the particular tightness with which television was controlled, see Androunas, *Soviet Media in Transition*, 40, and Muratov, "Soviet Television." An indication of the relatively liberal attitude of the Soviet authorities toward theater is the establishment of "studio theaters" in the mid-1970s attached to institutions of higher education and thus relatively free of central supervision. See Condee and Padunov, "Outposts of Official Art," 94. On the early relaxation of the distribution of heterodox visual art outside the authorized sector, see, for instance, McLure, *Politics of Soviet Culture*.

114. Golovskoy, *Behind the Soviet Screen*, 73.

115. The state kept access to cameras and editing facilities under tight control. In the early 1980s even Mikhalkov had difficulty obtaining a camera to shoot the interviews with his daughter that eventually became part of his "home movie" *Anna from Six to Eighteen*.

116. Shlapentokh, *Soviet Intellectuals*, 133–36; Brown, *Russian Literature since the Revolution*, 238–40.

117. Cushman, *Notes from Underground*.

118. Downing, *Internationalizing Media Theory*, 75.

119. A point argued by Andrei Sinyavsky: see Brown, *Russian Literature since the Revolution*, 292.

120. Bushnell, "Urban Leisure Culture in Post Stalin Russia," n. 43.

121. Tarkovsky, *Time within Time*, 10.

122. Condee and Padunov, "Frontiers of Soviet Culture," 5–6.

123. A term heterodox Soviet intellectuals used to characterize psychological withdrawal from involvement in the official structures of Soviet life.

Chapter 3

1. Christie, "The Cinema."

2. Take this entry from Tarkovsky's diary: "I telephoned Kulidzhanov yesterday about a flat. He said the Union of Cinematographers should be having two flats by the beginning of the [Union] Congress, and that the first would go to me" (*Time within Time*, 37). Cf. Vladimir Voinovich's satirical account of his difficulties getting housing through the Union of Writers, *The Ivankiad*.

3. Tarkovsky, *Time within Time*, 19.

4. Ibid., 14.

5. Ibid., 106.

6. Ibid., 211. We can assume that in the political climate of those times, any officially sponsored Soviet film dealing with dissidents would have taken the form of a savage attack.

7. Golovskoy, *Behind the Soviet Screen*, 143.

8. Olga Sezneva, personal communication.

9. Golovskoy, *Behind the Soviet Screen*, 83. Although this may have had as much to do with the turgidity of Soviet television as the dynamism of Soviet cinema.

10. Klimov, "Learning Democracy," 235.

11. Golovskoy, *Behind the Soviet Screen*, 137.

12. Ibid., 34. Clearly the Soviet Army was not yet ready for the "Rambo" model of patriotism.

13. Yevgeny Surkov, "You Have to Pay for Everything," interviewed by Viktor Matizen, *SF*, no. 12 (1989): 29.

14. Golovskoy, *Behind the Soviet Screen*, 15.

15. Ericson, "Classical Soviet-Type Economy."

16. Maya Turovskaya, personal interview.

17. Strangely enough, one of Yermash's first acts was to bring to an end the "Experimental Studio," which had been set up in 1963 in accordance with Kosygin's economic reform policy in an effort to speed up production time. The production team was paid according to ticket sales. Golovskoy states tantalizingly that "Yermash was pleased with the results of the Experimental Studio but concluded that the innovative concepts of compensation were not appropriate to the motion-picture industry of the USSR" (*Behind the Soviet Screen*, 96). It is possible that this decision was motivated by the impossibility of offering filmmakers substantial economic incentives for more efficient work without significantly increasing labor costs and thus reducing the state's share of the profit. Alternatively, the authorities may have felt that this form of production organization was incompatible with the maintenance of ideological supervision. In either case the studio transgressed the limits set by the system.

18. "Grigory Loves Aksinya," *KG*, no. 1 (1992): 24.

19. Bourdieu, *Field of Cultural Production*, 42.

20. Ibid., 45.

21. Valery Zalotukha, personal interview.

22. Tarkovsky, *Time within Time*, 78.

23. Ibid., 54.

24. In *Sculpting in Time*, written during his exile in the West, he remarks, for instance: "And the longer I live in the West the more curious and equivocal freedom seems to me. Freedom to take drugs? To kill? To commit suicide?" (Tarkovsky, *Sculpting in Time*, 180).

25. Bourdieu, *Field of Cultural Production*, 67–69.

26. Zorkaya, *Illustrated History of Soviet Cinema*, 271.

27. Tarkovsky, *Time within Time*, 62.

28. Ibid., 73. In *Mirror* Tarkovsky expresses his sense of personal and familial identification with Russian cultural tradition by juxtaposing his father's poems to references to wider Russian literature.

29. Quoted in Tarkovsky, *Time within Time*, 280–81.

30. Tarkovsky, *Sculpting in Time*, 164.

31. Ibid., my emphasis.

32. Ibid.

33. Ibid.,174.

34. Tarkovsky, *Time within Time*, 58.

35. Tarkovsky *Sculpting in Time*, 164.

36. Ibid., 165.

37. Tarkovsky, *Time within Time*, 212–17.

38. Johnson and Petrie, *The Films of Andrei Tarkovsky*, 11.

39. Tarkovsky, *Sculpting in Time*, 172. No doubt such individuals could be found, but it seems extremely unlikely that there was no statistical correlation between educational level and capacity to appreciate Tarkovsky's work.

40. Take for instance his reaction to the belated release of *Andrei Rublev*: "There's no announcement in any paper about *Rublev* being on. Not a single poster in the city. Yet it's impossible to get tickets. All sorts of people keep phoning, stunned by it, to say thank you" (*Time within Time*, 46). He expresses his wider conviction that "those responsible for cultural policy" are responsible for the "poor taste" of the average cinemagoer (*Sculpting in Time*, 174). He presumably intends his strictures to apply to both socialist and capitalist societies.

41. Tarkovsky, *Time within Time*, 9.

42. Other late-Soviet directors we might place within the messianic-elitist camp are Alexei Gherman, Sergei Parajanov, Otar Ioselani, Kira Muratova, and Alexander Sokurov.

43. Golovskoy, *Behind the Soviet Screen*, 59.

44. Horton, *Inside Soviet Film Satire*, 171.

45. Quoted in Lawton, *Kinoglasnost*, 15.

46. Ibid.

47. Val Kichin, "Ecstasy in Combat: On Eldar Ryazanov's New Film, *Forgotten Melody for a Flute, MN*, May 15, 1987, reprinted in *CDSP* 39, no. 47 (1987): 29.

48. Golovskoy, *Behind the Soviet Screen*, 117.

49. Quoted in Golovskoy, *Behind the Soviet Screen*. The accusation that filmmakers stood to profit by deliberately making their films obscure is on the face of it a puzzling one, unless Ryazanov has in mind the potential financial advantages that might stem from foreign critical acclaim (e.g., offers of coproduction deals, trips abroad to attend festivals, etc.).

50. Ibid.

51. See Timofeevsky, "Scherzo—Suite—Nocturne," 72.

52. During this period, entry to VGIK was more open to talented students from diverse social backgrounds than it subsequently became. This was especially true of Romm's workshop where Shukshin, his classmate Tarkovsky, and a disproportionate number of other prominent late-Soviet directors studied (Natalya Ryazantseva, personal interview).

53. Eduard Efimov, "The Story of How Ivan Made the Journey to the Black Sea," in Efimov, *Vasily Shukshin*, 108.

54. Ibid.

55. Efimov, "The Impact of Truth," in Efimov, *Vasily Shukshin*, 196–97. Another late-Soviet director with equally uncompromising views on the superiority of the auteurist ideal was the Georgian director of *Repentance*, Tenghiz Abuladze, who declared: "The more a director is in command of the film, the more interesting it becomes. Believe me, cinema is the art of a single person" (quoted in Gerber, "Two Meetings," 11).

56. Efimov, "Impact of Truth," 197.

57. Quoted in Efimov, "The Story," 103–4.

58. Garrard and Garrard, *Inside the Soviet Writers' Union*, 9–10.

59. The extent of Shukshin's personal popularity is indicated by the following account of the response to his sudden death in 1974: "This unexpected sorrow came as a shock to millions of people in the Soviet Union who had sincerely and ardently come to love his books and films. More than 160,000 letters of condolence were sent in to the newspapers, the film studio, to the Union of Writers and the Union of Cinema Workers and his family" (Efimov, *Vasily Shukshin*, 183).

The contrast between the artistic reputations of Shukshin and Vladimir Menshov, another filmmaker from an uneducated, provincial social background, is interesting. Shukshin achieved the status of a true *intelligent* by identifying himself and his work with the ideals of intelligentsia culture, whereas Menshov's work satirized the intelligentsia's pretensions.

60. Mark Slater, personal interview.

61. Karen Shakhnazarov, personal interview.

62. Marina Tsurtsumia, personal interview.

63. Anonymous source, personal interview.

64. Reported by Golovskoy, *Behind the Soviet Screen*, 83.

65. Lawton, *Kinoglasnost*, 17.

66. Golovskoy, *Behind the Soviet Screen*, 77.

67. A prominent late-Soviet actor, who later headed the Theaterworkers' Union during perestroika.

68. Vladimir Menshov, "Vladimir Men'shov: esli vyiti s takim fil'mom, to vsye uvidyat, chto u natsii est' eshcho potentsiya," interviewed by Alla Bossart, *IK*, no. 7 (1995): 8.

69. Ibid. Menshov is referring here quite literally to the practice standard in Soviet medicine of withholding such information from patients in the belief that if they have hope they might still recover (Olga Sezneva, personal communication). This image may work as a metaphor for Soviet official propaganda, but it is definitely off the mark as a characterization of, at least, unofficial Russian and Soviet cultural production. The term *"kheppi end"* was, after all, coined in the 1920s to describe one of the features Russian commentators found peculiar about American cinema.

70. However, *Moscow* also attests to the power of this claim, as the film upholds the importance of the ideal of *intelligentnost* itself, by suggesting that, despite his low professional status, Gosha combines his moral probity with an impressive—if empirically somewhat improbable—level of high cultural knowledge. At one point, for instance, he cites the example of the Roman emperor Diocletian to explain his way of dealing with the street toughs who are harassing Katya's daughter.

71. Menshov made no film during the perestroika era or its immediate aftermath. His 1995 comedy-thriller *Shirly Myrli* was his first work in ten years: his return to directing may have been stimulated by a shift in the climate of opinion within the film world (see Chapter 5).

Chapter 4

1. Shalin, "Intellectual Culture," 87.

2. Lane and Ross, "CPSU Ruling Elite," 35.

3. Quoted in Lovell and Marsh, "Culture and Crisis," 7.

4. Condee and Padunov, "Outposts of Official Art," 87.

5. Condee and Padunov, "Soviet Cultural Politics and Cultural Production," 1–2, 12–13.

6. For instance, the Theaterworkers' Union set up a disputes commission to deal with "unqualified, subjectivist and administrative interference in the creative process by local authorities, theatre officials, the mass media, etc." (Condee and Padunov, "Outposts of Official Art," 93).

7. Speech by A. Rekemchuk at the Sixth Plenary Session of the Board of the Russian Republic Writer's Union. Reported in Vyacheslav Sukhnev, "Life, Books and the Writer's Position," *Literaturnaya Rossia*, December 1, 1989, reprinted in *CDSP* 42, no. 1 (1990): 5.

8. Burawoy, "A View from Production," 184.

9. Simon Clarke makes this argument in relation to the general economy. See his "Privatization and the Development of Capitalism in Russia," 6–8.

10. For an account of how official ideology used the terminology of Marxist economics to explain to workers the purpose of their labor, see Humphrey, *Karl Marx Collective*, 76.

11. For comparative accounts of the response of each creative union to perestroika, see Nepomnyashchy, "Perestroika and the Creative Unions," and Condee and Padunov, "Outposts of Official Art," 59–106. On theater, see Glenny, "Soviet Theatre," 78–87.

The Theaterworkers' Association took the opportunity to raise its status to that of "creative union." The Architects' Union stole a march in the rush toward perestroika by being the first to strike allegiance to socialist realism from its charter. By contrast there was little response to perestroika in the Artists' and Composers' Unions (despite reformist speeches), perhaps because by then, the more nonconformist creative workers had already given up on the authorized sphere.

12. Condee and Padunov, "Frontiers of Soviet Culture," 5.

13. On television during perestroika, see McNair, "Media in Post-Soviet Russia"; Vartanov, "Television as Spectacle and Myth"; Muratov, "Soviet Television"; and Dingley, "Soviet Television and Glasnost." Interestingly, a central feature of the swing toward conservatism in television was a drive to prioritize entertainment over news. Perhaps the Soviet leadership had learned some useful lessons from their recent exposure to the ways of the West.

14. Thus the character of television programming reflected Gorbachev's belated swing toward conservatism from late 1990, as controversial new programs were axed and an increasing share of airtime given over to entertainment. These moves attracted protests from the more independent media.

15. Vladimir Motyl, "Appealing to Conscience," *Sovetskaya Rossia*, December 2, 1985, reprinted in *CDSP* 38, no. 7 (1986): 8. Given that Motyl had directed one of the highest-grossing of all Soviet movies—*The White Sun of the Desert*—which adapted the genre conventions of the Western to Soviet Central Asia during the Civil War—his charge of "grayness" cannot be seen as merely another manifestation of cultural elitism.

16. Grigory Chukhrai, "What 'Feeds' a Film Studio," *Pravda*, February 14, 1986, reprinted in *CDSP* 38, no. 7 (1986): 9–10.

17. In 1989 *Variety* lists the committee chiefs of the secretariat as including the following directors in addition to Klimov: Andrei Smirnov, Gleb Panfilov, Rolan Bykov, Igor Gelein, Sergei Solovyov, Eldar Ryazanov, and Grigory Chukhrai. "Who's Who in Soviet Film Industry," *Variety*, July 5–11, 1989, 68.

18. Gladilshchikov, "America Gave Russia a Steamship," *Literaturnaya gazeta*, April 4, 1990, reprinted in *CDSP* 42, no. 31 (1990): 15.

19. Verdery, *What Was Socialism*, 107–8.

20. Lawton, *Kinoglasnost*, 53–54.

21. Quoted in Condee and Padunov, "Frontiers of Soviet Culture," 5.

22. Christie, "The Cinema," 62.

23. Yuri Karyakin, quoted in "Renewal: Soviet Filmmakers Choose Their Deputies in the Nation's Highest Body of Power," *SF*, no. 7 (1989): 12.

24. Alexander Kiselyov, "Why Care about Hecuba?" *SF*, no. 11 (1990): 4–5, 8–9.

25. Klimov, "Learning Democracy," 240.

26. Elem Klimov, "Film Union Head Scores Stale Bureaucracy," interviewed by G. Kapralov in *Pravda*, June 5, 1986, reprinted in *CDSP* 38, no. 32 (1986): 5.

27. Elem Klimov, "Elem Klimov: 'Creativity Is the Watchword,' " interview in *SF*, no. 5 (1987): 1.

28. Klimov, "Learning Democracy," 240.

29. Ibid., 234.

30. On Mosfilm, see "Reform of Mosfilm Studios," *SF*, no. 5 (1988): 12–17; on Lenfilm, see "The Face of the Studios: Notes on Cinema in Leningrad," *SF*, no. 8 (1988): 16–17.

31. "Reform of Mosfilm Studios," 14.

32. Ibid., 13.

33. Alexei Gherman, "The Challenge of Freedom," interviewed by Sergei Dobrotvorsky, *SF*, no. 8 (1988): 14. Cf. Vladimir Dostal's upbeat assessment of the prospects for art cinema under the new model: "Of course the question has come up: What will we do with films of a high intellectual content? We came to the conclusion that it is precisely economic independence that enables a [creative] association that knows how to make money to raise the funds that provide it the freedom of creativity to make avant-garde films and films that are geared toward a narrow audience . . . no one has forgotten that what is needed is not just money but prizes in Venice also." Vladimir Dostal, "Moscow Film Studio Is Learning to Count Money," interviewed by N. Kishchik, *Izvestia*, February 7, 1989, reprinted in *CDSP* 41, no. 6 (1989): 28.

34. "State Group Goskino Faces New Role in Shifting Soviet Film Industry," *Variety*, July 5–11, 1989, 66.

35. Klimov, "Film Union Head," 5 (see note 26).

36. Christie, "The Cinema," 46–53.

37. Ibid.

38. See Mosfilm head Vladimir Dostal's remarks quoted in "Mosfilm Not Just a Studio—It's a Cinematic Empire," *Variety*, July 5–11, 1989, 69.

39. Lawton, *Kinoglasnost*, 59. Since the film subsequently became an object of ridicule among filmmakers and critics, Kulish might have done better not to fight this particular case.

40. "Though Subject to New Market Principles, Filmers' Union Finds Itself Breathing Less 'Restricted' Air," *Variety*, July 5–11, 1989, 66.

41. Lawton, *Kinoglasnost*, 56, 242n. Censorship remained permissible on certain grounds, namely national security, prevention of pornography, and encitement to ethnic conflict; we should also note that the late- and post-Soviet state continued to intervene extensively in the news and information media. Yeltsin's suspension of the nationalist and Communist press after the October 1993 rising is a case in point. The state has not, however, subjected *fictional* media forms to such supervision because it has rather narrow political aims such as ensuring the president's reelection, rather than the far-reaching "artistic and ideological" goals of the Soviet past.

42. Valery Zalotukha, personal interview.

43. Karen Shakhnazarov, personal interview; my emphasis.

44. Lawton, *Kinoglasnost*, 76–78.

45. Alexander Rybin and Vladimir Portnov, "Studiia Gor'kogo: perestroika prodolzhaetsia," interviewed by Viktor Matizen, *KG*, no. 2 (1995): 18.

46. Ibid.

47. Ibid.

48. "Liza," personal interview.

49. See, for instance, the comments of Oleg Rudnev, director of Sovexportfilm on "the wretched visual quality and sound" of Soviet films. Oleg Rudnev, "Sovexportfilm: 'If Everybody Goes Into Commerce, Who Will Make Films?' " interview in *SF*, no. 8 (1989): 28.

50. Kopetas, *Bear Hunting with the Politburo*; Jones and Moskoff, *Ko-ops*.

51. Deborah Young, "The Name of the Game Is Capitalism," *Variety*, July 8, 1991, 39.

52. "Pic Production Up, But So Are Costs," *Variety*, July 8, 1991, 44.

53. The 1995 Roskomkino figures. "Proizvodstvo padaet, gospoderzhka rastet. Komy daiut—neiasno," *KG*, no. 2 (1995): 1.

54. Writing at the beginning of the 1990s, Lawton (*Kinoglasnost*, 78–81) and Brashinsky and Horton (*Zero Hour*, 18–21) were generally upbeat about the independents' promise to revitalize the industry.

55. "Panorama Goes it Alone," *Variety*, July 5–11, 1989, 80. To give another example of this process: director Vasily Pichul formed the *Podarok* production association with producer Mark Levin because he was disgruntled by the small return he saw from his massively successful 1988 film, *Little Vera*. He continued, however, to work at the Gorky studios where *Little Vera* had been made. "First USSR Indie Feature 'Black Sea' Hopes to Be Ready for Venice Fest," *Variety*, July 5–11, 1989, 76.

56. Taped discussion with Valery Zalotukha, Lena Zalotukha, and Alexander Chernykh, Moscow, February 1995.

57. Vasily Pichul, "Ya—za nezavisimoe kino," *IK*, no. 4 (1990): 24.

58. Ibid.

59. In 1989 the average cost of shooting a feature film stood at 450,000 rubles, $650,000 at official exchange rates but around $100,000 at black-market rates ("Soviet Film Industry at a Glance," *Variety*, July 5–11, 1989, 59). By the beginning of 1994 it had reached 50–70 million rubles, that is, $300,000–$500,000 (Dondurei, "After the Empire," 8). The rise in costs was caused in part by a rise in salaries fueled by money-laundering itself, in part by the need to import virtually all film and equipment, and in part by the tendency of studios, who still controlled most production facilities, to charge monopolistic prices for their services. By 1995 I was told it actually cost more to shoot in Moscow than the West ("Maria," personal interview).

60. Golovskoy, *Behind the Soviet Screen*, 93.

61. Lawton, *Kinoglasnost*, 80.

62. Berman, "Controversy over Coproductions," 10.

63. Dondurei, "After the Empire," 7.

64. Sergei Solovyov, "To Coin Pots of Money by Selling Balalaikas Is Not My Style," interviewed by Viktor Matizen, *CE*, no. 1 (1991): 23.

65. Ibid.

66. Valery Todorovsky, personal interview.

67. Rudnev, "Sovexportfilm," 28.

68. In 1988 Soviet films received sixty international awards ("State Group Goskino Faces New Role in Shifting Soviet Film Industry," *Variety*, July 5–11, 1989, 66).

69. The actor and director Stanislav Govorukhin argued after the Fifth Congress of the Filmmakers' Union that the union's leadership was "elitist" and more interested in international film festivals than in the national audience. Bogomolov, "Stanislav Govorukhin," 28–30.

70. Yevgeniya Tirdatova, "The Berlin Model," *CE*, no. 3 (1994): 42.

71. Dondurei, "Filmmakers Versus Filmmaking: Creativity without Censorship Is a Colossal Test for Russia." *Nezavisimaya gazeta*, 10 April, 1993, reprinted in *CDSP* 45, no. 15 (1993): 27–28.

72. "The Franc Helps Those Who Help Themselves," *CE*, no. 3 (1994): 4.

73. The fund may have played a more constructive role in enhancing the future prospects of the Russian film industry by introducing Russian directors to the unaccustomed rigors of being subjected to a producer (one of the conditions of the grant was that the producer be French) as well as by giving them access to more up-to-date technical facilities, such as direct sound recording. At least one director who had shot a film with CNC money, Valery Todorovsky, considered these experiences valuable lessons for the future.

74. Jowett and Linton, *Movies as Mass Communication.*

75. "Boris," personal interview.

76. Lawton, *Kinoglasnost*, 84.

77. Dondurei, "After the Empire."

78. Oleg Rudnev, "What Kind of Cinema Will Dr. Tagi-Zade Prescribe for Us?" *Izvestia,* May 6, 1991, reprinted in *CDSP* 38, no. 18 (1991): 11. See similar accusations made by Kinotavr president Mark Rudinstein. "Mark Rudinstein: I'm Making Myself a Name. The Name Will Make Me Money," interviewed by Viktor Matizen, *CE*, no. 1 (1992): 33–34. AVKIN appears to have faded as a force by 1992, perhaps because it lost its protection from on high when the Soviet Union broke up. At any rate, the trade press cease to mention it after this date.

79. Valery Todorovsky, personal interview; "Dmitri," personal interview.

80. Valery Todorovsky, personal interview.

81. Anne Barnard, "Good-Bye Van Damme, Mayor Wants 'Quality,' " *MT*, 20 May 1994 (Lexis-Nexis, Academic Universe).

82. "Ksenya," personal interview.

83. Condee and Padunov, "ABC of Russian Consumer Culture," 141. On the decline of the audience for the underground rock scene in the later years of perestroika, see Cushman, *Notes from Underground*, 233. On reactions to the declining market for serious literature, see Marsh, "Death of Soviet Literature."

84. Lowe, "Book Business in Postcommunist Russia; From Marx to Mills and Boon," *The Economist*, October 25, 1997, 68.

85. For a discussion of these trends in popular music in the immediate post-perestroika period, see Cushman, *Notes from Underground*, 246–74. He gives the impression that rock musicians essentially gave up on reaching a mass market in this period, leaving the field to pop artists in the pockets of the mafia.

86. Condee estimates that American dramas and films made up 70 percent of primetime viewing in 1997 ("Dream of Well-Being," 18). In 1995, Sergei Blagovolin, the head of the largest television network, claimed that Russian programming only occupied 10 percent of airtime (Mickiewicz, *Changing Channels*, 234).

87. Guback, *International Film Industry.*

88. In television, the most popular programs of all in this period were Latin American *telenovelas.*

89. Quoted in Cushman, *Notes from Underground*, 272; interestingly, Russian rock music, which as we have seen was dominated by "artistic" considerations, fared far less well from a commercial standpoint in the post-perestroika period.

90. Viktor Matizen, "Armen Medvedev—kormiashchii otets," *KG*, no. 1 (1993): 11.

91. Anonymous source, personal interview.

92. Giving exact dollar equivalents is impossible because the ruble was depreciating so rapidly during this period, but note that this sum is less than the average production budget of a *single* Hollywood picture today.

93. Dondurei, "After the Empire," 25.

94. "Proizvodstvo padaet," 1.

95. Anonymous source, personal interview.

96. "Liza," personal interview. One distributor I spoke to claimed that Pyotr Todorovsky's recent heart attack was brought on by his struggle to get the Roskomkino officials to actually fork out the money he had been awarded to make *What a Wonderful Game.*

97. Karen Shakhnazarov, personal interview.

98. Anonymous source, personal interview.

99. "Liza," personal interview.

100. Karen Shakhnazarov, personal interview.

101. Alexander Rybin, "Studiia Gor'kogo: perestroika prodolzhaetsia," interviewed by Viktor Matizen, *KG*, no. 2 (1995): 19. He does not here suggest a return to censorship or the Goskino production plan, but he does believe that given that most filmmaking is dependent on government orders, the state should have a coherent policy for the kinds of cinema it supports.

102. See, for instance, the published interview with Vladimir Dostal, director of Mosfilm. Vladimir Dostal, "What's Happening with Mosfilm," interviewed by Gennady Belostotsky, *Izvestia*, January 5, 1994, reprinted in *CDSP* 46, no. 1 (1994): 14.

103. Semyon Riabikov, head of "Ass-Video" association, "Semen Riabikov: Srochno trebuetsia videopolitsiia!" interviewed by Pyotr Chernyaev, *KG*, no. 1 (1995): 23. In a 1997 article, Condee states that pirate copies made up 73 percent of the video market ("Dream of Well-Being," 73).

104. Jane Albrecht, vice-president of the American Motion Picture Association, "Rossiiskie Piraty—ne Robin Gudy," interviewed by Sergei Fiks, *IK*, no. 4 (1995): 104–7.

105. Stephen Shenfield, "On the Threshold of Disaster," 2 July 1998 (http://www.trud.org/index7-4.htm).

106. Stephen F. Cohen, "Why Call It Reform?" *The Nation*, September 7–14, 1998, 6.

107. On the general fall in educational standards: Shenfield cites figures claiming that only 30 percent of army conscripts are now judged competent in elementary mathematics, as compared to over 90 percent in the Soviet period (Shenfield, "On the Threshold of Disaster"). On the decline in applications to study subjects that have become economically marginalized, see Azhgikhina, "High Culture Meets Trash TV," 43, and Ellen Barry, "Class of 94's Hard Lesson," *MT Review*, April 2, 1995.

108. See also Chinyaeva: "In 1995 the average monthly salary of a bank employee was 1.4 million rubles [c. $300], while for those in the cultural sphere it was only 232,000 [c. $50]" ("Soviet Mass Culture in Russia," 62).

109. "Natalya," personal interview.

110. "Who Are the New Russians?" *Commersant*, September 8, 1992, 19. The reference is to the English-language edition of the Russian original.

111. "Andrei," personal interview.

112. Alexei Levinson, "What the Old Intelligentsia Didn't Give the 'New Russians,' " *IK*, no. 1 (1995): 29.

113. "Max," personal interview. People would often make these kinds of declarations to me in response to being teasingly accused of being a "New Russian" by friends.

114. "Andrei," personal interview.

115. Another striking example of New Russian-disavowal is offered by Fyodr Bondarchuk, son of Sergei, who as head of the rock and television advertising studio "Art Pictures" became one of the most successful figures in the new commercial media in the 1990s. In a press interview he stated, "I am not a New Russian. . . . New Russians have no concept of the past. For them, money is the most important thing. I have culture. I am a member of the intelligentsia" (David Stern, "Video-Generation Son Takes Cue from Dad," *MT*, June 10, 1995, 7).

116. Rutland, "Some Russians Are Learning to Be Rich."

117. On television, see McNair, "Television in Post-Soviet Russia"; Mickiewicz, *Changing Channels*; on newspapers, see McNair, "Media in Post-Soviet Russia"; for a general account of the oligarchs' ownership of the Russian media in the mid-1990s, see Fossato and Kachkaeva, "Russia's Media Empires."

118. On the cult of the *metsenatsvo*, see Condee and Padunov, "ABC of Russian Consumer Culture," 142–51.

119. Quoted in Chris Klein, "A Cultural Affair," *MT Review*, October 1, 1993; see also Vladimir Turchin, "Banki smotriat na iskusstvo—isskustvo sledit za bankami," *Bank*, no. 1 (April 1994): 22–23.

120. Valery Zalotukha, personal interview.

121. "Anastasia," personal interview.
122. Valery Todorovsky, personal interview.
123. Daniil Dondurei, "Kinematografisty o 'novykh russkikh,' " *IK*, no. 1 (1995): 27.

Chapter 5

1. Alexei Gherman, "The Challenge of Freedom," interviewed by Sergei Dobrotvorsky, *SF*, no. 8 (1988): 14.
2. "Ksenya," personal interview.
3. At the 1995 Kinotavr Festival, for instance, no clear direction was detectable in the types of films to which prizes were awarded. Art cinema was recognized in Sergei Selyanov's prize for best director, popular cinema in the prize for best film given to Rogozhkin's comedy *Peculiarities of the National Hunt in the Autumn Period* (*Osobennosti natsional'noi okhoty v osennii period*).
4. Anonymous source, personal interview.
5. I take this phrase from the title of a press article discussing the 1989 plenum of the Filmmakers' Union devoted to "artistic problems" in contemporary cinema: "With What Shall We Lure the Viewer?" by Grigory Simanovich, in *SF*, no. 10 (1989): 24–25.
6. Horton and Brashinsky, *Zero Hour*, 11. This sense of creative crisis was not confined to filmmaking. Tatyana Tolstoya, considered one of the most promising writers to emerge during the 1980s, confessed, for instance, "I know I can write, but I can't seem to find anything to write about" (quoted in Marsh, "Death of Soviet Literature," 122). See also the comments of Leonid Zhukhovitsky, a well-known heterodox but officially published author of the late-Soviet period: "My books used to have press runs of 200,000 copies and still the next day they would be gone from the stores. I knew who I was writing for. I received up to 30,000 letters a year. Today I can print and write whatever I like. If I don't proofread the galleys myself, they will even preserve all my typos. But to be honest, I do not know who I write for anymore. The press runs are very small" (quoted in Gessen, *Dead Again*, 28).
7. The term "elite cinema" (*elitnoe kino*) was widely, if sometimes sarcastically, used in the post-Soviet film world. The most common term for mass-oriented filmmaking was "commercial" (*kommercheskoe*) cinema.
8. Simanovich, "With What Shall We Lure the Viewer?" 25.
9. Christie, "The Cinema," 58.
10. Johnson and Petrie, *The Films of Andrei Tarkovsky*, 16.
11. Quoted in Christie, "The Cinema," 57.
12. Yevgeniya Tirdatova, "The Recesses of the Heart," *CE*, no. 3 (1994): 41.
13. *Second Circle* (*Krug vtoroi, 1990*) won the main prize at the art-cinema-oriented Rimini festival in 1992. Sokurov made *The Whispering Pages* and his 1997 film *Mother and Son* (*Mat i syn*) with a German producer and financing.
14. See, for instance, Natalya Rtishcheva, "Kriminal Sokurova," *KG*, no. 1 (1991): 36.
15. Zalotukha's own scripts, like those for *Makarov* (1994) and *The Muslim* (1995), directed by Vladimir Khotinenko, reflect his ambivalence about the legacy of Tarkovsky in that they attempt to address major "philosophical" issues facing Russia but employ many of the formal conventions of Hollywood thrillers to do so. These films have been highly successful in garnering prizes at Russian film festivals.
16. Valery Zalotukha, personal interview. See also Horton and Brashinsky, *Zero Hour*, 10.
17. Originally established under the auspices of the Filmmakers' Union, the Kinocenter (Kinotsentr) is Moscow's equivalent to such institutions as the British National Film Theatre: in the 1990s it maintained a diverse exhibition repertoire, which gave Moscow's cinema buffs the opportunity to see both domestic and foreign art films not otherwise in theatrical release.
18. Marina Tsurtsumia, personal interview.

19. Other prominent directors active in the post-perestroika period who can be placed within the messianic-elitist camp include Sergei Selyanov and Konstantin Lopushansky. In a published interview, regarding his 1990 film *Visitor to a Museum*, the latter declared, for instance, in terms that almost exactly parallel Tarkovsky's artistic rhetoric, that his intention was to "help the viewer to open up his soul for compassion, for understanding religious truths, for a desire to comprehend them and apply them to his own fate." Konstantin Lopushansky, "Road to Kindness," interviewed by Tatyana Mushtakova, *SF*, no. 6 (1990): 8.

20. See, for instance, the essay by the film critic Alexander Timofeevsky, himself a prominent representative of this generation, "The Last Romantics." In the sphere of rock music, Cushman finds a similar generation gap within the Leningrad underground scene between the older advocates of message-oriented rock and a younger generation who reject it as "primitive protest music." Cushman, *Notes from Underground*, 254–59. See also Gessen, *Dead Again*, 15.

21. I have avoided using the term "postmodern" as an analytical category in this study, since it is even harder to define in the Russian context than it is in the West. One young director who saw herself as a "postmodernist," for instance, spoke of her eagerness to set right in her films what she saw as twentieth-century cinema's neglect of moral issues.

22. Kira Muratova, "I Make Films about What Is in Me," interviewed by Viktor Bozhovich, *SF*, no. 4 (1990): 19.

23. Ibid. The Russian critic, Lev Karakhan, marks this break to her first feature of the perestroika era, 1987's *Twist of Fate*, which, he writes, "avoided any direct social implications. It spelled out her newfound distrust in 'messages' and faith in 'film for film's sake' " (Karakhan, "Jobless Prophets," 33).

24. When Roman Balayan was questioned about his purpose in producing in *First Love* (*Pervaya Lyubov'*), yet another screen adaptation of Turgenev, he declared that "I didn't think about the money, or whether it was needed, I just did it." Alexei Uchitel's response to similar doubts expressed by a film journalist regarding his ballet biopic *Mania Zhizeli* was still more lordly: "I don't find that question interesting."

25. Alexei Balabanov, personal interview.

26. Ibid.

27. In the years following our interview Balabanov appears not so much to have resolved the tension apparent in his discourse between his aspiration to make "energetic and interesting" films and his desire to pursue "art" cinema as to have given creative expression to both impulses. In 1997 he released the critically and commercially successful crime thriller *Brother* (*Brat'*), and in 1998 the "pathological" project he was attempting to raise funding for when I met him, *Of Freaks and Men* (*Pro Urodov i lyudei*).

28. Alexander Chernykh, personal interview.

29. Valery Todorovsky, personal interview.

30. Ibid.

31. Ibid.

32. Ibid.

33. Marina Kniazeva, for instance, applies the term *chernukha* to the theater of the mid-1980s, although she uses the term to describe a somewhat different trend from the one I focus on in the case of cinema, seeing it as "marked by hyperbole and the grotesque, absurdity and caricature" (Kniazeva, "Theater on the Market," 5). Thomas Cushman uses the term *chernukha* to characterize the lyrics and persona of Kostya Kinchev, lead singer for the cult rock band Alisa, who in Cushman's words "sees himself as the evil which is necessary for any good to come from Soviet existence" (Cushman, *Notes from Underground*, 153).

34. Horton and Brashinsky, *Zero Hour*, 163–64. Another Western film scholar who uses the term to describe the dominant trend in Soviet filmmaking in the years around 1990—coupling it with the other pejorative neologisms used to describe films of this period: *pornukha* ("porn-

stuff"—my translation) and *bytovukha* (everyday-life stuff)—is Vida Johnson. See Johnson, "Search for a New Russia."

35. On the origins of the term *"kheppi ending,"* see Youngblood, "Americanitis," 149.

36. This point was made regarding literature, for instance, by the scholar Galina Belaya. See Pittman, "Writers and Politics," 665.

37. "From the Editors' Point of View," *SF*, no. 10 (1989): 6.

38. Marina Tsurtsumia, personal interview.

39. Graffy, "Literary Press," 135.

40. Muratov, "Soviet Television," 172.

41. According to Rosalind Marsh, a common complaint of literary critics during the perestroika period was that publishers were only selecting works with socially sensational themes. Marsh, "Death of Soviet Literature," 123.

42. "From the Editors' Point of View," *SF*, no. 10 (1989): 6.

43. The large audiences for *Little Vera* and *Intergirl* can almost certainly be explained in terms of the new ground they broke in terms of sexual explicitness rather than any general hunger for social problem cinema.

44. Vladimir Dostal, "Mosfilm Not Just a Studio—It's a Cinematic Empire," interviewed in *Variety*, July 5–11, 1989, 68.

45. Nichols, *Representing Reality*.

46. The novelist Viktor Erofeev, for instance, argued that politically oriented literature was creatively dead. Pittman, "Writers and Politics," 665.

47. Valery Zalotukha, personal interview.

48. Daniil Dondurei, "Cinema, Cinema! Turn Your Face to Film-goers," *CE*, no. 1 (1992): 27.

49. The resurgence of national sentiment has of course been common throughout postsocialist Europe. As, for instance, Verdery argues, far from "suppressing" primordial nationalist sentiments, socialism did much to create the conditions for its subsequent renaissance (*What Was Socialism*, 83–103). The unique feature of the Russian situation is the country's postimperial breakup and humiliation and status as the only East European nation in which Communism could not be seen as an alien imposition. See Urban, "Politics of Identity."

50. See Shlapentokh, *Soviet Intellectuals*, 203–23. The accommodation between Brezhnevism and russophilism was not always as cosy as Shlapentokh tends to suggest, however; in cinema, a number of films by directors such as Tarkovsky, Konchalovsky, Klimov, and Panfilov provoked official disapproval despite their russophile ideological tendencies. The most prominent russophile of all, of course, was Solzhenitsyn, most of whose works were banned and who was forced into exile in 1971.

51. A personal experience may illustrate the pervasiveness of this sense of humiliation. In the summer of 1993 I went for a drink with a young Moscow labor activist, who described himself to me as an anarcho-syndicalist. Under Gorbachev he had been arrested for protesting a state visit by Deng Xiaoping shortly after the Tiananmen massacre. Several drinks into the evening he began talking bitterly of how humiliated he felt by the recent killing of Russian troops by rebels in Tadjikistan, an incident which he regarded as symptomatic of the humiliation of his country.

52. See, for instance, Nepomnyashchy, "Perestroika and Creative Unions," 141, and Pittman, "Perestroika and Soviet Cultural Politics." If true, this would illustrate Verdery's point that bureaucratic centralization and national chauvinism tended to march hand in hand in late state socialism. However, it is also possible that the thesis of what we might call a "gray-brown" alliance in which nationalist ideology was used to defend bureaucratic privilege was in part a rhetorical ploy devised by liberals to better discredit both factions. The dominant figures in the Soviet Writers' Union tended to forswear anti-Semitism, while, however abhorrent their politics, before perestroika many of the russophile writers had enjoyed a high artistic reputation among their peers as well as a wide readership.

53. Yevgenia Albats, "Yeltsin at the Manege—A Strange Political Gesture," *Izvestia*, July 22, 1994, 4, reprinted in *CDSP* 46, no. 29 (1994): 19–20.

54. Cushman, *Notes from Underground*, 315–16.

55. Kolesnik, "Advertising and Cultural Politics," 52. See also Yekaterina Karsanova, "Will Pushkin Peddle Purina Dog Chow?" *MN*, November 27–December 3, 1997, 14. The latter writer comments on this trend, "Lost Russian spirituality may lie in places one would never expect to find it."

56. Maya Turovskaya, personal interview.

57. Nancy Condee remarks of this wave of period cinema: "The grand style portrayed in these nostalgic films conferred on the newly wealthy the mantle of legitimacy it sorely needed" ("Dream of Well-Being," 21).

58. Viktor Matizen, "Mosfilm Will Not Shelve Its Teeth—Even If It Shelves Its Films," *CE*, no. 1 (1994): 28.

59. Ibid.

60. Valery Zalotukha, personal interview.

61. Svetlana Khokhryakova, "Screen Test for Mayor," *MN*, August 14–20, 1997, 1, 2.

62. Valeria Korchagina, "Preview of Luzhkov Film Horrifies Critics," *MT*, 1997 (Lexis-Nexis, Academic Universe).

63. Ibid.

64. Yevgeniya Tirdatova, "I dol'she veka dlitsia den'," *KG*, no. 1 (1995): 40.

65. Ibid.

66. Daniil Dondurei, "Tonkaya Frantsuzskaya igra," *IK*, no. 8 (1994): 15–18.

67. Nikita Mikhalkov, "Mne khotelos' ikh zashchitit'," interviewed by El'ga Lyndina, *Ekran*, no. 1 (1995): 1–8.

68. Nikita Mikhalkov, "Rezhissor ne dolzhen dolgo nakhodit'sia pod obayaniem svoei kartiny. Eto opasno," *IK*, no. 3 (1995): 9–13.

69. Lyndina, "Mne khotelos' ikh zashchitit'," 4.

70. He did not, however, take up his seat in the Duma.

71. Anonymous source, personal interview.

72. Alessandra Stanley, "Mikhalkov's Vision of the Terrifying Past of Russia," *International Herald Tribune*, March 22, 1995 (Lexis-Nexis, Academic Universe).

73. *Burnt by the Sun* was funded by French sources as well as the Russian government.

74. Nikita Mikhalkov, "Khochu byt' Oblomovym, a prikhoditsia zhit', kak Shtol'ts," interviewed by Pyotr Vail, *IK*, no. 9 (1995): 16.

75. In contemporary Russian slang the term *krysha* is generally used to refer to an entity such as a criminal organization (or sometimes the state authorities acting in a private capacity) that provides a business or an individual with protection.

76. Barthes, *Mythologies*, 165.

77. Condee and Padunov, "Not by *Bred* Alone," 3–6;

78. The technique of promoting a film by personally touring the country and turning its exhibition into an "event" was first used by Sergei Solovyov to market his 1988 movie *Assa*. See the interview with Solovyov by Viktor Matizen, "Sshibat' kush raspisnoi lozhkoi—ne nash variant," *KG*, no. 1 (1991): 22. Solovyov, however, created what he himself called a "carnivalesque" atmosphere (apparently he knows his Bakhtin), tapping into the vitality of the then flourishing "underground" youth culture, whereas Mikhalkov has used the technique to appeal to more "traditional" cultural/political values.

79. Lyndina, "Mne khotelos' ikh zashchitit'," 7.

80. Mikhalkov, "Rezhissor," 9.

81. According to legend, the state of Rus was founded when Slavic chiefs offered the throne to the Varangian leader Rurik in the hope that he would bring order to their land.

82. Leonid Pavlyuchik, " 'Lord of the Manor' Mikhalkov Undertakes to Clean Out the Film-Industry Stables," *Trud*, December 25, 1997, reprinted in *CDSP*, 49, no. 52 (1997): 16–17.

83. Anna Borotnikova, "Est' problemy? Zvonite Mikhalkovu!" *Moskoskie novosti*, May 24–31, 1998, 29. "Extrabudgetary" in Russian parlance means not funded from the federal budget. Because even the juridically private studios that survived the collapse of the early 1990s lease their production facilities from state-owned studios, this implies that almost the entire industry would come under the fund's supervision.

Conclusion

1. See Becker, *Art Worlds*, and Crane, "Reward Systems." For a Marxian critique of the "positivist" tendencies of American sociological approaches to cultural production, see Wolff, *Aesthetics and the Sociology of Art*.

2. Bourdieu, *Field of Cultural Production*, 112.

3. Ibid., 130–31.

4. Ibid., 44–45.

5. Bourdieu, *Distinction*, 317.

6. Staiger, *Studio System*.

7. Condee and Padunov, "Not by *Bred* Alone."

8. Condee, "Dream of Well-Being."

9. Veronika Kosenko, "Moscow Movies Move to Pull Crowds," *MN*, April 30–May 6, 1998, 15. In early 1998 ticket prices at the *Kinomir* ranged from 20 to 170 rubles (at early 1998 exchange rates, roughly $4–$30), that is from one day's to one week's earnings for the average Russian. On plans to build more new cinemas, see Igor Tolstunov, "Na tseremoniyu 'Oskara' zvezdy priletayut na vertoletakh," interviewed by Stanislav Komarov, *Moskovskii komsomolets*, April 6, 1998.

10. His estimates by source are $250,000–$300,000 from video, $100,000 from theater distribution, and $70,000–$100,000 from television (Tolstunov, "Na tseremoniyu 'Oskara' ").

11. See *Carnival of Images*, Michele and Armand Mattelart's account of how the Brazilian media company Globo consolidated a virtual monopoly over Brazilian television under the patronage of the state in the 1970s and 1980s, giving it the financial resources to invest in the large-scale production of television drama (in particular the *telenovelas*, so popular in post-Soviet Russia).

12. Appadurai, "Disjuncture and Difference." The theoretical model of cultural life Bourdieu sets out in *The Field of Cultural Production* and *The Rules of Art* gives no place to transnational forces. This omission is problematic even in the case of France, where the state's intervention in cultural affairs in the twentieth century has been powerfully influenced by anxieties regarding "Americanization."

Appendix

1. A list of interviews cited, giving locations, language of interview, and brief biographical details of my informants is given below.

2. Women are far more strongly represented in the film industry as distributors, scriptwriters, and critics than as directors. Several women in the industry I spoke to claimed that the former two roles were particularly suited to what they held to be women's essentially nurturing and supportive psychological makeup, whereas they characterized direction as an inherently "masculine" profession. Such views are typical of contemporary Russian gender ideology. On the role and representation of women in late-Soviet and perestroika cinema, see Attwood, *Red Women on the Silver Screen*.

3. As what is known as "nationality" can be a rather sensitive subject in Russia today, I never explicitly questioned my informants about their ethnicity or what role it played in their life. My estimate of my interview group's ethnic makeup is based either on my informants themselves mentioning their ethnicity, someone else mentioning it, or their having an obviously non-Russian surname. Compared to many other sectors of Russian society, including some other areas of cultural production, I came across rather little evidence of extreme ethnic chauvinism in the film world, either in discourse or in films themselves.

4. I spoke to only two filmmakers based outside Moscow, Alexei Balabanov from St. Petersburg and Natalya Andreichenko from Kiev.

5. One incident from teaching that stands out in my mind took place during a pre-vacation game of "hangman" with my class of adults. A student gave as a clue "Something that's bad here but good in the West," to which another shouted out, to universal laughter, "The word must be 'everything!' " (The correct answer, incidentally, was "service.")

BIBLIOGRAPHY

Althusser, Louis. "Ideology and the Ideological State Apparatuses." In *Lenin and Philosophy and Other Essays*. New York: Monthly Review Press, 1971.

Androunas, Elena. *Soviet Media in Transition: Structural and Economic Alternatives*. Westport, Conn.: Praeger, 1993.

Ang, Ien. *Desperately Seeking the Audience*. New York: Routledge, 1991.

Appadurai, Arjun. "Disjuncture and Difference in the World Cultural Economy." *Theory Culture and Society* 7 (1990): 295–310.

Attwood, Lynne, ed. *Red Women on the Silver Screen*. London: Pandora, 1993.

Azhgikhina, Nadezhda. "High Culture Meets Trash TV." *Bulletin of Atomic Scientists* 49, no. 1 (January–February 1993): 42–47.

Babitsky, Paul, and John Rimberg. *The Soviet Film Industry*. New York: Praeger, 1955.

Barber, John. "Working Class Culture and Political Culture in the 1930s." In *The Culture of the Stalin Period*, ed. Hans Gunther, 3–14. New York: St. Martin's Press, 1990.

Barthes, Roland. *Mythologies*. Trans. Annette Lavers. London: Paladin, 1971.

Bauman, Zigmunt. *Legislators and Interpreters: On Modernity, Postmodernity and Intellectuals*. Ithaca, N.Y.: Cornell University Press, 1987.

Becker, Howard S. "Art as Collective Action." *American Sociological Review* 39 (1974): 767–76.

———. *Art Worlds*. Berkeley and Los Angeles: University of California Press, 1982.

Berlin, Isaiah. *Russian Thinkers*. Harmondsworth: Penguin, 1978.

Berman, Boris. "Controversy over Coproductions." *SF*, no. 9 (1988): 10–11.

Bogomolov, Yuri. "The Revitalization of the Soviet Film Industry." In Seifert, *Mass Culture and Perestroika*, 39–45.

———. "Stanislav Govorukhin: The Victory of a Professional or the Defeat of a Moralizer?" *CE*, no. 1 (1993): 28–30.

Bordwell, David, Janet Staiger, and Kristin Thompson. *The Classical Hollywood Cinema: Film Style and Mode of Production to 1960*. New York: Columbia University Press, 1985.

Bourdieu, Pierre. *Distinction: A Social Critique of the Judgement of Taste*. Trans. Richard Nice. Cambridge: Harvard University Press, 1984.

———. *The Field of Cultural Production*. Ed. Randal Johnson. New York: Columbia University Press, 1993.

———. "The Forms of Capital." In *Handbook of Theory and Research for the Sociology of Education*, ed. John G. Richardson, 241–58. New York: Greenwood, 1986.

———. *The Rules of Art: Genesis and Structure of the Literary Field*. Trans. Susan Emanuel. Stanford, Calif.: Stanford University Press, 1995.

Boym, Svetlana. "Paradoxes of a Unified Culture: From Stalin's Fairy Tale to Molotov's Lacquer Box." *South Atlantic Quarterly* 94, no. 3 (Summer 1995): 821–36.

Brashinsky, Michael, and Andrew Horton, eds. *Russian Critics on the Cinema of Glasnost*. Cambridge: Cambridge University Press, 1994.

Brooks, Jeffrey. "Russian Nationalism and Russian Literature: The Canonization of the Classics." In *Nation and Ideology: Essays in Honor of Wayne S. Vucinich*, ed. Ivo Banac, John G. Ackerman, and Roman Szporluk, 315–34. Boulder, Colo.: East European Monographs, 1981.

———. "Socialist Realism in Pravda: Read All About It!" *Slavic Review* 53, no. 4 (Winter 1994): 973–91.

Brown, Edward J. *Russian Literature since the Revolution.* Cambridge: Harvard University Press, 1982.

———. "Trifonov: The Historian as Artist." In *Soviet Society and Culture: Essays in Honor of Vera S. Dunham*, ed. Terry L. Thompson and Richard Sheldon, 109–23. Boulder, Colo.: Westview, 1988.

Burawoy, Michael. "A View from Production: The Hungarian Transition from Socialism to Capitalism." In Smith and Thompson, *Labour in Transition*, 180–97.

Burawoy, Michael, and Janos Lukacs. *The Radiant Past: Ideology and Reality in Hungary's Road to Capitalism.* Chicago: University of Chicago Press, 1992.

Burg, David. "Observations on Soviet University Students." *Daedalus* 89, no. 2 (Summer 1960): 520–39.

Bürger, Peter. "Literary Institution and Modernization." In *The Decline of Modernism*, trans. Nicholas Walker. University Park: Pennsylvania State University Press, 1992.

Bushnell, John. "Urban Leisure Culture in Post-Stalin Russia: Stability as a Social Problem." In Thompson and Sheldon, *Soviet Society and Culture*, 58–86.

Chanan, Michael. *The Dream That Kicks: The Prehistory and Early Years of Cinema in Britain.* London: Routledge, 1980.

Chinyaeva, Elena. "The Fate of Soviet Mass Culture in Russia." *Transition*, 22 March 1996, 22–25.

Christie, Ian. "Canons and Careers: The Director in Soviet Cinema." In Taylor and Spring, *Stalinism and Soviet Cinema*, 142–70.

———. "The Cinema." In Graffy and Hosking, *Culture and the Media*, 43–77.

Churchward, L. G. *The Soviet Intelligentsia.* London: Routledge, 1973.

Clarke, Simon. "Privatization and the Development of Capitalism in Russia." *New Left Review*, no. 196 (1992): 3–27.

Cohen, Louis. *The Cultural-Political Traditions and Developments of the Soviet Cinema 1917–1972.* New York: Arno, 1974.

Condee, Nancy. "The Dream of Well-Being." *Sight and Sound* 7, no. 12 (December 1997): 18–21.

———. "Introduction." In Condee, *Soviet Hieroglyphics*, vii–xxiii.

———, ed. *Soviet Hieroglyphics: Visual Culture in Late Twentieth-Century Russia.* Bloomington: Indiana University Press, 1995.

Condee, Nancy, and Vladimir Padunov. "The ABC of Russian Consumer Culture: Reading, Ratings and Real Estate." In Condee, *Soviet Hieroglyphics*, 130–72.

———. "The Frontiers of Soviet Culture: Reaching the Limits?" *Harriman Institute Forum* 1, no. 5 (May 1988): 1–8.

———. "The Outposts of Official Art: Recharting Soviet Cultural History." *Framework* 34 (1994): 59–107.

———. "Perestroika Suicide: Not by *Bred* Alone." *Harriman Institute Forum* 5, no. 5 (January 1992): 1–15.

———. "Soviet Cultural Politics and Cultural Production." *IREX Occasional Papers* 1987:1–21.

Connor, Walter. *The Accidental Proletariat.* Princeton: Princeton University Press, 1991.

Crane, Diana. *The Production of Culture: Media Culture and the Urban Arts.* Newbury Park, Calif.: Sage, 1992.

———. "Reward Systems in Art, Science and Religion." In *The Production of Culture*, ed. Richard A. Peterson, 43–65. Beverly Hills, Calif.: Sage, 1976.

Cushman, Thomas. *Notes from Underground: Rock Music Counterculture in Russia*. Albany: State University of New York Press, 1995.

Daniels, Robert V., ed. *A Documentary History of Communism*. Vol. 1. Hanover, N.H.: University Press of New England, 1988.

De Maegda-Soep, Carolina. *Trifonov and the Drama of the Soviet Intelligentsia*. Brugge, Belgium: Ghent State University, Russian Institute, 1990.

DiMaggio, Paul. "Social Structure, Institutions and Cultural Goods: The Case of the United States." In *Social Theory for a Changing Society*, ed. Pierre Bourdieu and James S. Coleman, 133–55. Boulder, Colo.: Westview and Russell Sage Foundation, 1991.

Dingley, James. "Soviet Television and Glasnost." In Graffy and Hosking, *Culture and the Media*, 6–25.

Dobrenko, Evgeny. "The Disaster of Middlebrow Taste, or Who 'Invented' Socialist Realism?" *South Atlantic Quarterly* 94, no. 3 (Summer 1995): 773–806.

Dondurei, Daniil. "After the Empire." In *Catalogue, Russian Films 1991–1994*, ed. Evgenii Margolit, trans. Marina Lapina, 3–26. Moscow: Dubl-D, 1994.

———. "Artistic Culture." In Shalin, *Russian Culture at the Crossroads*, 259–78.

———. "Cinema, Cinema! Turn Your Face to Film-goers." *CE*, no. 1 (1992): 27.

Downing, John. *Internationalizing Media Theory: Transition, Power, Culture. Reflections on the Media in Russia, Poland and Hungary, 1980–95*. London: Sage, 1996.

Dunham, Vera. *In Stalin's Time: Middle-Class Values in Soviet Fiction*. Durham, N.C.: Duke University Press, 1990.

Efimov, Eduard. *Vasily Shukshin*. Trans. Avril Pyman. Moscow: Raduga, 1986.

Enzensberger, Maria. " 'We Were Born to Turn Fairy Tale into Reality': Grigory Alexandrov's *The Radiant Path*." In Taylor and Spring, *Stalinism and Soviet Cinema*, 97–108.

Ericson, Richard. "The Classical Soviet-Type Economy: Nature of the System and Implications for Reform." *Journal of Economic Perspectives* 5, no. 4 (1991): 11–27.

Farmer, Kenneth C. *The Soviet Administrative Elite*. New York: Praeger, 1992.

Feher, Ferenc, Agnes Heller, and Gyorgy Markus. *Dictatorship over Needs: An Analysis of Soviet Societies*. New York: Blackwell, 1983.

Filtzer, Donald. "Economic Reform and Production Relations in Soviet Industry, 1986–1990." In Smith and Thompson, *Labour in Transition*, 110–48.

Fisher, Wesley A., and Solomon Volkov. "The Audience for Classical Music in the USSR: The Government as Mentor." *Slavic Review* 38 (1979): 481–83.

Fitzpatrick, Sheila. *The Cultural Front: Power and Culture in Revolutionary Russia*. Ithaca, N.Y.: Cornell University Press, 1992.

———. *Cultural Revolution in Russia, 1928–1931*. Bloomington: Indiana University Press, 1978.

Fossato, Floriana, and Anna Kachkaeva. "Russian Media Empires," Special Report, Radio Free Europe / Radio Liberty, 26 September, 1997 (http://www.rferl.org/nca/special/rumedia4/index.html).

Foucault, Michel. *The History of Sexuality, Volume 1: An Introduction*. New York: Random House, 1978.

Friedburg, Maurice. "Literary Culture." In Shalin, *Russian Culture at the Crossroads*, 239–57.

———. *Russian Classics in Soviet Jackets*. New York: Columbia University Press, 1962.

Gans, Herbert. *Deciding What's News*. New York: Vintage, 1979.

Garnham, Nicholas. *Capitalism and Communication: Global Culture and the Economics of Information*. London: Sage, 1990.

Garrard, John, and Carol Garrard. *Inside the Soviet Writers' Union*. London: I. B. Taurus, 1990.

Gazso, Ferenc. "Cadre Bureaucracy and the Intelligentsia." *Journal of Communication Studies* 8, no. 3 (September 1992): 76–90.

Gerber, Alla. "Two Meetings with Tenghiz Abuladze." *SF* 5 (1987): 11, 14.

Gessen, Masha. *Dead Again: The Russian Intelligentsia after Communism*. London: Verso, 1997.

Getty, J. Arch, and William Chase. "Patterns of Repression Among the Soviet Elite in the Late 1930s: A Biographical Approach." In *Stalinist Terror: New Perspectives*, ed. J. Arch Getty and Roberta T. Manning, 225–46. Cambridge: Cambridge University Press, 1993.

Gitlin, Todd. *Inside Prime Time*. New York: Pantheon, 1983.

Gleason, Abbot, Peter Kenez, and Richard Stites, eds. *Bolshevik Culture: Experiment and Order in the Russian Revolution*. Bloomington: Indiana University Press, 1985.

Glenny, Michael. "Soviet Theater: 'Glasnost' in Action—With Difficulty." In Graffy and Hosking, *Culture and the Media*, 78–87.

Golding, Peter, and Graham Murdock. "Ideology and the Mass Media: The Question of Determination." In *Ideology and Cultural Production*, ed. Michele Barrel et al., 198–238. London: St. Martin's Press, 1979.

Golovskoy, Val S., with John Rimberg. *Behind the Soviet Screen: The Motion Picture Industry in the USSR, 1972–1982*. Ann Arbor: Ardis, 1986.

Gouldner, Alvin. *The Future of Intellectuals and the Rise of the New Class*. New York: Seabury Press, 1979.

Graffy, Julian. "Cinema." In Kelly and Shepherd, *Russian Cultural Studies*, 165–91.

———. "The Literary Press." In Graffy and Hosking, *Culture and the Media*, 107–57.

Graffy, Julian, and Geoffrey A. Hosking, eds. *Culture and the Media in the USSR Today*. New York: St. Martin's Press, 1989.

Groys, Boris. *The Total Art of Stalinism: Avant-Garde, Aesthetic Dictatorship, and Beyond*. Princeton: Princeton University Press, 1992.

Guback, Thomas. *The International Film Industry: Western Europe and America since 1945*. Bloomington: Indiana University Press, 1969.

Hall, Stuart. "Notes on Deconstructing 'the Popular.' " In *People's History and Socialist Theory*, ed. Raphael Samuel, 227–40. London: Routledge, 1981.

Haraszti, Miklos. *The Velvet Prison: Artists under State Socialism*. New York: Basic Books, 1987.

Havel, Vaclav. "Six Asides about Culture." Trans. E. Kohak. In *Living in Truth*, ed. Jan Vladislav, 123–35. London: Faber & Faber, 1986.

Hebdige, Dick. *Hiding in the Light*. London and New York: Routledge, 1988.

Heller, Leonid. "A World of Prettiness: Socialist Realism and Its Aesthetic Categories." *South Atlantic Quarterly* 94, no. 3 (Summer 1995): 687–714.

Horkheimer, Max, and Theodore Adorno. *Dialectic of Enlightenment*. Trans. John Cumming. New York: Herder & Herder, 1972.

Horton, Andrew, ed. *Inside Soviet Film Satire: Laughter with a Lash*. Cambridge: Cambridge University Press, 1993.

Horton, Andrew, and Leonid Brashinsky. *The Zero Hour: Glasnost and Soviet Cinema in Transition*. Princeton: Princeton University Press, 1992.

Hough, Jerry. *The Soviet Prefects: The Local Party Organs in Industrial Decision Making*. Cambridge: Harvard University Press, 1969.

Humphrey, Caroline. " 'Icebergs,' Barter and the Mafia in Provincial Russia." *Anthropology Today* 7, no. 2 (1991): 8–13.

———. *Karl Marx Collective: Economy, Society and Religion in a Siberian Collective Farm.* Cambridge: Cambridge University Press, 1983.

Jameson, Frederic. "Third World Literature in the Era of Multinational Capitalism." *Social Text* 4 (1986): 65–87.

"John Ford's *Young Mr. Lincoln.*" A collective text by the editors of *Cahiers du cinéma*, trans. Helen Lackner and Diana Matias. *Screen* 13, no. 3 (Autumn 1972): 5–44.

Johnson, Vida. "Search for a New Russia in an 'Era of Few Films.' " *The Russian Review* 56, no. 2 (April 1997): 281–85.

Johnson, Vida, and Graham Petrie. *The Films of Andrei Tarkovsky.* Bloomington: Indiana University Press, 1994.

Jones, Anthony, and William Moskoff. *Ko-ops: The Rebirth of Entrepreneurship in the Soviet Union.* Bloomington: Indiana University Press, 1991.

Joravksy, David. "Cultural Revolution and the Fortress Mentality." In Gleason, Kenez, and Stites, *Bolshevik Culture*, 93–113.

Jowett, Garth, and James M. Linton. *Movies as Mass Communication.* 2d ed. Newbury Park, Calif.: Sage, 1989.

Jowitt, Kenneth. "Soviet Neo-traditionalism: The Political Corruption of a Leninist Regime." *Soviet Studies* 35, no. 3 (1983): 275–97.

Karakhan, Lev. "Jobless Prophets: Glasnost and the Auteurs." In Brashinsky and Horton, *Russian Critics*, 30–34.

Kawin, Bruce. *How Movies Work.* Berkeley and Los Angeles: University of California Press, 1987.

Kelly, Catriona, and David Shepherd, eds. *Russian Cultural Studies: An Introduction.* Oxford: Oxford University Press, 1997.

Kelly, Catriona, Hilary Pilkington, David Shepherd, and Vadim Volkov. "Introduction: Why Cultural Studies?" In Kelly and Shepherd, *Russian Cultural Studies*, 1–17.

Kenez, Peter. *Cinema and Soviet Society, 1917–1953.* Cambridge: Cambridge University Press, 1992.

———. "Soviet Cinema in the Age of Stalin." In Taylor and Spring, *Stalinism and Soviet Cinema*, 54–68.

Kenez, Peter, and David Shepherd, " 'Revolutionary' Models for High Literature: Resisting Poetics." In Kelly and Shepherd, *Russian Cultural Studies*, 19–55.

Kepley, Vance. "The Origins of Soviet Cinema: A Study in Industry Development." In Taylor and Christie, *Inside the Film Factory*, 60–79.

Klimov, Elem. " 'Learning Democracy': The Filmmakers' Rebellion." In *Voices of Glasnost: Interviews with Gorbachev's Reformers*, ed. Stephen F. Cohen and Katrina van den Heuvel, 230–45. New York: W. W. Norton, 1989.

Klinka, Ivan. "Writing from the Empire behind the Wall." Trans. James Naughton. In *Description of a Struggle*, ed. Michael Marsh, xix–xxiv. London: Picador, 1994.

Klugman, Jeffry. *The New Soviet Elite: How They Think and What They Want.* New York: Praeger, 1989.

Kniazeva, Marina L. "Theater on the Market." *Journal of Communication* 41 (1991): 31–38.

Kolesnik, Svetlana. "Advertising and Cultural Politics." In Seifert, *Mass Culture and Perestroika*, 46–54.

Konrad, George, and Ivan Szelenyi. *The Intellectuals on the Road to Class Power: A Sociological Study of the Role of the Intelligentsia in Socialism.* New York: Harcourt Brace Jovanovich, 1979.

Kopetas, A. Craig. *Bear Hunting with the Politburo.* New York: Simon & Schuster, 1991.

Kornai, Janos. *The Economics of Shortage.* Amsterdam: North-Holland Publishing, 1980.

———. "The Soft Budget Constraint." *Kyklos* 39, no. 1 (1986): 3–30.

Lahusen, Thomas. "Thousand and One Nights in Stalinist Culture: *Far from Moscow.*" *Discourse* 17, no. 3 (Spring 1995): 58–74.

Lamont, Michele. *Money, Morals and Manners.* Chicago: University of Chicago Press, 1992.

Lane, David. *Soviet Society Under Perestroika.* Boston: Unwin Hyman, 1990.

Lane, David, and Cameron Ross. "The CPSU Ruling Elite, 1981–1991: Commonalities and Divisions." *Communist and Post-Communist Studies* 28, no. 3 (1995): 339–57.

Lapsley, Robert, and Michael Westlake. *Film Theory: An Introduction.* Manchester: Manchester University Press, 1988.

Lawton, Anna. *Kinoglasnost: Soviet Cinema in Our Time.* Cambridge: Cambridge University Press, 1992.

Lenin, V. I. *On Literature and Art.* Moscow: Progress Publishers, 1967.

Lewitt, Marcus. *Russian Literary Politics and the Pushkin Celebration of 1880.* Ithaca, N.Y.: Cornell University Press, 1989.

Liehm, Antonin. *Politics of Culture.* Trans. Peter Kussi. New York: Grove Press, 1967.

Liehm, Mira, and A. Liehm. *The Most Important Art: Eastern European Film after 1945.* Berkeley and Los Angeles: University of California Press, 1977.

Lipset, Seymour Martin, and Richard B. Dobson. "Social Stratification and Sociology in the USSR." *Survey* 19, no. 3 (Summer 1973): 114–85.

Lovell, Stephen, and Rosalind Marsh. "Culture and Crisis: The Intelligentsia and Literature after 1953." In Kelly and Shepherd, *Russian Cultural Studies*, 56–87.

Lowe, David A. "The Book Business in Postcommunist Russia: Moscow Year One (1992)." *Harriman Institute Forum* 6, no. 5 (1993): 1–8.

Malia, Martin. "What Is the Intelligentsia?" *Daedalus* 89, no. 2 (Summer 1960): 441–58.

Mandel, David. "A View from Within: Interview with a Soviet Auto-Worker." In Smith and Thompson, *Labour in Transition*, 149–79.

Marsh, Rosalind. "The Death of Soviet Literature: Can Russian Literature Survive?" *Europe-Asia Studies* 45, no. 1 (1993): 115–39.

Marshall, Herbert. *Masters of the Soviet Cinema: Crippled Creative Biographies.* London: Routledge, 1983.

Mattelart, Michele, and Armand Mattelart. *The Carnival of Images: Brazilian Television Fiction.* Trans. David Buxton. New York: Bergin & Garvey, 1990.

Matthews, Mervyn. *Privilege in the Soviet Union: A Study of Elite Life-Styles under Communism.* London: Allen & Unwin, 1978.

McClelland, James C. *Autocrats and Academics: Education, Culture and Society in Tsarist Russia.* Chicago: University of Chicago Press, 1979.

McClure, Timothy (pseud.). "The Politics of Soviet Culture, 1964–67." *Problems of Communism* 16 (1967): 175–204.

McNair, Brian. "Media in Post-Soviet Russia: An Overview." *European Journal of Communication* 9 (1994): 115–35.

———. "Television in Post-Soviet Russia: From Monolith to Mafia." *Media Culture and Society* 18 (1996): 489–99.

Mickiewicz, Ellen. *Changing Channels: Television and the Struggle for Power in Russia.* New York and Oxford: Oxford University Press, 1997.

———. *Media and the Soviet Public.* New York: Praeger, 1981.

Muratov, Sergei. "Soviet Television and the Structure of Broadcasting Authority." In Seifert, *Mass Culture and Perestroika*, 172–84.

Nahirny, Vladimir C. *The Russian Intelligentsia: From Torment to Silence.* New Brunswick, N.J.: Transaction Books, 1983.

Nepomnyashchy, Catherine Theimer. "Perestroika and the Creative Unions." In *New Perspectives on Russian and Soviet Artistic Culture,* ed. John O. Norman, 131–51. New York: St. Martin's Press, 1994.

Nichols, Bill. *Representing Reality: Issues and Concepts in Documentary.* Bloomington: Indiana University Press, 1991.

O'Dell, Felicity. "Socialisation in the Literature Lesson." In *Home, School, and Leisure in the Soviet Union,* ed. Jenny Brine, Maureen Perrie, and Andrew Sutton, 92–109. London: Allen & Unwin, 1980.

Peterson, Richard A. "Culture Studies through the Production Perspective: Progress and Prospects." In *The Sociology of Culture: Emerging Theoretical Perspectives,* ed. Diana Crane, 163–89. Oxford and Cambridge: Blackwell, 1994.

———, ed. *The Production of Culture.* Beverly Hills, Calif.: Sage, 1976.

Pipes, Richard. "The Historical Evolution of the Russian Intelligentsia." *Daedalus* 89, no. 2 (Summer 1960): 487–502.

Pittman, Ritta H. "Perestroika and Soviet Cultural Politics: The Case of the Major Literary Journals." *Soviet Studies* 2, no. 1 (1990): 111–32.

———. "Writers and Politics in the Gorbachev Era." *Soviet Studies* 44, no. 2 (1992): 665–85.

Powdermaker, Hortense. *Hollywood, the Dream Factory: An Anthropologist Looks at the Movie-Makers.* Boston: Little, Brown, 1950.

Raeff, Marc. *The Origins of the Russian Intelligentsia: The Eighteenth-Century Nobility.* New York: Harcourt, Brace & World, 1966.

Remchuk, A. "Russian Writers Wage Internecine War." *CDSP* 42, no. 1 (1990): 5–9.

Rice, Christopher. "Soviet Music in the Era of Perestroika." In Graffy and Hosking, *Culture and the Media,* 88–106.

Riordan, Jim. *Soviet Youth Culture.* Bloomington: Indiana University Press, 1989.

Robertson, Roland. "Globalization Theory and Civilizational Analysis." *Comparative Civilizations Review* 17 (1987): 20–30.

Rutland, Peter. "Some Russians Are Learning to Be Rich." *Transition* 3, no. 5 (21 March 1997) (http://www.ijt.cz/Publications/Transition/Features/Feature.V03N05-2.html).

Ryan, Bill. *Making Capital from Culture: The Corporate Form of Cultural Production.* New York: Walter de Gruyter, 1992.

Sakwa, Richard. *Russian Politics and Society.* London: Routledge, 1993.

Schiller, Herbert. *Mass Communications and the American Empire.* New York: A. M. Kelley, 1969.

Seifert, Marsha, ed. *Mass Culture and Perestroika in the Soviet Union.* Oxford: Oxford University Press, 1991.

Shalin, Dmitri. "Intellectual Culture." In Shalin, *Russian Culture at the Crossroads,* 41–98.

———, ed. *Russian Culture at the Crossroads: Paradoxes of Postcommunist Consciousness.* Boulder, Colo.: Westview, 1995.

Shatz, Marshall. *Soviet Dissent in Historical Perspective.* Cambridge: Cambridge University Press, 1980.

———. "Stalin, the Great Purge, and Russian History: A New Look at the 'New Class.' " *Carl Beck Papers in Russian and East European Studies,* no. 205 (1984).

Shenfield, Stephen. "On the Threshold of Disaster: The Socio-Economic Situation in Russia," 2 July 1998 (http://www.trud.org/index7-4.htm).

Shlapentokh, Dmitry, and Vladimir Shlapentokh. *Soviet Cinematography 1918–1991: Ideological Conflict and Social Reality*. New York: Aldine de Gruyter, 1993.
Shlapentokh, Vladimir. *Soviet Ideologies in the Period of Glasnost*. New York: Praeger, 1988.
———. *Soviet Intellectuals and Political Power: The Post-Stalin Era*. London: I. B. Tauris, 1990.
Shukshin, Vasily. "The Impact of Truth." In *Vasily Shukshin*, ed. Eduard Efimov, 195–208. Moscow: Raduga, 1986.
Simis, Konstantin. *USSR: Secrets of a Corrupt Society*. London: Dent, 1982.
Slater, Thomas. "The Soviet Union." In *Handbook of Soviet and East European Films and Filmmakers*, ed. Thomas J. Slater, 1–68. New York: Greenwood Press, 1992.
Smith, Chris, and Paul Thompson, eds. *Labour in Transition: The Labour Process in Eastern Europe and China*. London: Routledge, 1992.
Smith, G. S. *Songs to Seven Strings: Russian Guitar Poetry and Soviet "Mass Song."* Bloomington: Indiana University Press, 1993.
Sochor, Zenobia. *Revolution and Culture: The Bogdanov-Lenin Controversy*. Ithaca, N.Y.: Cornell University Press, 1988.
Sokurov, Alexander. "The History of the Artist's Soul Is a Very Sad History." Interviewed by Paul Schrader, *Film Comment* 33, no. 6 (November–December 1997): 20–26.
Solomon, Andrew. *The Irony Tower: Soviet Artists in a Time of Glasnost*. New York: Knopf, 1991.
Staiger, Janet, ed. *The Studio System*. New Brunswick, N.J.: Rutgers University Press, 1995.
Stark, David. "Coexisting Forms in Hungary's Emerging Mixed Economy." In *Remaking the Economic Institutions of Socialism: China and Eastern Europe*, ed. Victor Nee and David Stark, 137–68. Stanford: Stanford University Press, 1989.
Stites, Richard, *Revolutionary Dreams*. Oxford: Oxford University Press, 1989.
———. *Russian Popular Culture: Entertainment and Society since 1900*. Cambridge: Cambridge University Press, 1992.
———, ed. *Culture and Entertainment in Wartime Russia*. Bloomington: Indiana University Press, 1995.
Tarkovsky, Andrei. *Sculpting in Time*. Trans. Kitty Hunter-Blair. London: The Bodley Head, 1986.
———. *Time within Time, The Diaries 1970–1986*. Trans. Kitty Hunter-Blair. London: Verso, 1993.
Taylor, Richard. *Film Propaganda: Soviet Russia and Nazi Germany*. London: Croom Helm, 1979.
———. "Ideology as Mass Entertainment: Boris Shumyatsky and Soviet Cinema in the 1930s." In Taylor and Christie, *Film Factory*, 193–216.
Taylor, Richard, and Ian Christie, eds. *The Film Factory: Russian and Soviet Cinema in Documents*. Cambridge: Harvard University Press, 1988.
———, eds. *Inside the Film Factory: New Approaches to Russian and Soviet Cinema*. London: Routledge, 1991.
Taylor, Richard, and Derick Spring. "Red Stars, Positive Heroes and Personality Cults." In Taylor and Spring, *Stalinism and Soviet Cinema*, 69–89.
———, eds. *Stalinism and Soviet Cinema*. London: Routledge, 1993.
Thompson, Terry L., and Richard Sheldon, eds. *Soviet Society and Culture: Essays in Honor of Vera S. Dunham*. Boulder, Colo.: Westview, 1988.
Timofeevsky, Alexander. "The Last Romantics." In Brashinsky and Horton, *Russian Critics*, 24–29.

———. "Scherzo—Suite—Nocturne." In Brashinsky and Horton, *Russian Critics*, 70–76.

Trifonov, Yuri. *Obmen (The Exchange)*. Ed. Robert Russell. Oxford: Blackwell, 1990.

———. "Taking Stock." In *The Long Goodbye: Three Novellas*, trans. Helen Burlingame and Ellendea Proffer. New York: Harper & Row, 1978.

Turovskaya, Maya. "The 1930s and 1940s: Cinema in Context." In Taylor and Spring, *Stalinism and Soviet Cinema*, 34–53.

———. "The Tastes of Soviet Moviegoers during the 1930s." In *Late Soviet Culture: From Perestroika to Novostroika*, ed. T. Lahusen and G. Keuperman, 95–107. Durham, N.C.: Duke University Press, 1993.

Urban, Michael. "Elite Stratification and Mobility in a Soviet Republic." In *Elites and Political Power in the USSR*, ed. David Lane, 127–44. Cambridge: Cambridge University Press, 1988.

———. "The Politics of Identity in Russia's Postcommunist Transition: The Nation Against Itself." *Slavic Review* 53, no. 3 (Fall 1994): 733–65.

Vartanov, Anri. "Television as Spectacle and Myth." In Seifert, *Mass Culture and Perestroika*, 162–71.

Verdery, Katherine. *National Ideology under Socialism: Identity and Cultural Politics in Ceauşescu's Romania*. Berkeley and Los Angeles: California University Press, 1991.

———. *What Was Socialism, and What Comes Next?* Princeton: Princeton University Press, 1996.

Voinovich, Vladimir. *The Ivankiad*. Trans. David Lapeza. New York: Farrar, Straus & Giroux, 1976.

Williams, Raymond. *The Sociology of Culture*. Chicago: University of Chicago Press, 1981.

Wolff, Janet. *Aesthetics and the Sociology of Art*. London: Allen & Unwin, 1983.

———. *The Social Production of Art*. London: Macmillan, 1981.

Youngblood, Denise. "Americanitis, The *Amerikanshchina* in Soviet Cinema." *Journal of Popular Film and Television* 19, no. 4 (Winter 1992): 148–56.

———. *Movies for the Masses: Popular Cinema and Soviet Society in the 1920s*. Cambridge: Cambridge University Press, 1992.

Zassoursky, Yassen. "Mass Culture as Market Culture." In Seifert, *Mass Culture and Perestroika*, 13–18.

Zinoviev, Alexander. *The Yawning Heights*. Trans. Gordon Clough. New York: Random House, 1979.

Zorkaya, Neya. *The Illustrated History of Soviet Cinema*. New York: Hippocrene Books, 1989.